ERASMUS OF ROTTERDAM

☞ Books in the RENAISSANCE LIVES series explore and illustrate the life histories and achievements of significant artists, rulers, intellectuals and scientists in the early modern world. They delve into literature, philosophy, the history of art, science and natural history and cover narratives of exploration, statecraft and technology.

Series Editor: François Quiviger

Already published

Artemisia Gentileschi and Feminism in Early Modern Europe *Mary D. Garrard*

Blaise Pascal: Miracles and Reason *Mary Ann Caws*

Botticelli: Artist and Designer *Ana Debenedetti*

Caravaggio and the Creation of Modernity *Troy Thomas*

Giorgione's Ambiguity *Tom Nichols*

Donatello and the Dawn of Renaissance Art *A. Victor Coonin*

Erasmus of Rotterdam: The Spirit of a Scholar *William Barker*

Hans Holbein: The Artist in a Changing World *Jeanne Nuechterlein*

Hieronymus Bosch: Visions and Nightmares *Nils Büttner*

Isaac Newton and Natural Philosophy *Niccolò Guicciardini*

John Donne: In the Shadow of Religion *Andrew Hadfield*

John Evelyn: A Life of Domesticity *John Dixon Hunt*

Leonardo da Vinci: Self, Art and Nature *François Quiviger*

Michelangelo and the Viewer in His Time *Bernadine Barnes*

Paracelsus: An Alchemical Life *Bruce T. Moran*

Petrarch: Everywhere a Wanderer *Christopher S. Celenza*

Piero della Francesca and the Invention of the Artist *Machtelt Brüggen Israëls*

Pieter Bruegel and the Idea of Human Nature *Elizabeth Alice Honig*

Raphael and the Antique *Claudia La Malfa*

Rembrandt's Holland *Larry Silver*

Rubens's Spirit: From Ingenuity to Genius *Alexander Marr*

Titian's Touch: Art, Magic and Philosophy *Maria H. Loh*

Tycho Brahe and the Measure of the Heavens *John Robert Christianson*

ERASMUS OF ROTTERDAM

The Spirit of a Scholar

WILLIAM BARKER

REAKTION BOOKS

For Anthony, Madeleine, Lucy and Elinor

Published by Reaktion Books Ltd
Unit 32, Waterside
44–48 Wharf Road
London N1 7UX, UK
www.reaktionbooks.co.uk

First published 2021

Printed and bound in India by Replika Press Pvt. Ltd

A catalogue record for this book is available from the British Library

ISBN 978 1 78914 451 2

COVER: Hans Holbein the Younger, *Roundel Portrait of Erasmus of Rotterdam*,
c. 1532, oil on wood. Photo Kunstmuseum Basel (Amerbach Cabinet
1662, inv. 324).

CONTENTS

Introduction: Fame and the Humanist Scholar

ou might have first seen him from a distance, hurrying along a street in Antwerp or Louvain or some other town, a servant following closely; or perhaps he had just left a church after mass; or you had come across him at the edge of town walking with a friend or two; or seated on a boat, reading a book, on his way across the Channel to England. He was a slender man who looked prematurely old, dressed in the black of a priest with tufts of his whitening hair showing at the edges of his scholar's hat. He had none of the usual markers of a particular order. He had rings on several of his fingers, but his overall presence was modest, not at all showy, though his clothing was of good quality. You might have thought him a bit frail, but even at rest his thin lips were pressed in thoughtful concentration, and if you saw him move you would see a sudden energy and determination, a kind of impatience, and perhaps a sign of arthritic pain would flash across his face. In some ways, just another priest, but if your friend had excitedly said, 'That's Erasmus of Rotterdam!', you would remember having seen him for the rest of your life.

By 1520, Erasmus was in his mid-fifties and had become the embodiment of an ideal: the humanist scholar. Such an

Hans Holbein the Younger, *Portrait of Erasmus of Rotterdam Writing*, 1523, oil on paper, mounted on pine.

ideal might strike most people today as a bit odd. Few people today would place a scholar at the pinnacle of the social hierarchy. So it helps to compare Erasmus's fame with that of an Einstein or a Stephen Hawking, an intellectual who by pure intelligence and skill appears to dominate a field of enquiry, to have achieved the force of an institution, and to be no longer just an ordinary person. Erasmus the scholar, in his own lifetime, had become one of the gods; catching sight of him walking down the street would have been just as memorable as noticing one of our intellectual heroes casually strolling by in public today.

We tend to focus on famous people, but by concentrating on a single figure, too often still a male, we forget there would be no fame without a field or people to dominate. Erasmus was famous in his own time for advancing in northern Europe the very field for which he became the exemplar. Beginning in Italy in the fourteenth century, a European professional class was evolving. This professional elite was now increasingly trained in an education based on the study of *literae humaniores*, 'humane letters' or classics, the literature and culture of ancient Greece and Rome. Latin had long been the language of education and the Church. But now the educated class – the doctors, lawyers, priests and administrators – were increasingly drawn to an immersion in and imitation of the language of Cicero and Seneca and Virgil, some to such an advanced level that even the ancients would have been impressed, and they were also tackling the Greek texts, often through translation into Latin, but increasingly in Greek itself.

In Erasmus's time, 'humanism' referred directly to this programme of *literae humaniores*, not at all to any developed 'philosophy of the human', even though the idea of the individual being, the new man or woman of the Renaissance, had already been over a century in the making, with fourteenth-century Petrarch (Francesco Petrarca) its first great exemplar. The books of the humanists encouraged the renewal, a rebirth or renaissance, of an old idea of 'the human', which included notions of ethical behaviour in public life, the importance of history, and an ideal of beautiful style in writing. The movement had travelled north slowly, and Erasmus, born in 1466, belonged to a generation in his region that was already beginning to receive the early benefits of its education.

Today we live in a period that was shaped to some extent by that same curriculum, even if we are now in the midst of our own transition away from its ideals of elegant writing, sacred canonical texts and the significance of history to a new kind of humanities curriculum, something that still does not have a name, a reaction to the way the old curriculum and canon no longer seem to serve the needs of today – part of a continuous renewal that Erasmus also encouraged in his own time. The contemporary world of humanities struggles with the new media and newer forms of narrative, gender, race, politics and community, environment, and even a notion of the post-human that Erasmus would find mysterious. Nevertheless, the old tradition is woven through all the new discussions.

Erasmus was recognized from an early age as a good scholar, even if his performance at school was, by his own account, mixed. He detested the old Church Latin he was taught by some of his teachers, and loved the Classical Latin taught by others. Not yet a teenager, we are told, he had memorized the

poems of the Roman poet Horace and all the plays of Terence.
He was a bit of a show-off with Latin among his friends – he
could, largely self-instructed, write in a sparkling style, sometimes using amusing words or obscure turns of phrase that
he had found in his late-night reading of books outside the
usual curriculum. He was not the most learned of his school-
mates or other scholars of his generation. A scholar of the

Petrarch appearing to his humanist friend Giovanni Boccaccio in a dream,
inspiring him to resume work on his book, miniature by Boucicaut Master
in Boccaccio's *Concerning the Fates of Illustrious Men and Women*, c. 1413–15,
the J. Paul Getty Museum, MS 63 (96.MR.17), fol. 243.

Bible, he never mastered Hebrew. But in him there was a mixture of qualities that led to his fame: a remarkably playful Latin style that invited a reader's interest, a passion for encyclopaedic erudition coupled with an amazingly receptive memory, a grammarian's literal way of attending to the actual words of older texts (including the Bible), a sharp eye for social injustice and hypocrisy, an extraordinary capacity for hard work and swift completion, a strong sense of his own worth, and — perhaps most important to his time — an unusually individual and ethical Christian faith that had not been broken or tamed by his unpleasant experience in a monastery or by theological instruction in Paris.

By the time Erasmus was in his late thirties and, in his own view, something of an old man, he had learned a lot but written little. About then he found his path forward, and he started to publish. Over the next twenty years scores of books tumbled out of him, and he turned himself into the famous figure known as Erasmus. He published a hugely influential edition and translation of the New Testament, and with it provided a masterful and controversial commentary. He became a powerful force in religious debate during the contentious years of the Reformation. He published his *Praise of Folly*, an outrageous satire of the world around him and at the same time a defence of a personal Christianity. Well before he died in 1536 (at the age of 69) he had become known as 'the prince of scholars' — the most famous scholar in northern Europe, a correspondent with kings and popes, and someone publicly hated by the most notorious man in Europe, the reformer Martin Luther. Of course, the people to whom he was best known were all Latin scholars or were advised by such scholars.

They were not that many in number in a society that was still largely rural and illiterate, but they were the ones who managed the Church, cities, states and empire. The members of this elite were what the English writer Thomas Elyot (*c.* 1490–1546) called the 'governors' – some (but far from all) members of the nobility, lawyers, magistrates, city counsellors, chancellors, bishops, priests, physicians, bankers, ambassadors, and increasingly their wives and daughters. They are the cultural ancestors of a vastly larger and more diffuse professional and intellectual elite that exists today.

Erasmus is interesting for the path he took in his life, for the impact he had, for his ideas, but also in the way he became famous. In the early sixteenth century fame could happen by virtue of birth, for instance to Henry VIII of England or Francis I of France, who were first known simply as reigning monarchs. Of course, their fame was enhanced by the rhetoric of flattery that an army of writers (including Erasmus) directed towards them, even from their childhood. In previous ages the fame attributed to writers and artists was largely limited to local regions, but that was changing. Because of the rise of the printing press, which provided faster-moving knowledge networks over greater distances, a reputation could be built across countries in a short time. Erasmus, who came from a modest background, turned out to be a master builder of fame. Other writers in prior centuries had achieved a local fame that spread widely only after their death. Erasmus is the earliest author to have constructed in his own lifetime an international persona in print, and in this he was quickly followed by Martin Luther. He used the wide distribution of the printing press to entertain and instruct readers – and at the same time he informed his readers of his own struggles and importance, how this importance was recognized by others, and why it was deserved. He published his own correspondence, sometimes mere months after the letters had been exchanged, and he often used the prefaces of his books to present his own life as a series of dramatic episodes that continued over decades of publication. Even if all of this was written in Latin, many of his works were quickly translated into the many vernacular languages of Europe. The wide distribution of his letters and the story of his life, parts of which were even embedded in his scholarly and controversial writings, helped to generate his fame.

Erasmus's self-fashioning may strike lovers of sincerity as suspect, possibly repellent. But we should pause in this judgement. He had in his life made his own success from very modest origins in a society driven by class and wealth, and he steadfastly remained outside the usual hierarchies of Church and State. He never took up the offers to become a bishop or a lifetime professor at a university. He remained an autonomous sole operator by accepting gifts, allowances and pensions which were the result of his celebrity. Of course such benefits created obligation to his patrons, yet at the same time these gifts gave him a form of independence, because he was not dominated by one single patron or institution. Thus his self-fashioning not only provided him with material rewards but gave him the freedom to try to refashion the world around him – to encourage his readers to become more tolerant of their enemies, more suspicious of hypocrisy, less greedy for material success, more committed to literature and religious writing, and more generous in spirit to others.

At times he appears to be very knowing in his manipulation of compliments and his seeking of the attention of the great and powerful. At other times we read in his works surprisingly forthright, almost naive expressions of desire for better ways of being in the world. His scholarship resonated with his contemporaries and, I will argue, continues to do so because of the ethical and spiritual framework in which it was offered.

In this short biography I am interested in what Erasmus had to say to us about his own life and times, in which he was a participant-reporter. Biography has a way of engaging and coordinating many strands of a historical period through the lens of a single person, and can provide an accessible introduction to a complex time. Erasmus lived in an intensely transitional era, in which travel, communications and religion all underwent profound and sudden shifts. The Late Middle Ages had already seen the transformation of cities into modern centres of power, but now there was the beginning of continuous global travel and trade, a shift in communications with the rise of the printing press, and a traumatic breach in Western Christianity after the publication of Luther's Theses in 1517 and the resultant fragmentation of the Christian Church.

Erasmus was a witness to an early version of our modern world, which now depends greatly on the kind of advanced education and knowledge networks that he helped to develop in his own time. Even though we have left much of the material and social world of Erasmus behind us, we continue to ask a few of the same questions: how do we connect with others in a shared community of ideas? How do we study the past? What are we to make of tradition and how can we read and interpret it? How, in all of this, do we make sense of our spiritual longings? With Erasmus we see these questions being struggled with, in a time and place and language different from our own.

Erasmus often told his readers that we know a writer best through the writer's own works – not through biographies like this one. How do we read, then, a 'life in books'? Indeed, why do we even seek to know the life of the author? Erasmus gives us an example in his own biography of St Jerome, which he wrote to accompany an edition of his works. We know the saint's life by the way he presented himself to us, especially in his letters. And what St Jerome had to say in his writings was, in Erasmus's view, more vital and pertinent than any words he might have spoken directly to us. In his biography of St Jerome, Erasmus says that the authors of books

> converse with us, instruct us, tell us what to do and what not to do, give us advice and encouragement and consolation as loyally and as readily as anyone can. In fact, they then most truly come alive for us when they themselves have ceased to live. For such is my opinion: if a man had lived in familiar discourse with Cicero (to take him as an example) for several years, he will know less of Cicero than they who do by constant reading of what he wrote converse with his spirit every day.[1]

This claim is quite extraordinary. Surely we can never know the long-dead maker of a book better than we know the living. Yet Erasmus is arguing that writing can present the living spirit of the writer. It is one thing to see and speak with someone, it is another to read his words: 'The mind', he says, 'has its own eyes'; 'the most cordial affection sometimes unites men who have never exchanged a word or set bodily eyes on one another.'[2] I would argue that Erasmus is on to something. After all, part of our act of reading – of reading anything – is to situate the text in time and place, to ask about the source of the written work, what literary theorists call 'enunciation'. We seek, and in some ways we create, the sense of an author. Often the writing will encourage this sense. The author in a book or letter is nothing more than a string of words. Yet if these words are written and read in a certain way, the author comes alive for us – more tangible in some ways than if the author were standing before us, as Erasmus claims. More alive, because the writings give us access to the author's mind, to sustained patterns of thought that we can return to again and again.

A good writer is able to engage the reader with this stylistic presence. It is, if you wish, a kind of psychological trick that allows us, even after centuries have passed, to feel a living presence within a piece of writing. It doesn't matter if this sudden presence is a projection or conjures up an imagined character akin to fiction: we feel 'the other' in some ways as perfectly real. This idea of empathy is found in many humanist writers, from Petrarch onwards, who in turn felt an immediate relationship with their classical predecessors. Here is a famous comment by Niccolò Machiavelli in a letter to Francesco Vittori (written in 1513, only three years earlier than Erasmus's comment above):

On the coming of evening, I return to my house and
enter my study; and at the door I take off the day's
clothing, covered with mud and dust, and put on gar-
ments regal and courtly; and reclothed appropriately,
I enter the ancient courts of ancient men, where,
received by them with affection, I feed on that food
which only is mine and which I was born for, where
I am not ashamed to speak with them and to ask them
the reason for their actions; and they, in their kind-
ness, answer me; and for four hours of time I do not
feel boredom, I forget every trouble, I do not dread
poverty, and I am not frightened by death; entirely I
give myself over to them.[3]

This connection with the past through writing is a continuous
theme in humanist literature. Many humanist writers learned
from the ancients how to craft personas in their writings to
familiarize themselves to their readers. Erasmus is a strikingly
present author; he refers often to himself and his own expe-
riences, and part of his success as a writer comes from the
intimacy he creates between his words and the reader.

There is a famous engraving of Erasmus made by Albrecht
Dürer in 1526, about five years after the two men had met in
Antwerp. The portrait does not look at all like Erasmus, as
Erasmus himself noted, even though he was delighted to be
memorialized by the most famous Northern painter of the
time. On the wall plaque behind Erasmus, who is standing
pen in hand at his desk, is a Latin inscription that reads 'The
image of Erasmus of Rotterdam by Albrecht Dürer, drawn
to a living likeness.' Just below, in Greek, another inscription

IMAGO · ERASMI ROTERODA-
MI · AB · ALBERTO · DVRERO AD
VIVAM · EFFIGIEM · DELINIATA ·

ΤΗΝ · ΚΡΕΙΤΤΩ · ΤΑ · ΣΥΓΓΡΑΜ
ΜΑΤΑ · ΔΕΙΞΕΙ

· M D X X V I ·

says, 'His writings show him better.' It is as though the portrait,
claimed to be drawn precisely to life, cannot match the living
presence of the written text. This claim was actually one
made by Erasmus himself, on a coin he had commissioned
from the Antwerp artist Quentin Metsys. It is the same assertion that he had made about St Jerome. Yet it is a declaration

Albrecht Dürer, *Erasmus of Rotterdam*, 1526, engraving.

that we do not easily accept in our own time. For us, no text is perfectly transparent; it is a performance, a construction, that can reveal or equally well conceal a writer's motivations, intentions and personal beliefs. Erasmus is asking us to put aside our suspicion. As I hope to show, this 'living presence' of the written Erasmus is an essential part of the humanist programme, which depends on friendship and close alliances with others. Erasmus in his writing creates a character for us, and we are asked to accept this character as Erasmus himself.

So we must ask, if Erasmus has created the *character* of Erasmus, how does this character appear to us? Is it possible to find a narrative arc in the life and work of Erasmus? Unlike collections of letters, or the sequence of books in a writer's career, biographies are often constructed in the form of a novel or epic poem. Many of them even begin *in medias res* (that exciting moment in the midst of the action that was proposed by Horace in his *Art of Poetry*), an approach I suggest in the opening paragraph to this Introduction.

Many biographies contain a narrative that is typical of heroic legends or fairy tales, the monomyth – the protagonist is of obscure birth, but is marked with very obvious signs of exceptional greatness, undergoes a period of training, then is presented with a challenge that may lead him to the under-world or to some form of temptation, and the story often ends with an assumption of power and possibly, at death, an eleva-tion to godhood.[4] (One might think primarily of Hercules or Jesus Christ, but there are also female versions of this quest narrative.) One can see aspects of the monomyth hinted at in the story of Erasmus. Erasmus, for instance, progressed from obscurity to renown – he was marked by early signs of genius, then entered a 'golden age' (his words) of humanism and fame before reaching a final condition that one biographer, Marie Barral-Baron, has called hell, and another, Stefan Zweig, a tragedy.[5] This closing stage of Erasmus's life was brought on by his battles with Martin Luther and other critics. It is as though the narrative of a life almost demands the inevitable plot structures of fiction. And it may be that Erasmus himself encouraged us to think this way about him, such as when he referred to his great projects, like his *Adagia* (Adages) or his editions of St Jerome and the New Testament, as 'my labours of Hercules', casting himself as a figure from mythology.

Despite our longing to give shape to his life, even following the cues provided by the subject himself, Erasmus did not live a life in or through a narrative. We readers and biographers tend to lay a narrative over what is really an episodic life that returns to the same themes over and over again, so that Erasmus never, after his earlier years, really moves forward. This is not to say that he does not change, that his thought does not evolve (it certainly does). The argument I am making follows from an observation made some fifty years ago by Joseph Coppens, a Dutch scholar, who referred to the initial 'evolution' in the life of Erasmus in the years up to his middle age, and the 'constants' of his life afterwards.[6]

In a 2004 essay, 'Against Narrativity', the British philosopher Galen Strawson asks if we all have a 'life story' that follows the pattern we find so often in biographies.[7] We are urged by psychologists and moralizers to 'find our story', or to 'tell our story'. But what happens if I have no story, if I proceed through my life day by day? My life may then be described as a series of repetitions, of circling around certain characteristic themes or actions, now and then shaken by some unexpected event that demands a response.

Much of Erasmus's writing is in what are called short forms: letters, prefaces, poems, prayers, little treatises, orations, dialogues, essays, annotations and paraphrases. Often his writing is directed to a particular individual under specific circumstances, and he constantly rewrote or revised his works as circumstances or the world around him changed. He loved the rapid, condensed language of the proverb and apophthegm. He was, moreover, restless: he would up and move suddenly, and change his plans as he went. He was an episodic writer who lived an episodic life. There are certainly themes to which he returns constantly in relation to his grammatical work or his philosophy of Christ. Later in his life, the short forms evolved into longer works, some of them encyclopaedic in scope (the project of the New Testament; the ever-growing *Adages*; even his response to Luther in the two-part *Hyperaspistes* or his final work on preaching, the *Ecclesiastes*). The temptation to the biographer to find a pattern, a story with an arc, is strong. But Erasmus did not lead a life with a grand narrative. His life, as he tells us, is in his writings – a series of books that flow from his characteristic themes.

Martin Luther called Erasmus an 'eel', a most slippery character.[8] Erasmus himself in his *Adages* had written a short essay on the ancient proverb 'To catch an eel in a fig leaf', the idea being that you can use the roughly textured fig-leaf to wrap around and seize the eel. Andrea Alciato, a learned contemporary and friend of Erasmus, wrote a poem in 1531 about seizing the elusive eel in a fig-leaf. For each biographer

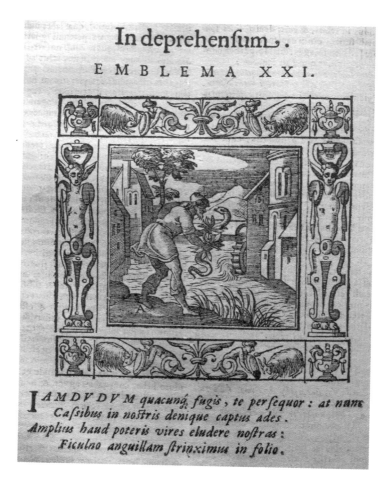

of Erasmus there is the question, what is the fig-leaf we will use to seize him? In this book, I look at Erasmus as a scholar first and foremost. I do this in part to define what a scholar in the humanities actually does, to show how much of our current practice is descended from our great predecessor, and how and why we have moved away from him.

Illustration for Andrea Alciato's emblem poem, 'In deprehensum' (Caught), in the 1621 edition of *Emblemata*.

A scholar, as Erasmus can show us, is someone who is interested in research, who appears to be focused on a narrow path but must be extraordinarily broad in interests to be effective. A great scholar is not buried in the past; he or she seems immersed in the past, yet speaks directly to his or her own time, and will attempt to tackle the broadest possible issues, even if the work is sometimes done with a care and attention that seem absurdly obsessive. A scholar may seem timid to the onlooker because a scholar is always aware of error and its relation to truth. Scholarship, often pursued in solitude, at the midnight hour, is seen by some as an anti-social activity. Yet it requires a complete engagement with other minds, even if these minds present themselves through the written word, as Machiavelli has told us and as Erasmus well understood. A scholar never operates on his or her own, but comes into being through community, whether that community exists as living friends or written works from another time. And for most scholars the corollary is that one needs friends, often a lot of them – family, patrons, publishers, colleagues, assistants, students – to pursue the work most effectively, even if sometimes only a very few of these friends actually understand the work that is being undertaken. Erasmus set a standard in his challenges to the normal expectations of the academic life of his own time, in his ability to create networks around himself, and in the breadth of his scholarly vision, which we can still recognize five centuries later.

I say that the life of Erasmus is found in his books and his letters, but the sheer quantity of his publications and correspondence is dizzying. Of course, to a scholar, such abundance is also exciting. The many surprises and secret avenues of research are everywhere. But it is difficult to compress it all into a short, comprehensive and comprehensible study. So, to help you, as well as myself, I have broken Erasmus's life into three parts, which sounds a lot like what Aristotle proposes in his *Poetics*, with a beginning, middle and end, and a lot like the life story that Strawson rejects. But for Erasmus this division provides clarity.

For the first part of his life, despite signs of remarkable ability, Erasmus is mainly interesting for what he was to become. I am calling this period his *preparation*, even if he only seems in retrospect to have been training to become 'Erasmus'. This is the period in which he lived with his family, attended school and engaged in his first attempts to make his way in the world – what we know of this part of his life emerges from works by Erasmus himself.

In 1500, at the age of 34, he seems to have undergone a change: he decided to launch a serious programme of study and writing, and the reform of his church. This period I call *publication* – his books at that time were being published, but in another sense he himself was also published. This is when he became a public figure. In a mere sixteen years he transformed himself into the leading scholar of northern Europe. This part of his life is also largely written by him for us.

In the last decades of his life, from 1516 to his death in 1536, Erasmus stopped his travels, partly because of his health but also because of the religious conflict brought about by the Reformation, which he had unintentionally helped to start. This last part of his life I call his *affirmation*, because this is when he doubled down on his earlier programme of humanist studies of language and Christian piety through not only a greatly expanded and now published correspondence, but continuous revision of his works, and new publications, not the least of which were sustained defences against attacks by his enemies who were so offended by his ideas. We now see him in a different dimension, in direct relation to others. The culmination of this part of his career is his collected works, a legacy that he himself planned, even though the great collection appeared in print after his death. As I shall try to show, Erasmus's writings, represented by his extraordinary publications, do in fact 'show him better' – for it is in his abundant books that we find his life and spirit.

ONE

Preparation, 1466–1500

uring his life Erasmus wrote thousands of letters to hundreds of correspondents.[1] In the beginning the recipients were his family and a small circle of friends, but as he became older the correspondence broadened first to other humanists, and then to important figures in the Church and in Europe's political realm. By 1515, when he was 49 years old and had become famous for works like the *Adages*, his collection of proverbs, and his satire *The Praise of Folly*, he began to gather his letters together for publication. His many published collections of these letters became widely read and brought Erasmus into an intimate relation with many readers. His letters told the details of his life (tales about a fall off a horse and a bout of dysentery, for example), they presented his controversial ideas on politics and religion, and they gave readers an inside look into the world of humanist scholars and their powerful patrons. There are flashes of anger, pages of moral musing or instruction, self-justification and humorous anecdotes. All this writing on such disparate topics has an extraordinary effect. We get to know Erasmus in the same way that we know the ancient writers Cicero or Pliny the Younger. Through their letters, we sense their living presence. Of course, by virtue of his composing and later careful curating of his letters, readers came to know Erasmus as Erasmus wished to be known. What follows is the story he has decided to tell us about his early years.

Erasmus was born in Rotterdam, then a small town in Holland, part of the Burgundian Empire, on the night of 27–28 October 1466. His father, Gerard (we now know his last name was Heyle), was a priest who had also worked as a scribe and had once lived in Italy. His mother, Margaret Roger, was the daughter of a physician from Zevenbergen, some 50 kilometres (30 mi.) from Rotterdam. His name was simply Erasmus; he was not given his father's name because as the son of a priest he was considered illegitimate (it was only when he was 34 years of age that he publicly named himself 'Desyderius Herasmus Roterodamus').[2] Erasmus had a brother named Pieter, who was three years older. When Erasmus was still very young, the family settled in Gouda in northern Brabant, a long day's walk from Rotterdam. By the age of four he was in school. When he was eleven, in 1478, he and Pieter were taken by their mother to St Lebuin's School in Deventer (also in Brabant), some 120 kilometres (75 mi.) west of Gouda.[3] This was an unusual move, a sign of the parents' commitment to the education of their boys, for the school at Deventer was already known as a superior institution.

Late medieval schools like St Lebuin's were intended to immerse students in Latin, a language that was only heard in church or in the classroom. The child would come in off the street speaking a variant of Middle Dutch and would enter the foreign world of Latin. The whole point of the technical side of the education was to get the student to read

overleaf: Rotterdam and nearby Gouda, views from Georg Braun and Frans Hogenberg, *Civitates orbis terrarum*, vol. III (1581).

ROTT
LAN

ROTT

ROTT

GOV
lam am
vrbs n

HOL.

VDE.

Opp. ad Isa-
nius, à quo
situm.

and write and speak the language. The instruction was based on memorization and rote, but over time students would begin to use it as a living, spoken language, though only within certain contexts with others who had received similar instruction. Many students must have struggled. To get the students sufficiently instructed, the teachers resorted to traditional classroom motivators – praise, humiliation, psychological fear and physical punishment. Because the schools were closely tied to the Church (priesthood was the common vocational aim), there was a heavy emphasis on prayer and moral behaviour, an important part of the curriculum. In the later years of their education, the boys would be introduced to philosophical texts that would lead to studies in theology. Even the literary texts were subject to a kind of ethical interpretation that would conform to a religious training. Some of Erasmus's moral and religious education may have come from teachers who belonged to the popular lay movement the Brothers of the Common Life, which promoted a distinctly personal piety that was emphasized in the houses in which the students boarded. Erasmus's ideas of personal piety show the influence of this movement, even though he was never (like Thomas à Kempis, *c.* 1380–1471) a follower of the Brothers.

During the years in Deventer Erasmus learned to read, write and speak Latin effectively, and may also have had some kind of elementary encounter with Greek. Though his studies by his own account were tied to the older medieval textbooks, it was at Deventer that he also had some form of contact with the new curriculum of Renaissance humanism that had already begun its travel northwards from Italy. These studies rejected the medieval schoolbooks, and encouraged direct contact with the great writers of ancient Rome (and, increasingly, Greece). By his own account Erasmus was an indifferent classroom student, but he claimed that 'a secret natural force [*occulta naturae vis*] swept me into liberal studies'[4] – to the prose of Cicero, the poetry of Virgil and Horace, the plays of Terence, and the joys of erudition. This was the beginning of a life dedicated to the study of texts and language.

His feeling for ancient literature may have seemed to him to have sprung up spontaneously as a mysterious or hidden force, yet such interests do not arise in total isolation. Erasmus's interest may have come in part from his father, who had lived in Italy and who as a scribe had copied out some of the great classical writings, or perhaps it was a master in his school who urged him along. Erasmus certainly befriended like-minded fellow students who were also drawn to ancient literature. He found much of his schooling to be a trial, as it can be for any child who knows he or she is brighter or more impassioned than the teachers, and his later essays on education should be read with his youthful disappointment in mind, as well as his evident precocity for learning outside the regular classroom. At the end of his schooling, he fell under the spell of Alexander Hegius, who became a famous teacher of humanities at Deventer, and he also claims to have seen (but not met) Rudolphus Agricola, the most learned northerner of the older generation, who visited the school. Agricola's work would prove transformative in the trans-European shift from scholastic philosophy to a literary culture.

By the time Erasmus was about sixteen years old, he had, certainly in his own mind, become a scholar. He was old enough to attend university, which for some students began as early as fourteen. At this essential moment, his mother died from the plague. The boys moved back to Gouda, and their father died from the plague soon afterwards. The death of both parents must have been a catastrophic event for Erasmus. Strangely, he never expressed any pain at the loss of his parents in his later accounts of the extraordinary change he underwent in this moment of his life. What did afflict him was falling under the control of three unsupportive guardians, one of whom was a relative who had taught him years earlier in Gouda.

The two boys, now orphaned, wanted to study in a university, but the guardians sent them to learn and work in a lay community in 's-Hertogenbosch, another small but prosperous town nearby, to the southwest of Gouda (the artist Hieronymus Bosch was then living in the city, whose name he had adopted as his own). Erasmus and his brother moved there in 1484, no longer advancing in their studies as they had at Deventer but apparently serving as assistant teachers in a school associated with the pietistic Brothers of the Common Life. The boys and their guardians engaged in an intense discussion over their future. There was no money, so there were few options. For scholars with no other prospects, the Church was the inevitable place for employment. Pieter opted to join a monastery. Soon after Erasmus also joined a monastery, of Augustinian canon regulars, in Steyn, a short walk from Gouda. He took his vows as a noviciate perhaps in 1487. In later life he expressed massive regret over his decision to become a cloistered Augustinian canon, and even after some twenty years he was still angry at his brother, his guardian, the canons at the monastery, and (to a lesser degree) himself for taking these vows. But the idea of the cloistered life had been seductive, because he was told he would have leisure time to pursue the humanistic studies that by then had come to be so important to him. Some six years later he was able to leave the monastery, even though he remained under the requirement to wear the habit and to report back regularly to his order.

When we look at these early years, we have to remember that most of this biography comes from Erasmus himself. Normally in a biography, readers appreciate how the subject's early years shaped the later years. But in Erasmus's life, we have to accept right from the start that the early years were carefully redescribed in his later years. We know a bit about the schools he attended, even though there exists no documentation for his attendance. Even the year of his birth is based on his own inconsistent correspondence (he exaggerated his youth in some accounts of his monastic vows). Although I confidently give his birthdate as 1466, the year is still contested by some scholars.[5] A principal source is his short autobiographical statement, called the *Compendium vitae*, or 'Summary of His Life', which is a letter to a friend dated around 1523, though not published until 1607.[6] This set of notes, apparently dictated when Erasmus was concerned about his health and possible death, and marked as a private document, is in a style unlike his usual polished prose. Yet this mysterious document fits so well with what is known elsewhere that most (but not all) scholars accept it as the work of Erasmus. It is from this document that we learn about his birth, and what his illegitimate status meant to him.

Erasmus tells us that he was the son of a priest. There were many children of priests at the time, but the Church considered those children to be marked with the 'stain' of illegitimacy. This mark had lifetime implications for them, giving them not only a reduced status in the Church and at university, if attending, but general social disapproval. In his *Compendium* Erasmus tells the affecting story of his own origin in such a way as to excuse his parents from any intentional misdeed. His father, he says, was destined for the priesthood, but he had fallen in love with Margaret. Forbidden to marry by his family, Gerard left her and travelled to Rome. Later he was told by his family that she was dead, and so became a priest. Margaret, however, was pregnant with Gerard's child, and it was only later that he discovered he had a son. The family was reunited, but Gerard, now under the priestly vow of celibacy, never after entered into physical relations with Margaret. This story of Erasmus's suffering parents and their tragic miscommunication was so good that it was later adapted into a hugely popular novel, Charles Reade's *The Cloister and the Hearth* (1861). But Erasmus's autobiographical account may also be in part a work of fiction, for it leaves out his brother, three years older, whose existence effectively contradicts the chronology of his tale.

The story of Erasmus joining the monastery is also laced with elements of fiction. By the age of fifty he was still under his full vows to the monastery, and his only way of achieving some kind of independence was to receive a papal dispensation. He made this application in 1516, and, as part of his request, he included a letter explaining his situation to an official named Lambertus Grunnius.[7] The name appears to be fictional, for it means 'Lambert the Oinking Pig'. This letter tells the sad tale of a boy named Florentius who was seduced into joining a monastery, how he took the perpetual vows under duress, and how he suffered as a monk. The letter, which could be entitled 'The Misfortunes of Florentius', is a portrait by Erasmus of his younger self.

The tale discloses that the parents of Florentius and his older brother Antonius had died, leaving the boys a small estate, which quickly disappeared to the trustees to whom they had been assigned. Though the boys were sufficiently prepared for university studies, having mastered 'a great part of the Dialectic of Peter Hispanus', a standard textbook of Aristotelian logic, their guardians, led by one overbearing hypocrite in particular (Erasmus's uncle Pieter Winckel, who taught him in his early schooling at Gouda), arranged for the boys to join a community of Collationary Brothers (another name for the Brothers of the Common Life). There the boys 'wasted two years and more' – a waste especially for Florentius, who, we are told, 'already knew rather more than his teachers themselves'.

After two years, as Erasmus tells it, the boys returned to their native place, and the guardians (who could see that the boys now had no other form of support) began to encourage them to join a monastery. The boys were reluctant, because the monastery would at some point require of them a lifetime vow of obedience. Together they planned to resist, but shortly afterwards Antonius gave in and took the vow as a monk, showing himself to be a Judas to his younger brother (to call your brother a 'true Judas' is a harsh accusation, especially in a letter written so many years after the event). Florentius continued to resist but was caught 'between the devil and the deep sea'.

At this point Florentius met Cantelius (now known to be Cornelius of Woerden), a monk in the Augustinian monastery at Steyn and a charming man a few years his senior, who had spent some time in Italy. Florentius was naturally drawn to this older friend, who described the marvels of the monastic life as 'a fellowship with angels', with leisure time to read and study. Florentius succumbed and joined the order. He was given many liberties, but when the time for the final vows came he recoiled, and the monks let him be for another period. Florentius came to realize that he loved the time for study, but he detested the community: 'Among these people, if a gifted mind appears that is born for the liberal arts, they suppress it . . . just imagine what torture it must be for a gifted nature born for the Muses to spend all of his life among men like that.' Florentius also found that the food and the regulated hours of sleep ruined his health. Why did the reverend fathers of the community not see the mismatch and convince him to leave? Instead they urged him to take the vows, which in the end he did and was miserable for years after.

Thus the life of Erasmus is retold to explain why he wished to escape from his monastic vows. A year later, in his 51st year, Erasmus was released from many aspects of these vows – he was allowed to accept multiple church livings, and he could live where he wished, even though he remained a member of his order until his death. He published the Grunnius letter (now perhaps revised) in the 1529 collection of his correspondence, so the letter became public. The early years of Erasmus are thus known, even in his own lifetime, uniquely from the account that he himself provides. We can sense his fragility, his fear of commitment to the monastic life, and his boldness in his attempt to fight against a life that had been imposed on him – all parts of the drama of Erasmus's life.

I have spent a bit of time on just two moments in his early years because they are part of the life story that all biographers like to retell, as though these moments seem to explain something about the young Erasmus: his fragility, his loss of family, his fear of institutional life. There is no reason to say that Erasmus lied about his early years; in his retelling the focus is on his status as an illegitimate child who has lost his parents, who is angry at his brother, and who is now trying to escape his vows. We do not hear about any suffering over the loss of his parents or any other details of his upbringing. Did he ever play games as a child? What did he think of his mother and father? The biography of the early years was clearly written in response to particular circumstances. His is not a 'narrative life', as I shall continue to argue, it is an 'episodic life' out of which a narrative can be composed.

'I TOOK THE HABIT, OR RATHER, HAD IT FORCIBLY PUT UPON ME'

In 1487 or so (the chronology is uncertain) Erasmus joined the monastery of Steyn, a community of Augustinian canon regulars, just a short walk from Gouda. (The monastery no longer exists.[8]) By 1489 he 'took the habit, or rather, had it forcibly put upon me',[9] committing his life to the rule of St Augustine and fealty to this particular monastery. Erasmus's days were spent in prayer, at meals, reading, copying manuscripts and in conversation with his fellow monks. During his time there, he tells us, he wrote a defence of monastic living,

On Disdaining the World (*De contemptu mundi*), a description of the possible contemplative pleasure to be found in the monastic life. This work was published much later, in 1521; by then, however, he had written a conclusion that contradicted the first eleven chapters. In the revised version, he advises the reader to proceed extremely carefully towards taking vows, because monastic life can in fact be very bad for one's spiritual life.[10]

Erasmus hated the food and the regulated schedule, later claiming both of these were bad for his health. He also disliked many of his fellow monks. In his letter to Grunnius he condemned the monastic vows, which he insisted are 'not found in either the New Testament or in Old', and he attacked the absence of religious discipline in the monasteries, which 'has fallen so low that in comparison with them there is more sobriety and more innocence in a brothel'.[11]

Erasmus depicted himself as suffering from loneliness, but we know that at this time he began to gather around him a close circle of friends. We get an unusual glimpse into his emotional life from a group of letters written to Servatius Rogerus, a fellow monk. This strange correspondence, which was never published by Erasmus himself, burns with pathetic longing. One letter reads: 'What is it that makes you so hardhearted that you not only refuse to love him who loves you so well but do not even regard him with esteem?' When he finally receives a letter in response, Erasmus is overcome: 'For as I was reading your very sweet letter, the effective proof of your love towards me which I long for, I wept as I rejoiced and in the same measure rejoiced as I wept.' How are we to take such an outpouring? Some readers proclaim this emotional outburst to be proof that Erasmus was homosexual and in love with Servatius; others call the writing an exercise in rhetoric. It is also possible to take a more nuanced position, for his language was typical of the kind of sentimental but non-sexual friendships that then existed.[12] Erasmus's awkward correspondence is clear evidence of a passionate longing for friendship in what sociologists now call a homosocial world, in some ways not that much different from sub-communities that exist today in which close relationships (not necessarily sexual) are found between men. For almost his whole life, Erasmus lived in this homosocial world. Of course he had female acquaintances, and he featured women in a later book of dialogues, his *Colloquies*, in a way that shows he clearly understood the power disparity of the time. Yet his life was organized around male friendships, male colleagues at work, male patrons, male students, male secretaries, male servants (except for Margarete, his strong-willed housemaid in later years). Of his 666 correspondents, only seven were women.

Despite the intense emotions, we cannot conclude from these letters to Servatius anything regarding the physical desires of the young Erasmus. He wrote many years later, in 1514, that 'I have never been a slave to pleasures, though I was once inclined to them.'[13] This comment was written to that same Servatius who had become the prior of the monastery at Steyn, and to whom Erasmus reported regularly on his activities in order to maintain his vows to the monastic order. Unlike the early letters, these later ones were published. Given Erasmus's cautious nature, and the fact that Servatius knew him well, these 'pleasures' must have been relatively innocent.

In matters of sexual behaviour Erasmus does not seem prudish, just uninterested. Elsewhere he says, 'I was never a slave to venery, and indeed had no time for it under the load of my researches.' But then he reopens the question: 'If ever I had a touch of that trouble, I was set free from that tyrant long ago by advancing years, to which on this account I am most grateful.'[14] The actual nature of that 'trouble' is not given. For present-day readers who like to get into bed with a biographical subject, this is as close as you are going to get. We can say with assurance that Erasmus always lived in the world of men, and he openly treasured their friendship, sometimes (as was the custom) in highly sentimental terms. He was certainly not fixated on celibacy; in a sample letter to a young man recommending marriage, he asks:

> why did nature assign us these members and add these incitements and this power of reproduction, if celibacy is to be considered praiseworthy? If someone gave you a splendid gift, a bow, or fine raiment, or a sword, you would seem unworthy of what you received if you were unwilling or unable to use it. Since everything else has been designed with a purpose, it hardly seems probable that in this one matter alone nature was asleep.[15]

HUMANISM VS SCHOLASTICISM

We have spent the past few pages on Erasmus's poorly documented early years because we are trying to find out how he presents his young self in his own letters, and how he came to be a great scholar and a force for change. In this auto-portrait, he is sensitive, easily wounded, awkward at times, sentimental, longing for friendship, and delicate in physique and in diet, but passionate about learning, enormously intelligent and well educated, and fully committed to his engagement with ancient literature, with an extraordinary determination to do things his own way. In his youth he lived a relatively private and confined life in the small world of Dutch culture and religious institutions. This changed in his mid-twenties. In 1493 he managed to break free of the monastery (but not the monastic vows) by becoming a secretary to Hendrik van Bergen, the Bishop of Cambrai, and on 25 April 1495 he was ordained a priest.[16] Erasmus had heard that the bishop might be travelling to Italy. And the bishop must have heard about this talented young man who could write so well. Owing to his mastery of the classics, Erasmus was beginning to be seen as a young man of interest.

Erasmus did not remain long in the court of the bishop, who never did get to Italy for his promised cardinal's hat. Later in 1495, still restless, Erasmus left for Paris, finally escaping from the Low Countries. He entered the Collège de Montaigu, claiming to seek a doctorate in theology, even though he must have known that such a degree would require many years of study. But such a claim might allow him to stay in Paris and not return to the monastery. His advanced studies were to be paid for by the bishop (who, he later said, never paid).

The rector of the small college was a well-known countryman, Jan Standonck, a strict disciplinarian. Even though Erasmus had now arrived at arguably the greatest university in Europe, he was not registered in the university proper, and the residential college where he studied was the worst of many disappointing institutions. Again, with a touch of the dramatic, he retrospectively claims that the 'rotten eggs and infected lodgings' made him sick, and he chafed under the discipline that he later described as cruelty. He left the college after only a year, and for the next few years lived in and out of Paris, much of the time working as a tutor of foreign students, continuing his own studies and writing. Now and then he may have stepped into a lecture, for he never seems to have relinquished the unlikely goal of the doctorate, even though he was as temperamentally unable to digest the curriculum as he was the rotten eggs of Montaigu.

Scholastic philosophy in the fifteenth century is difficult to characterize because it was such a complex and often embattled collection of philosophical positions. It did, however, rely on a methodological approach of dialectic (or logic) – that had yet to be integrated with the rhetorical method in the study of humanities. In dialectic the method of argument is by syllogism: 'Socrates is a man; a man is mortal; therefore, Socrates is mortal.' In rhetoric, by contrast, the argument is by enthymeme, that is by inference, by piling up testimonies, sayings, metaphors or images to win the reader over. To use an example from Plato's *Symposium* (and expanded by Erasmus in his *Adagia*, the famous collection of proverbs), we can make up our own enthymeme:

> Reader: look at this hilarious statue of the ugly Silenus, the friend of Bacchus! Now open it, and inside the statue you find many miniature and beautiful statues, all of gold: such is Socrates, an ugly old man who within him has the beautiful and supple mind of

youth. Therefore, we should never judge by external appearance.[17]

The conclusion is not reached by logic but by the seduction of comparison. Erasmus had a start in training for scholastic philosophy and theology about the time he was at 's-Hertogenbosch, as he had claimed in his letter to Grunnius, but he never completed studies for the bachelor's degree, and instead took the path of humanism, with its basis in classical style, storytelling and compelling mastery of rhetorical forms.

Erasmus described scholastic philosophy as distasteful, foreign. He did this enthusiastically in a letter of August 1497 (or thereabouts) to Thomas Grey, a pupil.[18] Erasmus did not attack the methodology, but instead (as a rhetorician) he told a story, comparing himself to Epimenides, the Cretan philosopher. Epimenides fell asleep for 47 years, and then abruptly woke up. 'Most of our present-day theologians never wake up at all,' Erasmus pointedly stated. Epimenides wandered about in a stupor (a predecessor of Rip Van Winkle), before finally some old friends took him in. The question is, what did Epimenides dream about in his 47 years of sleep? According to Erasmus, he dreamed the convoluted subtleties of the Scotist theologians (followers of Duns Scotus, 1266–1308). For that is the very sleep in which Erasmus now finds himself:

> If only you could see your Erasmus sitting agape among those glorified Scotists, while some foolish old pig lectures from a lofty throne. If you could but observe his furrowed brow, his uncomprehending look and worried

expression, you would say it was another man. They say the secrets of this branch of learning cannot be grasped by a person who has anything at all to do with the Muses or the Graces.

Erasmus swears that he is being destroyed by spending his time with men 'whose brains are the most addled, whose tongues the most uncultured, the wits the dullest, the teachings the thorniest, talk the most slanderous, and hearts the blackest on earth'. He presents himself as an amused and amusing intellectual who is naturally averse to the scholastic programme. He is not arguing against scholastic thought through theoretical argument, but by evoking sentiment and engaging the sympathy of readers, a technique he learned from the ancients and from his humanist predecessors.

HUMANISM AND FRIENDSHIP

By his early thirties Erasmus had made the shift from his family to the monastery to the life of a freelance tutor in Paris with relative independence, even if this life was now precarious. But along the way, as witnessed in the letters, he maintained himself in a community based on a sociability that was not domestic or institutional. Instead he turned to friendship with other young men of his generation. We have seen how he moved (or was moved) away first from his family because of his parents' death and then along the unwelcome path to the monastery. When he entered the monastery, he found himself in an uncongenial environment among the many monks and their regulated life. The letters to Servatius, whether rhetorical exercise or emotional release, were a plea for friendship. Other letters at the time show this longing, too.

The kind of community that Erasmus sought can be found in his letters. It is also dramatically presented in his earliest works. In the mid-1490s he wrote an imagined conversation between a group of friends and called it *The Antibarbarians*. The Antibarbarians are the enemies of the dominant 'barbarian' curriculum of the scholastics; they are five like-minded companions, all committed to the new humanistic learning. These devoted lovers of antiquity all speak beautifully, as though they had just stepped from the pages of a dialogue by Plato or Cicero.

With the plague ravaging whole regions, Erasmus, here a character in his own work, has moved from his monastery to 'a corner of Brabant' (Halsteren, the home of his bishop near the seaside town of Bergen op Zoom, 65 kilometres (40 mi.) to the south of Gouda). There he is visited by fellow monk and poet Willem Hermans, and Erasmus is so excited that he immediately contacts another friend, Jacob Batt, a talented writer and the town clerk in nearby Bergen. Jacob hurries over the next day and the three go out for a walk. As they are crossing a canal they run into two other friends, Jodocus (Joste van Schoonhoven), a cordial and philosophically learned physican, and Willem Conrad, the burgomaster, a leading citizen of Bergen, the least sympathetic to the humanist cause. These are all historical figures, and they accurately reflect the varied careers of that generation's humanist scholars. The usual pleasantries are exchanged and soon they move on to a topic that concerns them all: 'how did it happen that there is such an enormous distance between ourselves and the writers of antiquity?' Perhaps it was a fate directed by the stars, says the doctor, a keen astrologist. Maybe it was the impact of Christianity, and the ideal of unlearned simplicity provided by Christ, says Willem the burgomaster. Or perhaps it is a result of the natural ageing and decline of the world, says Willem the poet. Jacob now speaks up and says it all comes down to a single person. They pause in suspense. Jacob says it is the burgomaster, the very man standing before them. It is the burgomaster who arranged to hire the terrible teachers in the local school: 'You wonder at the death of letters, when even labourers and blockheads run schools!'[19] It is time to get rid of the terrible teachers and their outdated curriculum. The burgomaster begs to differ: was it not Jacob who hired the teacher? This accusation just fires up Jacob further.

The group agrees to listen to Jacob, who then proceeds with a full-on lecture, a defence of ancient learning, interrupted now and then by his friends, each of whom has particular questions regarding some of the details (thus maintaining the illusion that this is actually a dialogue). The true humanist is beset by enemies, those who 'pour scorn on the whole of what learned scholars toil for far into the night'. These barbarians reject ancient learning out of ignorance, unable to see how well such learning moulds character, quiets passions, checks uncontrolled impulses, and gives mildness to our minds in place of savagery. Even the great Church Fathers like Jerome and Augustine approved of the learning of the pagan thinkers, but nowadays the barbarians are unable to see the way that knowledge enhances religion. They claim, following St Paul, that 'knowledge puffeth up' – but 'Paul does not mean that knowledge should be non-existent, but that it should not exist alone, that is, without charity.'

Jodocus and the others praise Jacob's speech – he really should be a Dominican father, he speaks so well (an ironic touch, for Dominicans were devoted to scholastic philosophy). Even so, Jacob admits that he cannot explain the resistance to learning that he sees around him: learning is essential, not just for the individual, but for the community. In a passage that sums up Erasmus's programme, Jacob argues for a learning that will change the world for the better by being tied to the moral philosophy of the ancients:

> The man who lives an upright life is indeed doing a great thing, but it is useful only to himself, or at most to the few with whom he passes his days. If learning is added to his upright life, how much the power of his virtue will be increased, more brilliantly and more widely known as if a torch had been set before it! And if he is one of those who can put down in writing the most beautiful meditations of his heart, that is if he is eloquent as well as learned, the usefulness of this man must necessarily be widespread and pervasive, not only among his friends, his equals, his neighbours, but for strangers, for posterity, for the people at the uttermost ends of the earth. Worth without learning will die with its possessor, unless it be commended to posterity in written works. But where there is learned scholarship, nothing stops it from spreading out to all humanity, neither land nor sea nor the long succession of the centuries.[20]

This is a call to the reader to join a kind of crusade in favour of learning and scholarship, a learning that has a public goal, to improve society, to extend the 'charity' of learning. This learning is preserved above all in written form. It is, however, an emotionally engaged form of learning, maintained by a circle that begins with friends and radiates outwards. The believers in this new learning will have to overcome the barbarians, many of whom

> have been ordained in the church, they live on church stipends, they are old, white-haired, shrivelled, some even wear the cowl – and yet they seem to have entered into competition with Sardanapalus himself. Here am I, a young man and a layman, engaged in public affairs, and with a declared interest in literature which is itself secular, and they arraign me, they put me on trial as guilty of a nefarious crime, because I freely spend my time reading ancient philosophy, early history, the writings of the poets and orators.[21]

The humanist programme in northern Europe is here shown to reflect the restlessness and resentment of an evolving younger, urban educated elite that has turned away from the outworn values of the ruling Church and State hierarchy. *The Antibarbarians* is a call to those who belong to the emerging Republic of Letters to work together for a new order. This order can be brought about by a new education, by reading texts that promote a different relationship to the beauty of the world (now seen in more secular terms), to public morality (described by the ancient philosophers), to a better political state (found in the writings of Plato and Cicero) and a better Church (looking back to older writers such as Jerome and Augustine, who read the pagans, but were not the slaves of the hierarchy of present-day papal Rome). This new programme is based on the way friends communicate with other friends. The harmony that humane letters can bring is, moreover, seen in the generous way the friends are able to debate among themselves, indeed as evidenced by the dialogue in which all this is said.

Though the work had been written early in a period of intellectual formation, Erasmus revised and published *The Antibarbarians* years later, when he had achieved a position of leadership in the world of letters. It is a lovely portrait of the group of friends we know gathered around him when he was in his thirties. When he revised the book Erasmus claimed the dialogue was incomplete, missing a second part, but it is unclear how much further he could have taken his argument. It brilliantly demonstrates the centrality of friendship in the humanist programme. Friends are those who support the humanities, who encourage good writing, who value the ancient writers, who seek moderate social change and who above all seek reform in the Church. This is the same community that is mirrored in many of the letters.

In the Paris years of the late 1490s, Erasmus was living a life of intellectually virtuous obscurity. He seems to have been cut off from his allowance from the Bishop of Cambrai, yet he still resisted returning to the relative comforts of the monastic life. He was now looking for opportunities outside of the normal Church structure. On his arrival he sought out Robert Gaguin (1433–1501), a leading academic in Paris and

Trinitarian monk who had become the general of his order;
Gaguin had been to Italy and had strong humanist interests.
They exchanged the usual, mutually flattering letters, and
Erasmus sent him a draft of *The Antibarbarians*. Gaguin was
impressed. He encouraged Erasmus, and asked him, at the
last minute, to write a commendatory letter in the first edition of his patriotic historical chronicle, the *Compendium of the
Origin and Deeds of the Franks* (1495).[22] This was Erasmus's first
published piece of writing, and it is strikingly banal. At this
time, he was still struggling to find his voice as a writer. The
successful contact with Gaguin must, however, have been a
great confidence builder, an important introduction to a way
of relating to established scholars in the early years of the
northern Republic of Letters.

For most of that time in Paris Erasmus lived on the margins
as a tutor. This time of obscurity was, however, remarkably
productive. As part of his work as a tutor, he wrote a series
of instructional texts – on style, on letter-writing, and on proverbs and similes. We know about these works because every
one of them, starting with a collection of proverbs, was later
turned into a published book. Indeed, they were to become
some of the most widely used textbooks of the century
throughout northern Europe. As a tutor he seems to have
been well liked by some of his students. In November 1498
he took on a new adolescent pupil named William Blount,
who already by the young age of seven had inherited the title
Baron Mountjoy. When he was to go back to England the
following year, Mountjoy asked Erasmus if he would like to
go along with him.

Portrait engraving of Robert Gaguin from Isaac Bullart, *Academie des sciences et des arts*, vol. II (1682).

ENGLAND AND NEW FRIENDS

So far what we have learned about Erasmus's life has been built out of retrospective accounts and from letters sent to people within Erasmus's fairly small circle of friends. All this changes with a marvellous phase of his life, his first visit to England. When he arrived there, Erasmus had not yet entered what might be called an interconnected upper tier of writers and thinkers, though his connection to Gaguin and some others in Paris was a start. In England, in a matter of months, he entered a community of socially connected and sophisticated well-educated men with whom he immediately engaged. The well-placed young Lord Mountjoy was a perfect bridge to this educated world, but once let loose Erasmus did well on his own.

Erasmus clearly enjoyed his time in England. There is a jocular letter from him to Fausto Andrelini, an Italian friend in Paris (whom Erasmus had met through Gaguin). The letter contains, first, some unlikely news: 'The Erasmus you knew has already become quite an accomplished sportsman; he is not a bad horseman either, and quite a skilful courtier.' He even remarks that

> there are in England nymphs of divine appearance . . . and there is one custom which can never be commended too highly. When you arrive anywhere, you are received with kisses on all sides, and when you take your leave they speed you on your way with kisses. The kisses are renewed when you come back . . . If you too, Fausto, once tasted the softness and fragrance of these same kisses, I swear you would yearn to live abroad in England.[23]

One senses a desire to show off to and impress his friend
Andrelini. (No matter how 'rhetorical' the letter might be,
the present-day reader cannot help but observe that Erasmus,
now in his mid-thirties, may have been a bit slow to grow up.)

The biggest immediate impact on Erasmus in 1499 was
his discovery that he could join in mutually respectful friendship with highly accomplished men of standing and ambition.
The first was Thomas More, who took him to Greenwich to
see the young Prince Henry. Erasmus wrote a long poem to
Henry afterwards; in his accompanying letter, he boldly claims,
'Kings may indeed earn such fame by their glorious deeds, but
poems alone can confer it.'[24] A humanist must pay court to
the king, but the poets and writers are the real makers of fame.
You can sense Erasmus's new confidence. He and More immediately bonded, beginning a remarkable friendship based first
of all on a similar taste in classical literature and a shared sense
of ironic humour. This friendship, set out in many later letters,
was exceptional. More was a devoted supporter; Erasmus
would stay in More's household on his visits to London. The
relationship was reciprocal: Erasmus's *Praise of Folly* (1511) was
written for More, and Erasmus arranged for the publication
of More's *Utopia* (1516). Though there were periods in which
no letters were exchanged, the famous friendship lasted until
More's execution in 1535, a year before Erasmus's own death.

The second new friend was John Colet, who had studied
in Italy, and who later became Dean of St Paul's in London.
Erasmus met Colet in Oxford. The letters between the two
men begin with a vigorous but amicable dispute they had in
Oxford over the meaning of Mark 14:36: 'Father let this cup
pass from me; yet not as I will, but as thou wilt' (the passage

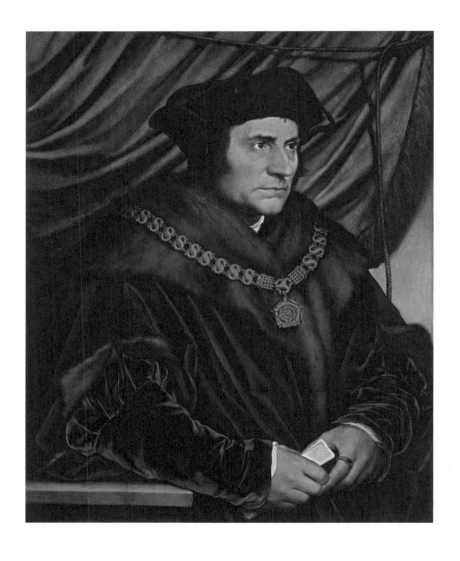

Hans Holbein the Younger, *Sir Thomas More*, 1527, oil on oak panel.

also appears in Luke 22:42 and Matthew 26:39). The 'cup' was often taken by commentators to mean a draught of poison. In this sense, does Christ fear death? Is this Christ admitting that he is human? Or is this the agony of a divine Christ who is expressing the disappointment he feels in the way the Jews have caused his death? Colet preferred the latter interpretation (which he derived from St Jerome's commentary on Christ's words), and Erasmus took the former position (thus unusually rejecting Jerome, whom he held to be the greatest of the Fathers of the Church). According to Colet, Erasmus was refusing Christ's divinity; Erasmus argues back that he is not rejecting Christ's divinity but accepting his humanity to be just as real as his divinity: this is Christ's dual nature. The approach shows that Erasmus finds a very human as well as divine Christ in the biblical text. Erasmus's response to Colet was expanded and published in 1503 as *Disputatiuncula de taedio, pavore, tristicia Iesu* (A Short Debate Concerning the Distress, Alarm, and Sorrow of Jesus). The debate is Erasmus's first written foray into theology, and it is interesting to see how it came out not as a formal exercise in dialectic, but as a rhetorical debate between two friends in informal letters. Theology as it was currently taught – 'niggling, nit-picking, threadbare, and thoroughly sophistical', as he says in the published text – was not the way the great theological truths should be argued between friends.[25]

England was transformational for Erasmus. When he summed up his experience there in a letter to his former pupil Robert Fisher, he did so in terms of the people he had met:

Hans Holbein the Younger, *John Colet, Dean of St Paul's*, c. 1535, black and coloured chalks, pen and ink, brush and ink, and metalpoint on pale pink prepared paper.

When I listen to Colet it seems to me that I am listening to Plato himself. Who could fail to be astonished
at the universal scope of Grocyn's accomplishments?
Could anything be more clever or profound or sophisticated than Linacre's mind? Did Nature ever create
anything kinder, sweeter, or more harmonious than
the character of Thomas More?[26]

William Grocyn and Thomas Linacre had both studied
Latin and Greek in Florence (one of their instructors had
been the great scholar Angelo Poliziano); both were leading
figures of early humanism in England, and Linacre was later
to gain a reputation on the continent for his translation into
Latin of short books by the ancient Greek physician Galen
(the principal source of Renaissance medical knowledge).
With these men, Erasmus was suddenly accepted not just by
individuals, but by an intellectual community that had a significant role in English public life. Moreover, he seems at this
point to have realized that the literary style that he had polished so well in correspondence could also be used for both
scholarship and theology. Even today, his writing does not
appear to be that of a narrow scholar using technical jargon,
but rather is meant to engage even the moderately informed
reader.
    Erasmus had begun to shift levels, now engaging with a
community that was already well established in politics and
religion at a high level. He found that he could flourish in
such a community. This meant that his notion of friendship
underwent a change, to become a bit more formal, more orientated towards public life. His community of friends was

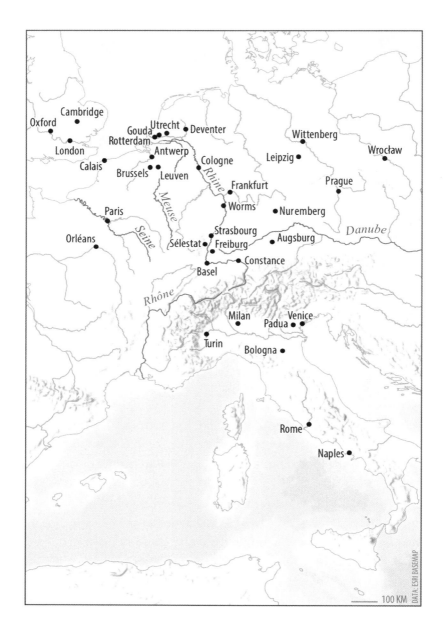

The Europe of Erasmus: he visited or lived in most of these towns and cities, with the exception of those to the east in Germany and Poland.

expanding into what might now be called a 'network', in which the friends related to each other independent of one particular central person, united by common purposes and interests.

Funerary statue of Anna van Borssele in Veere, mid-16th century.

TWO

Publication, 1500–1516

n 1500, despite his wide learning, remarkable talents and a small circle of admirers, Erasmus was, to put it bluntly, a nobody. Fifteen years later he was 'the prince of scholars'.[1] It was only after 1500 that he began, through extraordinary labour and boldness, to establish himself as a prodigy, a scholar whose learning was a match for the great Italians. This is a period for which we would like to have more correspondence. Much of what we have learned about him during his great climb comes from his books and later, retrospective comments. And even these books provide a complication. There is hardly a work that he published during this period which he did not revise and republish later on. The result is that the Erasmus we have during this period is still an Erasmus who was largely written, and revised, by Erasmus himself. During this period of increasing confidence, he not only published a lot, but worked towards an increasingly clear vision of the humanities and the Christian faith. He had clearly discovered what might be called an inner necessity, a focused sense of meaning and of himself.

THE TEACHER OF THE CLASSICS

When Erasmus returned to the continent, he faced two substantial challenges. He had no position, and he had no money. When he left England in early 1500 he had with him a substantial sum, enough to cover at least a year of expenses. At Dover, however, most of his money was confiscated, according to a law that forbade the export of gold or silver. This theft (as he saw it) was a major blow that he never forgot.[2] He raised some funds while in the Low Countries, but on his way to Paris he barely escaped an additional robbery by brigands along the road. On arrival he was broke, exhausted and feeling very unwell. His letters to Jacob Batt set out his situation. The Bishop of Cambrai, who had offered to support his earlier studies in Paris, 'goes so far as to turn his back on me'. Anna van Borssele, a potential aristocratic patron, whom Batt had encouraged Erasmus to approach, 'merely extends promises from day to day'.[3]

In spite of and also because of the sudden constraints, Erasmus was in a hurry to publish something, anything. In one letter to Batt (perhaps in March 1500), he wrote, 'I am engrossed in literature; I plan to compile a thesaurus of ancient adages, working in great haste, it is true . . . I shall dedicate them to your pupil Adolph [that is, Adolph of Burgundy, about ten years old at this time, who was the son of Anna van Borssele and was being tutored by Batt].' Erasmus continued: 'I shall bide my time for another month, supporting myself on credit, until some good news arrives from you.' In another letter, he tells Batt he will finish his *Antibarbarians*, and adds 'I have turned my entire attention to Greek. The first thing I shall do, as soon as the money arrives, is to buy

Deſyderii Heraſmi Roterdami veterũ maximeʒ inſi‑
gnium paroemiarũ id eſt adagiozum collect̃nea: opus
quin nouũ tum ad omne uel ſcripture uel ſermonis ge‑
nus uenuſtãdũ inſigniendũʒ mirũ in modũ cõducibile.
Id quod ita demũ intelligetis adoleſcĕtes optimi: ſi hu‑
iuſmodi delicüs et litteras veſtras et ozatiõe quotidia‑
nam aſſueſcetis aſpergere. Sapite ergo et hũc tam rarũ
theſaurũ tantillo nũmulo venalẽ vobis redimite: multo
pzeſtantioza propediẽ accepturi: ſi hec boni cõſulueritis.
Ualete.

Duobus in locis libellus hic proſtat: In magiſtri Iohãnis philippi offi
cina:cuius quidẽ tum induſtria: tum ſumptu nitidiſſimis formulis
eſt emaculatiſſime impreſſus: In via diui Marcelli ad diuine trinita‑
tis ſignum: Rurſũ in via diui Iacobi ad Pellicani quem uocant notam:

Title page of *Adagorium collectanea*, 1st edition (Paris, 1500).

some Greek authors, after that I shall buy clothes.'[4] This is the original version of the encouraging quotation from Erasmus that today appears on the walls of bookshops: 'When I have a little money, I buy books; and if I have any left, I buy food and clothes.'

The Antibarbarians, as we have already seen, was not published during this crisis. But in Paris, in June 1500, Erasmus did succeed with his book of proverbs. Proverbs are effective, focused linguistic units that can provide emphatic (if somewhat deceptive) clarity to moral debate and at the same time a sense of oral informality, making them ideal for written letters. At first Erasmus had proposed a collection of a few hundred ancient proverbs, but he managed to find some 820 of them, to make a small book of 152 pages called *A Gathering of Adages* (*Adagiorum collectanea*). He dedicated it to his former pupil Lord Mountjoy, instead of the young Adolph whose family had not been forthcoming with support. The title page, very much in the style of the time, explains the use of the book:

> This book not only has originality but is also a work that will be marvellously helpful for adding charm and distinction to every genre of the written or spoken word. You will be aware of this, young men, if you are in the habit of dropping such delightful gems into your letters and everyday conversation. If you are sensible, then, you will buy this rare treasure that is on sale at such a bargain price.[5]

The text itself is not much more than a list of proverbs (we would recognize expressions like 'To stir up hornets', 'Fire

follows smoke', 'You are entirely on the wrong road', 'To break
the ice').[6] Each is accompanied with a short explanation, for
often these old expressions are rather mysterious. What does
it mean to turn someone into Harpocrates? Erasmus explains:
to silence some normally garrulous individual and turn him
into the Egyptian god of silence with a finger on his lips.[7] To
hold a wolf by the ears? A writer today might say this about a
project that she can neither finish nor abandon.[8] These memorable expressions worked their way into regular Latin usage,
and then moved into the vernacular languages, sometimes
altered over time (for instance, in English we now say 'to have
a tiger by the tail'[9]). In his notes Erasmus not only explains
the proverb briefly, but now and then adds another unlisted
proverb that seems to pop into his mind as he proceeds.

There are occasional asides that the modern reader can
recognize as coming from Erasmus. For instance, 'service for
money is a fair exchange' is one of several proverbial sayings
in *The Comedy of Asses* by the ancient Latin playwright Plautus.
Here Erasmus cannot restrain himself from a topic then of
some concern to him:

> This saying will suit those boastful persons who think
> they have done a great kindness if they give some gift
> to a poor person; they brag about it and think they
> should get great credit for it. However, they do not
> remember how much the poor man has served and
> obliged them.[10]

There are few such interjections in the first text. But it was
a sign of what was to come. In later editions of the *Adages*

Erasmus personalizes, carrying into his historical explanations the kind of presence that he had in his letters, thereby enlivening what could be a purely technical account. In the preface addressed to Mountjoy he suggests the book was put together while Erasmus was ill, dictating the contents in a mere two months. The reader might be fooled by this and overlook that behind this casual mastery is more than a dozen years of relentless reading and study of ancient texts with, no doubt, many lists made along the way, most recently for his private pupils. Furthermore, Erasmus may have been aware of a possible model, the *Little Book of Proverbs* (*Proverbiorum libellus*) by Polydore Vergil, published in Venice in 1498. Erasmus later refused to acknowledge Vergil's work as a source or even as a predecessor to his collection, even though it seems likely he knew it (there are some eighty proverbs that overlap, some of which may well have come from Vergil).[11] Nevertheless, most of Erasmus's collection did come from his own work. The Greek – not yet one of Erasmus's strengths – came however from a collection ascribed to the ancient grammarian Diogenianus, which he found in a Paris library.[12] Erasmus was looking for proverbs that could actually be used by writers to refresh their prose, using these sparkling gems (as he called them) from ancient writers to brighten a composition, mainly in correspondence.

The little proverb book did not solve Erasmus's immediate financial problems. He wrote to Batt in 1501 that Anna van Borssele, who had promised 'never to behave like a woman . . . is now behaving in a more than feminine way, which causes me intense surprise' – in other words, she changed her mind and was no longer inclined to support him.[13] To readers today,

Erasmus sounds hostile and – typically for the times – sexist.
He moved on immediately to another book, while he continued to tutor and to pursue his studies (now mostly in Greek)
in and around Paris.

By April 1501 Erasmus was ready with an edition of *On
Duties* (*De officiis*), Cicero's last great work of ethical instruction.
It had already appeared in many editions, beginning with the
one produced in Mainz in 1465. Erasmus provided some
explanatory notes to this foundational text. He wrote a dedi-
catory letter to Jacob Voogd, a lawyer whom he had befriended
during a stay in Orléans a year earlier; this letter was attached
to a later printing. It lays out some of the challenges in 'improving the text' of the generally circulated Cicero:

> I found a great many flaws, as one would expect in such
> a familiar work; one scribe will throw the order into
> confusion as he copies, while another will replace a
> word, which perhaps had eluded him, with an approx-
> imation. These flaws are of course not monstrosities,
> but still they are intolerable in such a great author. I
> have corrected all of them, partly by collating editions,
> in which the disagreements are astonishing, partly by
> informed guesswork based on Cicero's style, so that at
> least I can promise the reader that no copy is closer to
> the original text then the present edition.[14]

Later, when we consider his editions of the New Testament and the letters of Jerome, we shall look more closely at
his scholarly methods. This Cicero is an early effort. Though
Erasmus claims to have corrected 'all' the errors in the Cicero,

his edition is not in any way authoritative because he relied so heavily on what he himself terms 'informed guesswork'. Today we call this 'conjectural emendation', a technical term for correcting a grammatical error or misspelling using the assumptions based on your own prevailing historical knowledge of orthography, grammar and the author's style (for instance, in the way you should correct 'then' to 'than' in the last few words of the short quotation I just gave you!). Of course, errors in manuscripts are sometimes the result of much more complex behaviour introduced over centuries of inaccuracies, as Erasmus himself was to discover as he learned to edit the Bible.

This same letter to Voogd also introduces an interesting word. Cicero's *On Duties* is a book that one should always keep nearby because, Erasmus says, it is a 'handbook' for morality. Moreover, he goes on to say, it is also a 'tiny dagger' – 'short, but neither Homer's Achilles nor Virgil's Aeneas was better equipped, though their arms were forged by Vulcan himself'.[15] The word he uses for both 'handbook' and 'dagger' is the Greek *enchiridion*, which is the title of his next book.

THE TEACHER OF RELIGIOUS LIFE

To avoid the plague in Paris, Erasmus had moved to Tournehem (in the very north of today's France), to be near his friend Jacob Batt. While he was in nearby Saint-Omer he met a Franciscan monk named Jean Vitrier. He was deeply impressed by Vitrier and under his advice began to read the work of Origen, the third-century Church Father, in the Greek that he was trying to master. It was at this time in the Low Countries

that Erasmus quickly wrote what was to become another popular work, the *Enchiridion militis christiani* (*Handbook of the Christian
Soldier*). This book directs readers towards a moral and religious renewal through Christ.

For readers of the short secular book of *Adages*, which leaves
out the many familiar sayings in the New Testament, it is hard
to tell that Erasmus is a canon and an ordained priest. There
can be no such confusion in relation to his *Enchiridion*. The
book is clearly directed to the 'Christian soldier' (it is strange
for us to see Erasmus, so opposed to war, take up that milita-
ristic image from 2 Timothy 2:3, still familiar in the memorable
hymn 'Onward, Christian Soldiers'). The book is written by
a priest, but it is directed, in the form of a familiar letter, full
of intimate advice, to an unnamed secular 'friend at court' who
is seeking to escape what Erasmus calls 'Egypt, with her sins
and allurements', in order to follow 'Moses on the road to virtue'.[16] Here he is teaching and preaching, using the form of
the personal letter (his virtuoso technique) to teach a central
lesson, first a dark picture of the world, 'which according to
the words of St John is given over entirely to vice', then a series
of 22 'rules' for moral and religious regeneration, followed by
'remedies' for lust, avarice, ambition and anger (four of the
seven deadly sins).

An eminent historian once wrote that the *Enchiridion* was
'the most boring book in the history of piety – at least that
was the judgement of his contemporaries, because it was a
publishing failure'.[17] This ironic assessment of one of Erasmus's
most famous books is only true of the early publication. The
Enchiridion had been published as part of a collection of religious writings called the *Lucubratiunculae* ('lucubrations' are,

literally, works made under lamplight, and the suffix -*ulae* means that they were a collection of 'little nightworks'). It was in this modestly titled book of *Small Meditations* (as *Lucubratiunculae* has also been translated) that Erasmus also included his response to Colet, *A Short Debate Concerning the Distress, Alarm and Sorrow of Jesus.*

Despite its inauspicious start, the *Enchiridion* remains one of the fullest and clearest expressions of piety written by Erasmus. It largely offers formal advice: Rule 4, 'Place Christ before you as the only goal of your life'; Rule 9, 'Your mind must be vigilant'; Rule 16, 'Take care that you do not immediately throw away your shield, lay down your weapons, and surrender to the enemy.'[18] But, as the address to 'you' indicates, it does offer advice in a direct manner. As one reads, an attainable vision of Christian faith comes into shape. At the beginning, the deeper message seems to be more a kind of ancient Greek 'Know thyself', advice that is an early sign of Erasmus's interest in Stoic philosophy.[19] In what follows, Christ is presented less as a judge, more as a model of charity and self-management. The faith is not described through the formal exercises and rituals of the Church so much as through personal behaviour marked by restraint and dignity. There are no scholastic authorities, and here and there we are directed to Jerome or Augustine; to help with a deeper understanding of Scripture, Erasmus relies on his recent discovery of Origen. As Erasmus was to say to Colet:

> The *Enchiridion* I composed not in order to show off my cleverness or my style, but solely in order to counteract the error of those who make religion in general

consist in rituals and observances of an almost more than Jewish formality, but who are astonishingly indifferent to matters that have to do with true goodness. What I have tried to do, in fact, is to teach a method of morals, as it were, in the manner of those who have originated fixed procedures in the various branches of learning.[20]

By 'Jewish formality', Erasmus is expressing a common understanding that the Jewish faith of the Old Testament was strictly bound to a narrow set of ritual behaviours, in contrast to a kind of liberty offered by the New Testament.

In his book Erasmus is presenting to us a kind of Christianity that seems deceptively modern: it is largely personal and it encourages ethical behaviour in day-to-day living. It takes many of the monastic ideals and proposes an orderly and managed existence for those living outside the monastery. Even if the ethical norms are hard to attain (there is for instance a requirement that one reject physical pleasure), this form of faith is welcoming. The focus on personal renewal through a direct knowledge and imitation of Christ has a relationship to the popular Dutch piety familiar to Erasmus from his own background and contact with the Brothers of the Common Life. He places Christ of the New Testament at the centre of his theology, and this Christ is not a guide to the afterlife, or to any kind of mystical experience, but to life as it is to be lived now. The *Enchiridion* is not a book of spiritual exercises (of the kind written by St Ignatius Loyola twenty years later, for example). It is what we would call a self-help book for the Christian who is seeking to reform and lead a better life.

It is hard for many of us today, in our secular world, to see how necessary such a guide might be. But if your whole social and psychological make-up is structured by the norms of Christian faith, and if you are aware of your failings, a clear path to personal reformation is crucial if you are unsure or faltering in your life and are seeking the reassurance of eternal salvation.

A feature of the book that is rarely remarked on is the rather hurried way the argument is presented, perhaps a sign of an informality that comes from the style of correspondence. There is a real imbalance between the many pages of discussion for rules 4, already mentioned, and 5 ('Progress always from visible things, which are usually imperfect or indifferent, to invisible'),[21] and the extremely short treatment of many of the other rules. The conclusion of the book works through four of the seven deadly sins, and Erasmus suddenly drops the final three: 'You see, my dear friend, what a vast sea of vices still remains to be discussed. But we will take in our sails in mid-course and leave the rest to your resourcefulness.' He goes on to recommend that the believer – who may think that the physical and moral restraint encouraged by most of the book is asking the reader to become a monk – not allow himself to be 'thrust . . . into a monastic order by means of the most impudent urging and threats and cajoleries, as if Christianity did not exist outside the monk's cowl . . . I merely advise you to identify piety not with diet, or dress, or any visible thing, but with what I have taught here.'[22] In other words, he proposes that aspects of monastic life be brought into one's personal life, while leaving the rule-bound monastery itself behind.

Erasmus explains in the first version of the *Enchiridion* that he is now in the midst of a larger project of study (of Greek and of the New Testament), and by 'putting aside this vast enterprise for just a few days, I have taken upon myself the task of pointing out to you, as with my finger, a short way to Christ.'[23] As with his *Collection of Adages*, written in a few weeks, Erasmus seeks to demonstrate his facility at writing, but also suggests that he is now in something of a hurry.

Despite the slow early reception of the 1503 *Enchiridion*, Erasmus strikingly repackaged it in 1518. He had it produced as a separate text by his Basel publisher Johann Froben, and for the new edition he wrote a long prefatory letter to Paul Volz, a Benedictine abbot.[24] In this letter, Erasmus offered an interpretation of the 'heavenly philosophy of Christ' found in the Bible that does not rely on monastic observances or on the arguments of the scholastic theologians ('who often fight each other until they are pale with fury').[25] This reformed religious faith can be followed by both the powerful people and the ordinary. By 1518 he had published his edition of the New Testament, and Luther had recently posted his 95 theses, so Erasmus's religious teachings had become of great interest to readers. The revived and even more personalized *Enchiridion* was now a best-seller. This work of Latin piety was soon translated into the vernacular languages across Europe – Czech, German, Low German, Dutch, Spanish, French, Italian, English (by William Tyndale, the Bible translator) – all during Erasmus's lifetime. It became a best-seller because it offered a meaningful and personal path at a time when believers were looking for a new way to Christ. And furthermore this was, as he said, 'a short way'.

Anonymous, *Philip the Handsome, Archduke of Austria, Duke of Burgundy,*
c. 1500, oil on panel.

THE TEACHER OF POLITICS

In late 1503 Erasmus, still in Louvain, was approached to write an oration in praise of Philip the Fair of Burgundy, son of the emperor Maximilian. Philip had just returned to the duchy of Brabant from a three-year trip to Spain, the home of his wife, Joanna, daughter of Ferdinand II of Aragon and Isabella of Castile. The point of his voyage abroad had been to establish the younger couple as inheritors of the joint crown (and indeed Philip became king of Spain the next year). The resultant *Panegyricus* was delivered as an oration to Philip now home at court, in January 1504. It is likely that Philip did not understand the Latin of this elaborate composition, though the ceremony of presentation would have been impressive. The work was published the next month by Dirk Martens, Erasmus's printer then in Antwerp.

This piece of public writing was difficult for Erasmus, who in the letter of dedication describes himself as 'a man who was not particularly curious and was always muttering over his books'.[26] He was embarrassed by the flattery he felt called upon to deliver. The *Panegyricus* has passages of enthusiastic praise that are openly sycophantic. It begins with 'transports of joy' over the return of the monarch, who surpasses 'Cecrops in nobility of birth, Polycrates in good fortune, Croesus in wealth, Xerxes in armies, Julius Caesar in victories, and Pompey in triumphs', marvellous compliments for the relatively untested 26-year-old Philip of Burgundy.[27] In places Erasmus reminds Philip of his sober obligation to his people to be an honest ruler (Philip had sworn an oath of service when he accepted the duchy of Brabant); he praises his modesty; and he emphatically and at length condemns the dangers and stupidity of war (a theme that later became paramount for Erasmus). But for the modern reader, and apparently for readers of Erasmus's own time, these admonitions seem less central than the over-the-top compliments.

Erasmus later defended himself against charges of excessive flattery by claiming that to make a monarch become an ideal ruler, it helps to describe him as ideal. As in the tradition of the medieval mirrors of princes, one must use honey to deliver the medicine of instruction. Nevertheless, the *Panegyricus* is a strong reminder of the role that flattery plays in the realm of politics. Erasmus understood that extravagant compliment is basic to the rituals of the court, whether in the ancient world (when Pliny the Younger praised Trajan in an earlier *Panegyricus*) or his own time. Situating the current prince in the context of ancient comparisons could provide a degree of dignity to the recipient of the praise. Of course, the deal was mutually beneficial. Humanist writers gained in prestige through their association with the rich and powerful, and would not have existed had it not been for their patronage. It is useful to remember that the humanities (even today) are not just critical of power but also celebrate wealth and power, in part to preserve their own position in the prevailing culture. Sometimes this ambivalent dependency on power can be embarrassing. Still, for his work, which was well received, Erasmus remembered twenty years later that he collected 50 gold florins from the Burgundian court.[28] He was also able to establish a toehold in the court culture. When the time came to repeat the performance, when Philip's son Charles (later Emperor Charles v) became ruler of the Burgundian Netherlands, Erasmus wrote a much more direct *Education of a Christian Prince* (1516).

BEGINNING HIS NEW TESTAMENT SCHOLARSHIP

In the same year of the *Panegyricus*, in a monastic library in Parc outside Louvain, Erasmus had spent time 'muttering over his books'. There, to his astonishment and joy, he discovered a manuscript that was to provide him with a powerful direction for his scholarship. This new find was Lorenzo Valla's (*c.* 1407–1457) famous series of notes that critiqued the commonly circulated text of the Vulgate or Latin New Testament.[29] Erasmus, who already knew Valla's textbook on Latin style, immediately transcribed the entire work (or had it transcribed), and soon afterwards took his copy to Paris, where the freshly discovered Valla was published by Josse Bade. Erasmus chose Bade because this printer was highly educated and also one of the few publishers who had the Greek types needed for the text (though the published book has an apology from Bade for the lack of accents). The *Very Useful Annotations by Lorenzo Valla on the Latin Translation of the New Testament from the Collation of Greek Exemplars* appeared in 1505. Valla had written his book in two versions, the second heavily revised; by serendipity Erasmus had unknowingly transcribed the only surviving copy of Valla's final revision.

This was a major find for Erasmus. By carefully comparing the language of the Latin Vulgate (the commonly used Bible of the Catholic Church) as it had descended from Jerome, and comparing the translation to different Greek manuscripts, Valla had come to a significant conclusion. As the text of the Latin Bible had been translated, sometimes mistranslated, then copied and recopied, and reinterpreted and even rewritten or 'corrected' along the way, the text had become corrupt. Valla's book is a series of notes that propose a recalibration of the text, as it were, by turning back to the original Greek sources to identify errors and to solve apparent confusions. In his work he moves book by book through the entire New Testament pointing out hundreds of corruptions and possible emendations. For instance, Luke 15:8 reads *evertit* ('she over-turns') for *everrit* ('she sweeps'), and John 18:28 reads *ad Caiapha* ('to Caiaphas') where it should read *a Caiapha* ('from Caiaphas').[30] The Bible has passages that had confused St Augustine a thousand years before; if only Augustine, like Valla, had known the Greek.

By present-day standards, Valla's approach was not sys-tematic; he never identified his particular sources or dealt directly with the very confusing history of the Greek text, which he accepted as relatively stable. For instance, Christians are familiar with different versions of the Lord's Prayer, which is found at Matthew 6:8-13. In the Greek manuscripts the end of the Lord's Prayer reads 'for thine is the kingdom and the power and the glory forever.' This passage does not appear in the Latin Vulgate. Valla was astonished to see this omission and sought to emend the text by adding it. What he did not know was that this part of the Lord's Prayer had long ago been incorrectly back-translated from the Latin into some of the Greek texts. With his revision, Valla was sure the error was fixed. In fact, the shorter Vulgate version was correct.[31]

Nevertheless, Valla was a remarkable scholar of Greek and Latin and a formidable trailblazer for Erasmus. By ques-tioning the actual language and style of the received text of the Latin Bible, proposing that Jerome had made errors in his translation, and insisting that a knowledge of Greek was

essential for the study of the New Testament, Valla alienated
the more traditional communities of Christendom, who were
already offended by his philosophical positions (he was known
as an enthusiastic Epicurean). Valla never shied away from
controversy. From his reading of Valla's *Annotations*, Erasmus
was thus not only given a methodological approach for a study
of the Scriptures, but he was emboldened by Valla's energy for
controversy and his ability to bring an enlightened historical
sense to the older texts. The new approach was, as Erasmus
said to Christopher Fisher in his prefatory letter to this edition
of Valla, not a challenge to theological ideas so much as a
clearer understanding of the practical problem of textual
transmission. The work was 'a grammarian's function', not a
theologian's.[32] As we shall see, it was work for both.

TRANSLATIONS

During 1505 Erasmus continued with his work on Greek, his
study of the Bible, his expanding collection of proverbs and
similar work. At the end of that year, he was in London. From
there he had written one of his regular reports to the prior of
his monastery, his old friend Servatius Rogerus. He tells
Servatius that he has been staying for a few months with Lord
Mountjoy. He has been in the company of 'five or six men in
London profoundly versed in Greek and Latin' (Thomas
Linacre, William Grocyn, William Latimer, Cuthbert Tunstall,
William Lily and Thomas More are names that come to
mind), and they all 'pay high tribute to my talents and learn-
ing'.[33] Although he claims to Servatius that he has come to
England 'that my scholarship may profit, and not to make my

own fortune', it would be correct to say that the two are in his mind intimately connected.

The continued attempt to profit from scholarship could sometimes lead to embarrassment. During his time in the Low Countries Erasmus had translated the challenging *Hecuba* of Euripides (a remarkable project considering his relatively short time with Greek). He chose as its patron William Warham, Archbishop of Canterbury (1503–32) and lord chancellor (1504–15), and soon chancellor of the University of Oxford (1506–32). Later Warham was enormously generous and supportive. But the first meeting did not go well. Erasmus met the archbishop through the introduction of Grocyn. Warham had handed over a gift, and on the way back by boat Grocyn asked Erasmus how much he had received. Reluctantly Erasmus had to admit that it was much less than he had expected. Grocyn then suggested that Warham must have thought that the book had several patrons:

> This took me aback, and when I asked him what on earth could have put that idea into his head, he laughed (and a mirthless laugh it was), and said 'It is the sort of thing you people do', suggesting that men like myself make a habit of it. This barbed shaft remained fixed in my mind, which was not used to such two-edged remarks.[34]

Erasmus, stung by the thought that he would be seen as a double-dipping supplicant, a year later sent Warham the published Euripides, but with the *Hecuba* came another play, the *Iphigenia*, which he had since translated.

Along with Euripides, Erasmus had also begun to translate
the short works of Lucian, the second-century satirist, who
wrote comic dialogues and mock orations, featuring ancient
gods, fools and sly operators. Erasmus entered into a light-
hearted partnership with Thomas More, who like him was a
late though enthusiastic student of Greek. The two translated
Lucian's *Tyrannicida*, a declamation by a man who killed the

Hans Holbein the Younger, *William Warham*, 1527, oil on panel.

son of a tyrant king and left the sword behind in the body. The king then came in, discovered his dead son, and in grief used the sword to kill himself. The murderer argues that he should be rewarded for having killed the tyrant, even if the death was not directly by his own hand. Both More and Erasmus translated the work and then each wrote their own versions of the already absurd speech. Both argue that the man did not actually kill the king, and therefore did not deserve a reward, and they managed to ring many changes on this comic performance. Lucian's playfulness and ironic sensibility had a profound impact on both Erasmus and More, fully evident in their respective *Praise of Folly* and *Utopia*.

With the Lucian translations, Erasmus landed on a new way to dedicate his work. For the first edition, each Lucian work was presented to a different patron. The recipients included a bishop and five other potential patrons.[35] One book, six patrons – a very effective distribution, but one done in a clever way that does not altogether avoid the assumption made earlier by Warham. Erasmus's actual financial return is not known. Later on, with his *Paraphrases* on the books of the New Testament (1517–24), he again used this system of distributing parts of a single work to multiple patrons, this time not for financial gain but to protect his project of the New Testament scholarship.

Early in 1506, as he was pursuing his efforts to find support, Erasmus received a dispensation from Pope Julius II, allowing him 'to accept and . . . to hold any ecclesiastical benefice whatsoever with or without cure of souls'.[36] Though he was now allowed to take a benefice, he had none on offer. It is therefore not surprising that he accepted with enthusiasm the request

of Giovanni Battista Boerio, Henry VII's physician, to serve
as a teacher to his sons Giovanni and Bernardo and accompany the boys on a trip to Italy. Another man, named Clifton,
would also accompany them as a tutor or guardian. Italy had
been the dream since 1493, when Erasmus had gone so hope-
fully to work for the Bishop of Cambrai. Thus, within a few
months, he was on the road again. On the way he stopped to
visit Mountjoy, who was now the commander at the castle of
Hammes near Calais, and he spent time in Paris preparing the
Lucian and the Euripides. By the end of the summer Erasmus,
the two boys, Clifton and retainers were on their way south
via Orléans, Lyon, and then through the Alps.

ITALY

Travel focuses the mind and often causes one to reflect. The
Alps were breathtaking to someone from the Low Countries.
Some fifty years later Pieter Bruegel the Elder crossed the
Alps, and the experience changed his art. But Erasmus did not
record his impressions of the trip, not even in the tradition of
Petrarch, who had written about his ascent of Mont Ventoux
in southern France a century and a half before. Erasmus's
thoughts instead turned inwards. As he travelled through the
vast and unfamiliar mountains, he wrote what many readers
consider his best poem. It is a long meditation on his realization of the passing years of his life, dedicated to his doctor
in Paris, Guillaume Cop.

Erasmus in this highly autobiographical account 'suddenly
begins to feel the curse of oncoming old age'.[37] He was turning
forty, and was aware of white hair beginning to show and time

slipping away. Once, when he was beardless, he 'burned for letters', and 'loved the figures of the rhetoricians and the charming fictions of poetry'. But he felt that 'sluggish old age secretly' had stolen over him and that 'the time of vigorous youth has now slipped away.' He had squandered his youth the way rich people wasted their money. Nothing can bring youth back, not even the charms uttered by ancient seers. Unlike the natural world, when spring follows winter, 'there is no hope that a past spring will return.' But after our hot summer has passed in our declining years, when gloomy winter has taken possession of our body, and after the stubble on our temples has turned white under a heavy snowfall, there is no hope that a past spring will return or that a new one will follow. Only death will end our afflictions. Like Trojans, we 'grow wise when it is too late' (a saying in Erasmus's *Collectanea*[38]), and we look back in horror at our 'shamefully spent years'. The past time cannot be recovered. The poem ends with a call to action: 'enough of this slumbering', 'now is the time to wake up', 'we must strive by vigilant effort to make good the loss of time past.'

The snowy Alps had reminded Erasmus of the approach of the winter of his own life. In the poem he reaffirms the direction he had taken after England: to dedicate his life to 'Christ alone', an affirmation he had already made to Servatius in one of his reports, some months earlier in April:

> For myself, I am deeply preoccupied with pondering how I can wholly devote to religion and to Christ whatever life remains to me . . . I am conscious how fleeting and insubstantial is the life of man, even the longest;

and I can see also that my own health is frail and has
been further weakened to a considerable degree by my
laborious studies, and to some extent also by misfor-
tune. I can see that those studies have no end, and every
day I seem to begin all over again. Therefore I have
made up my mind to be content with my present un-
distinguished fortune, especially when I have acquired
as much Greek as I need, and to pay attention to the
contemplation of my death and the state of my soul. I
should have done this long ago; I ought to have been
sparing with my years, the most precious possession
of all, what that possession was at its best. But, though
'too late to spare when the bottom is bare', still I must
husband it all the more carefully now that it is shorter
and poorer.[39]

Is Erasmus indulging in self-pity when he sees himself growing
'old' at forty? It is true that the average life expectancy of the
time was indeed around forty years, based on the high mor-
tality rate of early childhood. Yet, if you look at someone who
has survived those hazardous early years, and has attained the
age of twenty, the average life expectancy was actually around
sixty years or more (Erasmus died at 69). There were many
ways to divide up the 'seven ages of man', and some schemes
divided life into only four stages. The fourth and last stage,
which Erasmus felt he was prematurely entering, was called
by some writers 'decrepitude'.[40] It is no wonder, given his late
start in life, that he was concerned.

By and large, despite writing continuously in his letters
and his poetry about his situation and his activities, by being

the very source by which biographers choose to describe his life and to ponder his innermost thoughts, Erasmus is not given to much self-reflection. His approachable style gives us an intimate sense of a personality. He is an alert commentator on things around him, on people and their writing. But there is not much inwardness in his writing, little of the autobiographical reflection that we find in modern writers, and indeed will soon find in the work of an early modern like Montaigne. Though he reports on his health and his changing financial situation, Erasmus often seems blind to his own inconsistencies (unlike Montaigne). He rarely comments on his own closeness to Christ or to God; even his prayers are written with a degree of formality and distance. Thus this poem to Cop and a few other occasional autobiographical statements in his writing really stand out. Here he knows he is getting older, and, yes, he uses all the standard tropes to describe old age, but he applies them to himself. This poem marks an inward-looking moment, and it is one of the few such moments that we find in his writings.

For the educated elite of northern Europe, Italy was a dream destination. Scholars came for the living presence of antiquity scattered in ruins across the countryside, the lively commerce in the larger cities, the aura of moral corruption that both repelled and attracted travellers both young and old, the power of the Church that radiated from Rome, the art, the libraries, and the lively intellectual life of the major cities and their schools. Education was a major draw: 'To its ancient universities,' Percy Allen once wrote, 'students from the North swarmed like bees.'[41] Humanism had been alive since the time of Petrarch, and for more than a century Italian scholarship had led the way on the continent (though soon writers were to claim that Erasmus now held the top position among humanist scholars[42]). Many writers then and later have left excited accounts of their Italian journeys. Erasmus's correspondence thins out after his arrival in mid-summer of 1506, however, and we have hardly any first-hand accounts of this time. It is only after his return to the North that he wrote, 'I cannot without anguish recall the climate, the green places, the libraries, the colonnades, and the honeyed talks with scholars – the lights of the world, the position, the prospects.'[43]

Because of the conflicts among the Italian states, Erasmus could not travel freely. By November he was able to report back to Servatius that he was in Florence, having been blocked by a besieging army near Bologna, and so having gone on to Turin. There Erasmus received a doctorate, his first and only university degree. The process is described in 'How to Get a Degree in Fifteen Days', an informative and amusing article by the historian Paul Grendler.[44] The requirements for this doctoral degree were simple: once a candidate had been put forward by referees, there was a brief oral examination. Erasmus was declared by examination 'sufficient and fit' to receive the degree, and he became a doctor of theology 'on Friday, the fourth of September in the year from the Nativity of the Lord 1506'.

This degree was not Erasmus's noblest accomplishment. Turin was one of the worst of the eleven universities of Italy, and its avoidance of the long programme of the earlier degree requirements was called taking a degree *per saltum*, or 'by leaping'. Erasmus may have heard about this in England, as a number of Englishmen took their degree from Turin in a similar manner. Even Erasmus's own report to Servatius at the time is rather lukewarm: 'I have received my doctorate in theology; really I took this in disregard of my own inclinations and in response to my friends' insistence.' As Grendler concludes his account, 'If ever there was a scholar who did not fit into the academic mold, it was Erasmus.'[45]

Erasmus did make it to Bologna later in the year, and stayed there to the end of 1507, during which time he witnessed the triumphal entry of Pope Julius II into the city. He was still teaching the Boerio boys and pursuing his own academic projects in the libraries. In the autumn of 1507 he wrote a letter to Aldo Manuzio in Venice asking him to print a corrected edition of the two plays of Euripides that Bade had published in Paris the previous year. Aldus took the project, and the result was a small, elegant book printed in a fine italic.

Aldo Manuzio (often known simply as Aldus, his first name in Latin) was the premier printer in Italy, and in the twenty years or so since he had started his work he had become known across Europe.[46] His books were eagerly sought by readers in England, the Low Countries and the German states (often by those who had studied in Italy). These books, printed in new typefaces that Aldus had commissioned in the late 1490s, were beautifully designed. The texts were often prepared by leading scholars, in what today are called 'reading texts', without the usual massive commentaries. He mostly published in Latin and Greek, presenting classical texts that set a new standard of excellence. For Erasmus, Aldus was the perfect printer, with his beautiful layouts, fonts that were eminently readable (especially the Greek), and a household

ERASMI ROTERODAMI ADAGIORVM
CHILIADES TRES, AC CENTV-
RIAE FERE TOTIDEM.

ALD·STVDIOSIS·S·

Quia nihil aliud cupio, q̄ prodeſſe uobis Studioſi. Cum ueniſſet in manus meas Eraſmi Roterodami, hominis undecunq̄ doctiſs. hoc adagiorū opus eruditum. uanum. plenū bonæ frugis,
& quod poſſit uel cum ipſa antiquitate certare, intermiſſis antiquis autorib. quos pa-
raueram excudendos, illud curauimus imprimendum, tati profuturum uobis
& multitudine ipſa adagiorū, quæ ex plurimis autorib. tam latinis , quàm
græcis ſtudioſe collegit ſummis certe laborib. ſummis uigiliis , &
multis locis apud utriuſq̄ linguæ autores obiter uel correctis
acute, uel expoſitis erudite. Docet præterea quot modis
ex hiſce adagiis capere utilitatem liceat, puta quē-
admodum ad uarios uſus accōmodari poſ-
ſint. Adde, q̄ circiter decē millia uer-
ſuum ex Homero·Euripide, & cæ
teris Græcis eodē metro in
hoc opere fideliter, &
docte tralata ha
bētur, præ
ter plu
rima
ex Pla-
tone , De-
moſthene, & id
genus ali
is·An
autem uerus ſim,
ἰδοὺ ῥόδος, ἰδοὺ καὶ τὸ πήδημα.
Nam, quod dicitur, αὐτὸς αὐτὸν αὐλᾶ·

AL   DVS

Præponitur hiſce adagiis duplex index·Alter ſecundum literas
alphabeti noſtri·nam quæ græca ſunt, latina quoq̄
habentur, Alter per capita rerum.

of scholars, including Aldus himself (a grammar master before he turned to publishing), who were able to produce texts to the highest standard.

At the end of 1507 Erasmus concluded his teaching arrangements with the Boerio boys and made a move to Venice to undertake a new and vastly expanded edition of the *Adages*, so far his most successful book. It is not clear how he arranged this move, but soon he was a member of the printer's household (living with Aldus's father-in-law, whose cheapness he recalled in later years, and sharing a bed, a normal custom, with the equally poverty-stricken and much younger Girolamo Aleandro, later a cardinal who became one of Erasmus's great enemies). He remained there, toiling with 'untold effort and laborious nights',[47] for almost the whole of 1508, converting the earlier *Gathering of Adages* to a massive new collection now called *Adagiorum chiliades*, or *Thousands of Adages*; from a small pocket-sized book emerged an impressive folio that needed to be placed on a bookstand or desk. In his new edition Erasmus presented four times the number of proverbs, some of them now with long explanatory essays. He added further elaborations on ways to use the proverbs in writing. The work also included many asides, often of moral commentary. He must have had a working draft when he arrived in Venice, but he discovered many new sources, especially in Greek, now provided by the network of scholars associated with Aldus.

You get a sense of the scene in which Erasmus worked from an engraved image drawn in the 1590s by Jan van der Straet, known as Stradanus, for a work published in 1600 in Haarlem called *Nova Reperta* (New Discoveries). The work presents twenty of the significant inventions or discoveries of the age,

for instance the mechanical clock, gunpowder, refined sugar
and eye-glasses. The fourth in the series shows the printer's
shop in action; the nearby caption reads 'One voice can cap-
ture many ears; likewise, a single page of script can yield a
thousand pages.'[48] The image is not entirely accurate (for
instance, the printer in the foreground is printing from a plate,
not letters set in a metal frame) but the bustling interior is
convincing. The master of the shop is to the right, looking
over the presses, next to the compositor setting type we see a
proofreader (or corrector) wearing his glasses, and even a
small child is busy stacking printed sheets. Now, to imagine
the press of Aldus (or, later on, that of Johann Froben), add
several more presses and pressmen, more typesetters and
proofreaders, and turn up the volume. In Venice, Erasmus sat
in one corner, writing or revising the next day's text as fast as

Jan Collaert I, after Jan van der Straet, called Stradanus, 'The Invention
of Book Printing', plate 4 in the series *Nova Reperta* (*New Discoveries of Modern
Times*), *c.* 1600, engraving.

κύϐος,id eſt,Omnis iacta ſit alea,ad quod alludens Lucanus. Cadat alea ſati Alterutrū merſu
ra caput.Item Petronius Arbiter,Iudice fortuna cadat alea.Plato uitā humanā,teſte Plutar
cho ſimilem eſſe dixit,alearum ludo,in quo & iacere oporteat accōmoda, & iis,quæ cecide
rint recte uti. Quid cadat,id fortunæ in manu eſt,diſtribuere uero recte quæ forte ceciderūt
id in nobis eſt ſitum. Quā cōparatione imitatus fuiſſe uidetur Terentius in Adelphis.

Vela uentis permittere.   XXXIII
Neꝗ diſſimili figura dixit Quintilianus in præfatione inſtitutionū oratoriarum.Permitta
mus uela uentis,& oram ſoluentibus bene precemur,hoc eſt,editionis ancipitem euentū,ut
cūꝗ cadet,experiamur. Simillimū eſt illud apud Senecā in Agamemnone, Fluctibus dedi
tatem,hoc eſt,rem fortunæ arbitrio cōmiſi. Theognis οὐνεκα τῷ φερόμεϑα. καϑʼ ῖσια λύκα βαλόν
ης,id eſt,Quare nūc ferimur pendentes carbaſa uentis.

Sub omni lapide Scorpius dormit.   XXXIIII
τᾷ παντὶ λίθῳ σκορπίος ὑϐ᾽α,id eſt,Sub omni lapide Scorpius dormit.Admonet adagium ca
uendum eſſe,ne quis apud captioſos & calumnioſos temere loquatur,quicquid enim attigerit,periculum eſſe ne mordeatur.Cōſtat autē ſcorpios ſolere ſub ſaxis cubitare,que ſiquis tol
lat incautius,ſit ut ictus uulnus accipiat.Cōueniet & in moroſos,qui quiduis cauſari ſolet,uel
in pigros,ꝗ friuola quædā prætexentes,ſuffugiunt laborē.Ariſtophanes, ἐν Θεσμοφοριαζούσαις·
Τὴν παροιμίαν δ᾽ ἐπαινῶ τὴν παλαιάν,ὑπδλιϑῳ γαρῳ παντὶ πῳ χρὴ μὴ δάκῃ ῥήτωρ ἀϑρεῖν,id eſt,Sermo
mi uetus ꝓbatur, Nā decet lapide ſub omni Mordeat ne rhetor,obſeruare. Nicandri cō
mentator,hunc ſenariū citat,ex captiuis Sophoclis,ἐν παντὶ γαρῳ τις σκορπίος,φραϑᾷ λίθῳ.Etenim
ſub omni lapide ſcorpius excubat,id eſt,nihil tutum,& omnia cauenda.

Aſinus ad lyram.   XXXV
ὄνος λύϱας,ſubaudi ἀκροατὴς. Aſinus Lyræ auſculator.In eos,qui propter imperitiam nullo
ſunt iudicio,craſſiſꝗ auribus.Hūc titulum,puerbialem. M. Varro Satyræ ſuæ cuidā indidit.
Eiuſdē apud Gelliū extant hæc uerba e ſatyra,cui titulus,teſtamentū. Siquis mihi filius unus,
plures ue in decē mēſibus gignūtur,ſi erunt ὄνοι λύϱας,id eſt,aſini ad lyram,exhæredes ſunto.
ὄνους λύϱας appellat indociles bonarū artium,atꝗ intractabiles. Diuus Hieronimus ad Mar
cellam,Quos ego cū poſſem meo iure cōtēnere,aſino quippe lyra ſuperfluē canit,tamē ne
nos ſuperbiæ,ut facere ſolent,arguant.Et idem aduerſus Vigilantiū. Quāꝗ ſtulte faciā,magi i
ſtro cūctorū magiſtros quærere,& ei modiſ imponere,qui loqui neſcit, & tacere nō poteſt.
Verū eſt illud apud Græcos prouerbiū,ὄνος λύϱας.Lucianus de his, qui mercede ſeruiunt, τί
γὰ κοινὸν φασι λύϱα ἢ ὄνῳ,id eſt, Quid cōmercii aſino cū lyra? Idem aduerſus indoctū, ἀλλ᾽ ὄνος
λύϱας ἀκούεις κινῶν τὰ ὦτα, id eſt,ſed aſinus lyram audis,auriculas moues.Vnde & hoc pacto
effertur adagiū,ὄνος τὰ ὦτα κινῶν,id eſt,Aſinus auriculas mouens. Rurſum ad hunc modum,
ὄνῳ τις ἔλεγε μῦϑον,ἢ δ᾽ ταῦτα ἐκίνει,id eſt,Aſino quidā narrabat fabulam. At ille auriculas mo
uebat. In eos,qui cū nihil intelligant,tamē perinde quaſi nihil nō intelligant,ita nutibus allu
dunt,aut arrident dicētibus.Eſt autem aſino naturale,ſubinde mouere auriculas,ueluti ſigni
ficanti ſe iam intelligere,cum nihil etiam audierit.Aliquādo referunt ad aſinū nō auſculantē
lyram,ſed ipſum canere conantē.Lucianus,καὶ μάυσα ὁπότᾳρ ὧν ἢ ἀφρός τίνες δὴς,ὄνος αὐτὸν
ῥήνων φασί,id eſt,Maxime ſiquādo canit,cupitꝗ feſtiuus,ac lepidus uideri,aſinus,ut aiunt, ipſe
lyra canens. Idem in Pſeudologiſta,τοὺς δ᾽ ὰ τῷ λόγῳς ὄνῳ κυϐαϑόμῳ παρέμενον ὁρᾷμ, id eſt, Iuxta
hociſpum,quod uulgo dici ſolet,aſinū cōſpiciens cithara canere tentantē.Recte torquebit in
eos,ꝗ indecore tentant artificiū,cuius ſunt imperiti,& a quo natura abhorrent.

Sus tubam audiuit.   XXXVI
ςᾶλπιγγος ὗς ἤκους,id eſt,Tubam ſus audiuit.In eos quadrabit,qui res quidem egregias audi
unt,uerum eas,neꝗ intelligunt,neꝗ mirantur. Aut in eos,qui iis,quæ audiunt,neꝗ gaudent,
neꝗ commouentur. Equi tubarū clangore concitantur ad bellum. Suem abigat citius,ꝗ ani
met ad pugnam.Extat apud Suidam huiuſmodi ſenarius, ὄνος λύϱας ἤκουε,ꝗ σάλπιγγος ὗς,id
eſt,Aſinus lyram,Sus audiit ſtolidus tubam.

Nihil graculo cum fidibus.   XXXVII
Nihil graculo cum fidibus,id eſt,nihil ſtolidis & imperitis,cū bonis literis.Nā graculus auis
eſt ineptæ,moleſtæꝗ garrulitatis,atꝗ obſtrepera,adeo,ut a uoce qua ſonat,nomen inditū pu
ter,autore Quintiliano primo inſtitutionū libro. Tū ſui generis conuentus amat,quo mutuo
garritu,ſtrepitus fiat odioſior.Porro cithara ſilentiū poſtulat,& aures attentas.Aulus Gellius

Pro Heluonis Adagin [marginal note]

Symbola huir Duo [marginal note]

Graculus
Cithara [marginal note]

'An Ass to the Lyre' (1 iv 35), on ignorant people who lack judgement,
here illustrated by an early reader of the *Adages* (Basel, 1515).

he could, and Aldus, the master, sat in another reading the proofs; when he was asked a question he answered simply '*studeo*' ('I'm working').[49] Erasmus already had experience of printers' workshops, but it turned out that he also had the temperament and capacity to excel in the shop of Aldus. One of Erasmus's strengths as a scholar was his remarkably energetic response to the pressure of time. He could write and revise very quickly. And, unlike many scholars, he was not slowed down by the inevitable errors. As we shall see with his edition of the New Testament in 1516, he moved fast, and when things were finished, he made his corrections in a revised edition.

This expanded edition of the *Adages* was the one book before all others that made Erasmus's reputation. This great encyclopaedic work showed how he had total mastery even over the most obscure corners of ancient literature, including Greek texts that were still unpublished (thanks to the great resources of the Venetian libraries and collectors). It declared him the equal of any Italian humanist in his learning, the work having been published by the premier scholarly printer of Europe. And it was, for any reader of Latin at the time, not at all obscure, but playful, a joy to read. A typical entry includes several classical citations, advice on how to use the proverb, perhaps another proverb that this one seemed to parallel, and moral commentary. The internal citations open up a labyrinth of meaning, in which one proverb leads easily to another, a movement encouraged by word and topical indexes and an interpretive introduction. It presented Erasmus as a vastly learned scholar but also as a sensitive reader and an amusing and accessible writer who loved an adage so well that he could use one proverb to describe another. Even though (or perhaps because) the book was so impressively large and so packed with learning, it was not long before it began to be pirated and sold in different forms in other cities; we will look at the way it was expanded for its second edition in Basel in 1515. It was and still is an extraordinary gateway into the lore and language of the ancient world.

After less than a year in Venice, Erasmus was on the move again, this time to Padua.[50] There he undertook the instruction of James and Alexander Stewart, the illegitimate sons of James IV of Scotland. He was particularly close to Alexander, who, though sixteen years of age, was already named Archbishop of St Andrews – the kind of absurd ecclesiastical appointment (made so that his father could collect the income until the boy came of age) that Erasmus might ordinarily have scorned. Because of the threat of war, the three of them moved on to Siena. After a brief visit to Rome in Easter Week, Erasmus returned to the young men, and then travelled with Alexander as far south as Naples. They ended up back in Rome, where Erasmus, now the author of the extraordinary *Adages*, was feted by cardinals. Alexander had to return to Scotland, where, despite his youth, he was to become chancellor of state. Before he left he gave Erasmus, as a 'pledge of their undying friendship', a gold ring that held an engraved stone said to depict Terminus, the Roman god of boundaries.[51] Erasmus later interpreted the image as a warning of the limits of his own life and he adopted the figure of Terminus as a personal device, later adding the words *concedo nulli* – 'I yield to no one' (a phrase he picked up from Aulus Gellius, the ancient writer). The image of Terminus, very different from the figure on the ring, was used in his portraits – in a medal from 1519 created by Quentin Metsys and in the final print by Hans Holbein (who also did a small painting of a very different-looking Terminus, in part modelled on Erasmus's features). This device and its motto were taken by some as a mark not of death, but of Erasmus's obstinacy (which, we have seen, had been on display from a young age). When pressed to explain the motto, Erasmus however insisted that this device was a *memento mori*, a warning that death yields to no one, and that we should get on with things. This is the theme also of his *Declamation on Death* (*Declamatio de morte*) that he began while he was in Siena (it was later published in 1517). The thought of inevitable death can drive us forwards, as evidenced in Erasmus's poem to Cop. There was a poignancy in this gift, for Alexander was to die just four years after his time with Erasmus, at the Battle of Flodden, fighting for Scotland alongside his father.

Erasmus was in Rome in June 1509 when he received news from Mountjoy that Henry VII had died and that, with the

Erasmus's signet ring from Alexander Stewart, early 16th century, with a gem from the 1st century BCE.

ascension of Henry VIII, there had been some exciting changes, notably in patronage. Apparently 'generosity scatters wealth with unstinting hand.'[52] In July Erasmus left Rome and crossed the Alps through the Septimer Pass to Constance. He travelled down the Rhine back to Antwerp and Louvain, and arrived in London late in the summer of 1509.

ENGLAND, *THE PRAISE OF FOLLY*

> As I was returning lately from Italy to England, in order to avoid squandering upon vulgar and uneducated talk the whole time I had to spend on horseback, I sometimes preferred inwardly to savour some memory, either of the studies you and I shared once, or of the learned and congenial friends whom I had left behind in this country . . . since I thought I must at all costs occupy myself somehow, and since that particular time seemed hardly suitable for serious scholarly writing, I decided to compose a trifling thing, an *encomium moriae* or a 'praise of folly.' You will ask how some Pallas Athene came to put that idea into my head. First, I was inspired by your surname of More, which is as close to *Moria* (or Folly), as you are in fact remote from folly itself . . . Second, I guessed that this flight of fancy might find some especial favour in your eyes since you take immense pleasure in frolics of this kind.[53]

Here Erasmus is writing to Thomas More, in a letter of dedication to his friend at the head of *The Praise of Folly*, the book that is now recognized as his masterpiece. As he says, he conceived of this book during his travels, rather the way he had come up with his poem on old age almost three years earlier. This new work was however much bolder, enriched with the massive and abundant learning of the *Adages*, a clear sign of his increased confidence after his successful time in Italy. Erasmus says he completed a draft of his *Folly* in a week or so at the house of More and his family in Bucklesbury (a street east of St Paul's Cathedral). The first draft may have come to him very quickly, but we may assume that he continued, in his customary manner, to revise and expand it.

In his writing so far, Erasmus generally had aimed for clarity of composition, balance, acuity, humour and allusion. Even his poetry showed restraint. He had written academic commentaries, social criticism and a call to Christian charity and piety. He was a scholar, not a writer of fiction or a theological speculator on the mysteries of faith. Not so in this delirious work. He goes to the outer limit, to explore important social and religious themes with a *docta ignorantia* or learned ignorance that approaches mysticism. The work begins with social criticism, a kind of genial mocking, but it ramps up to direct attacks on various interest groups in the political, intellectual and religious worlds, and, in the amazing final move, suddenly turns inwards, and pulls the reader towards the abyss found in the complete loss of self through a total religious faith. There is a boldness and at the same time unusual humility to this argument. Erasmus is telling us that we are fools and that he too is a fool, for we are all fools if we follow Christ. It is as though the argument consumes itself and us by the end. If Erasmus shows himself in his own writings, as we argue is a central theme throughout his work, his *Praise of Folly* is a mysterious and challenging way to present himself to the reader, hovering as he does behind the remarkable figure of Dame Folly.

The Praise of Folly begins simply '*Stultitia loquitur*' — 'Folly speaks.' The entire work is a long quasi-academic speech by Folly, in praise of herself. Dressed in the clothing of a fool, her cap bearing the long flapping ears of an ass, she greets, gathered before her, a happy audience of fools (the reader with them too, it is understood). She does not tell a story, but presents an argument that proves that Folly is basic to all our lives. Her argument proceeds in three stages. The first is a kind of general proof that by her birth and status she is the most favoured of the gods and that all people are fools, both those who claim to be fools and, even more, those who do not know that they too are fools. 'Nothing happens in this world which isn't full of folly, performed by fools amongst fools.'[54] The second part of the argument is a sharper attack on those special groups who look down on fools. Greedy monks, ignorant priests and scholars, lawyers, doctors, theologians, monarchs and even popes all come under attack. This is the cadre of the learned and the powerful, the very people from whom Erasmus seeks recognition, acceptance and patronage. Why would Folly turn on them in this hostile manner? Because, as Erasmus knew so well, these are the ones who are most resistant to Folly. These serious and single-minded men 'have some reputation for wisdom among mortals', and by virtue of this reputation, they hold a power that they will not easily relinquish. They will never accede to Folly's argument that their work is foolish and that they too are fools. Yet, as Folly shows, the learned are greater fools than the fools they laugh at.

uſendum fuit. Sed quid ego hæc tibi, pa
trono tam ſingulari, ut cauſas etiam nõ
optimas, optime tamẽ tueri poſsis? Va
le diſertiſsime More, & Moriã tuã gna
uiter defende. Ex Rure, Quinto Idus Iu
nias.

ΜΩΡΙΑΣ ΕΓΚΩΜΙὸ N.i. Stulticiæ laus
Eraſmi Roterodami Declamatio.
Stulticia loquitur.

Ʈcũqʒ de me uulgo
mortales loquũtur,
(neqʒ enim ſum ne
ſcia, q̃ male audiat
ſtulticia etiam apud
ſtultiſsimos) tamen
hanc eſſe, hanc inquam eſſe unam, quæ
meo numine deos atqʒ homines exhila
ro, uel illud abunde magnũ eſt argumẽ
tum, quod ſimul atqʒ in hunc cœtũ fre
quentiſsimũ dictura prodij, ſic repente
omniũ uultus noua quadam atqʒ inſo
lita hilaritate enituerũt, ſic ſubito frõte
exporrexiſtis, ſic læto quodã & amabi
li applauſiſtis riſu, ut mihi pfecto quot
quot undiqʒ pſētes ſtueor, pariter deo
rum Home

eſt in dignitate rerũ
& ſermonũ, cuius præ
cipua ratio habetur in
tragœdijs, comœdijs,
& dialogis. Quid
ego hæc tibi,) ἀποσιώ
πησις eſt. Patrono tã
ſingulari) Patronº hic
ſignificat aduocatum
cauſarũ. Nã aliquan
do refertur ad libertũ.
Eſt aũt Morus præter
egregiam optimarum
literarum cognitiõem,
inter Britannicarum le
gum profeſſores, præ
cipui nominis.

DECLAMATIO
pte uo
cauit
decla
mati
onem
ut inl
telligas rem exercendi
ingenij cauſa ſcriptam,
ad luſũ, ac uoluptatẽ.
Porro Moriã fingit uel
terum more, ceu deam
quãdam, ſuas laudes
narrantem, idqʒ deco
re, quod hoc ſtultis pe
culiare ſit, ſeipſos ad
mirari, deqʒ ſeipſis glo
rioſe prædicare. Tar
men hanc eſſe.) Hanc
ſ ἐκτικῶς accipiendũ,
ut ſeipſam digito oſtẽ
dat. Frontem expor

Riſus ſtul
torum

rexiſtis) Frontem exporrigimus, cũ hilareſcimus. Contra mœſti frõte cõ
trahimus, quære in Chiliadibus Eraſmi. Deorum Homericorum.) Facet
te uocat Homericos, qui cum non ſint ulli in rerum natura, tamẽ ab Homel
ro ſingũ

B

The final and shortest argument concerns Christians. Taking her cue from passages in the Bible, especially from St Paul, Folly argues that the greatest fools are Christians. That is because in giving themselves over to Christ, they have taken a path away from all normal beliefs and behaviour in their single-minded drive for charity, love of neighbour and love of Christ.

The first two sections mix merriment and cruelty. Some of the attacks ring true:

> Picture the prince, such as some of them are today: a man ignorant of the law, well nigh an enemy to his people's advantage while intent on his personal convenience, a dedicated voluptuary, a hater of learning, freedom, and truth, without a thought for the interests of his country, and measuring everything in terms of his own profit and desires.[55]

Sometimes Folly's cruelty is excessive, such as the image of old women who are 'like corpses that seem to have risen from the dead', 'smearing their faces with make-up, always looking in the mirror, and taking tweezers to their pubic hairs, exposing their sagging, withered breasts'.[56] Nothing escapes the eyes of Folly or, apparently, the eyes of Erasmus.

The first two waves of the argument make it clear that we live in a fallen world. Given this – the dedication of the learned and the powerful to worldly pursuits, to greed, self-love and flattery – we are faced with a complicated question. If all people are fools, and I turn away from them to Christ, does this not make me a fool in their eyes? Falling on my knees in prayer, meditating on the divine – are these not foolish acts in the eyes of the foolish? We are thus led to that astonishing claim: the believing Christian is also a fool. Folly is taking the words of St Paul literally.

To make the transition to this most serious of Folly's claims, she eases us into accepting that she is really just playing a game: 'To play the fool in season is the height of wisdom,' she says, quoting a line that every schoolchild would have read in Cato's *Distichs*. After all, even Cicero claimed in one of his letters that 'The world is full of fools.' And Ecclesiastes in the Old Testament: 'The number of fools is infinite.' And does not Solomon in Proverbs say 'Folly is joy to the fool'? This is 'clearly an admission that nothing in life is enjoyable without folly'.[57] Ecclesiastes insists that we must accept folly as part of learning – 'And I gave my heart to know wisdom and learning, and also madness and folly.'

Folly has moved from the classical texts to the Bible, and from the Old Testament to the New, where St Paul says: 'I speak as a fool, I am more', 'because it is the privilege of fools to speak the truth without giving offence.'[58] But this, Folly goes on to say, is not a simple claim, but rather a recognition of Paul stripping himself down in his faith, the way Christ does when he urges his followers to remove everything except 'the sword of the spirit which penetrates into the innermost depths of the bosom and cuts out every passion with a single stroke, so that nothing remains in the heart but piety'.[59] It is in this sense of stripping away that Paul says 'We are fools for Christ's sake,' and 'Whoever among you thinks himself wise must become a fool to be truly wise.' Christ himself is humble when he enters Jerusalem on a lowly ass rather than a lion and is referred to as the Lamb of God. And Christ taught the people

'to shun wisdom, and made his appeal through the example
of children, lilies, mustard-seed, and humble sparrows, all
foolish, senseless things, which live their lives by natural
instinct alone, free from care or purpose'.[60] When Adam was
forbidden to eat of the tree of knowledge, there was a reason.
Knowledge is dangerous for religious faith.

The point becomes clear. Christian faith is a kind of stripping away, first of bodily concerns, then, more surprisingly,
of those of friendship and family. The ideal is Platonic, where
the essence of the soul is non-material, so that as you move
towards the truth, the physical world and the world of human
companionship fall away. But, unlike Plato, Folly takes you to
divine revelation in Christ and God. The truly pious 'regulate
all the remainder of life's duties, so that anything visible, if it
is not wholly to be despised, is still valued far less than what
cannot be seen'.[61] The passions are reduced, even the Eucharist
'seems to serve no useful purpose'. Normal people seek the
crowd, the words of the ritual. For the truly pious these things
have begun to fade away. The pious man is drawn to the 'eternal, invisible, and spiritual',[62] a more abstracted kind of faith
than we saw in the *Enchiridion*, which is more orientated to
ordering one's lived behaviour. *The Praise of Folly* makes man-
ifest the ultimate goal of transcendental 'learned ignorance'
that approaches mysticism.

Folly describes the final ecstasy using the language of Plato
in relation to love, in which the lover lives within the object
of his love, and thus is 'beside himself' and in that sense is
insane: 'The more perfect the love, the greater the madness.'
This state of self-abandonment is the foretaste of the final
assimilation of the soul into the eternal. The ecstatic believers

will 'speak incoherently and unnaturally, utter sound without sense, and their faces suddenly change expression'. They fall unconscious, and 'when they come to, they say they don't know where they have been, in the body or outside of it, awake or asleep.' They have attained perfect happiness and 'all they want is to be mad forever with this kind of madness.'[63] Even though they have been caught up in a violent transition with the acceptance of their own folly, they turn not to violence but to a higher state of understanding. Earlier in the book the 'others' are all fools, but when the Christian reader and the author are subsumed into this otherness, the irony is complete.

At this point, Folly stops. She says she has forgotten herself, she has 'overshot the mark'. She reminds her audience and the reader (who knows perfectly well that Erasmus made this book) that 'it's Folly and a woman who's been speaking.' So with these words she attempts to trivialize what we have just read, and, in doing so, draws attention to their loaded meaning. She refuses to give the peroration (the final part of a speech, summing up the argument) as she can barely remember what she has said. But she does remind her readers that 'I hate an audience which won't forget.'[64] These concluding remarks also draw attention to the fact that the speech that she will not summarize, and has by now herself more or less forgotten, is still there as a book in the hands of the reader, who will, by virtue of the written word, never forget the words of Folly (or Erasmus).[65]

I have focused on the final section of the book because here Erasmus broke convention. It is as though the logic of the whole book carries him to a point of revelation that even he does not seem to expect. He does not write like this anywhere else. In his writings he is normally intent on the social self – on teaching the self; on finding ways for us to express our selves most clearly; on social presentation of the self, his own included. The end of his *Folly* moves beyond, into a statement of selflessness.

The Praise of Folly was an instant hit, in an era that found great entertainment in fools and folly. The humanist scholar Sebastian Brant's *Ship of Fools*, published in 1494, was already in circulation in several languages. This earlier work catalogues many categories of human fool and seems close to what is called 'estates satire', medieval literature in which the nobility, clergy and peasants are satirized for their failures. Erasmus took the joke further. Folly includes *everyone* in her company, including the reader and the author. Needless to say, this resolute claim, even though it is an extension of St Paul's teachings, caused (and still causes) a violent tremor in many readers. Though he never returns to this idea, it remains Erasmus's most profound theological assertion. It is as though the unseriousness of his book freed him to break from convention and to express a darker and more complex emotion. Later we see this same phenomenon, though within a more social context, with his *Colloquies*.

The book sold well and was well received by the very objects of Folly's laughter; even Pope Leo X found it amusing. It had a complex effect on Erasmus's career. He was praised by some, and attacked by others. He was seen as brilliantly learned (the book is stuffed with allusions to ancient literature, especially with the adages from his 1508 edition, making it in some places a tough read for the present-day reader) and a brilliant writer (the delirious hyper-abundant style of his *Folly* was developed about the same time as the appearance in 1512 of his expanded textbook on *copia*, or abundance and variation in style). For many of his contemporaries, plenty of whom did not understand his irony, *Folly* was alien, heretical. Erasmus was thus seen as a serious critic by some and by others as someone who seemed flippant, even impudent, and therefore not to be trusted. Yet for us, even for non-believers, there can be nothing more serious, more humiliating or more ecstatic than the surrender to Christ that he proposes at the end of his *Folly*.

As we proceed in our account of Erasmus's life we want to keep testing the claim that 'his writings show him better.' We know Erasmus wrote the book, but here he manages both to disclose his ideas and to hide behind them. Erasmus defended himself against the critics of his book by pointing out that 'Folly speaks', not Erasmus himself. Moreover, the logic of the book insists that Erasmus too is a fool. The *persona* ('role', or sometimes 'mask') of Erasmus is concealed within another *persona*, that of Folly, a technique he also later uses in his *Colloquies*. The matter became even more complicated in 1515 when Erasmus and Gerardus Listrius, a younger scholar, together wrote a set of annotations to the work (for even his learned contemporaries needed to know that the Cave of Trophonius was a depressing place to visit, and that a fuller explanation could be found in the *Adages* of Erasmus). Oswald Myconius, a Basel schoolmaster, purchased a copy of this 1515 revision and commissioned two young artists to illustrate it (now in the library of the University of Basel). The 82 tiny pictures by Ambrosius and Hans Holbein that you can see in

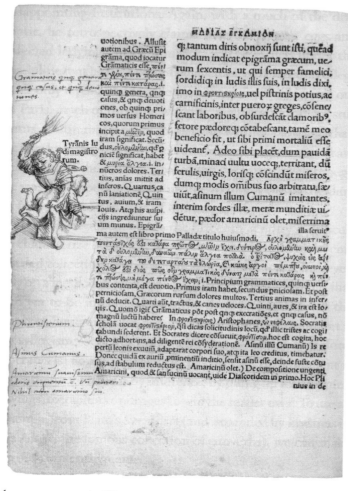

these pages are brilliant interpretations of the text, and they even include the first 'portrait' of Erasmus. On folio 51r there is a tiny Erasmus (who has been quoted by Folly in his own book) seated at a desk, and Myconius has written next to the sketch that when Erasmus saw this picture of himself in the

Hans Holbein the Younger, 'The tyranny of schoolmasters', drawing in a 1515 copy of *The Praise of Folly*.

margin, 'he exclaimed, Oh, Oh, if Erasmus looked like that to-day, he would at once find himself a wife' – an amusing irony from a celibate priest.[66]

In 1522 Erasmus added an index. *The Praise of Folly* is one of very few literary works to have a set of notes co-written

Hans Holbein the Younger, 'A scholar (Erasmus) at his desk', drawing in a 1515 copy of *The Praise of Folly.*

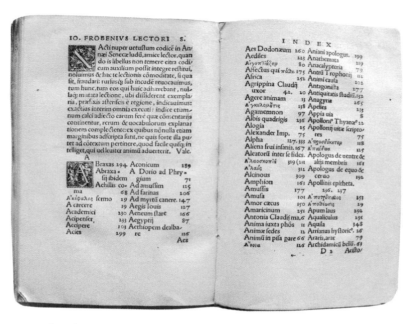

by the author, and it may well be the only one ever to have
an author-prepared *index vocum*, or index of key words. The
parody was now wrapped up in the scholarly trappings of an
ancient classic, further complicating and perhaps insulating
the presence of the author, who is both inside his book and
now outside it, commenting on it from the margins as though
he had not written it.

ENGLAND AND TEACHING OF THE YOUNG

Erasmus was in England, on and off, from 1509 to 1514. For
the first two years, there is no correspondence. There is spec-
ulation about how long he stayed with More, and about what
he may have otherwise been doing, but nothing certain is

An unusual addition to a work of fiction: Erasmus's index to the 1522
edition of *The Praise of Folly*.

known except for the books that he published. He was in Paris in 1511 (it was there that his *Folly* was first published), and for most of the time between 1511 and 1514 he was in Cambridge.

In 1509 John Colet had refounded St Paul's School with a new curriculum, a process that was later repeated in England in many schools that were founded or reorganized over the next century during an amazing expansion of the education system. All these schools – the old ones, including Eton and Winchester, and many new ones, such as Rugby, Harrow and Westminster – were reformed, refounded or founded during this century. These schools followed the humanist curriculum that emerged at this time, which was greatly influenced by Erasmus and his work for Colet at St Paul's. Erasmus outlined the ideal curriculum in his *Method of Study* (*De ratione studii*), which appeared with other works in Paris in 1512: a full programme of Latin and Greek that followed the ancient educational theorist Quintilian, but with a Christian direction. Erasmus also helped William Lily, the new high master of St Paul's School, to write a Latin grammar that was soon folded into the English authorized grammar book that survived, in various forms, until Benjamin Hall Kennedy's *Latin Primer* arrived in 1866. In addition, he wrote prayers for the boys.

When he was in Paris Erasmus had written a short intro-duction to Latin style for his pupils; this he transformed into a remarkable work on rhetoric, *On the Abundance of Both Words and Things* (known by the short title *Copia*), dedicating it to Colet in 1512. The work is a thorough discussion of style, aimed at producing the fluent, fast, amusing and attractive kind of

writing that one finds in his letters and *The Praise of Folly*. When
we write, we get stuck with certain phrases and we start repeating them. Over time, our writing seems to get thinner. Erasmus
shows how to vary our language, by expansion, contraction or
substitution. The book is still remembered for two lengthy
examples: 'Your letter pleased me mightily' and 'Always, as
long as I live, I shall remember you.'[67] The latter he varies in
154 different ways, for instance: 'You are too dear to my heart
ever to pass into forgetfulness, at least while I have life', or,
with a direct reference to his friend Thomas More, 'Only then
will Erasmus prove able to forget his beloved More, when he
ceases to be mindful of himself.'[68] The idea of bringing his
friend's name into this textbook is one of the personal touches
that remind us how important it was for Erasmus to present
himself as a visible subject in his own work and to demonstrate
the way that grammar is able to draw readers in to the scholarly Republic of Letters. The fancy stylistic variations were
standard in many textbooks; for instance, Aeneas Sylvius
Piccolomini (later Pope Pius II) gave similar variations at the
end of his *Precepts for the Art of Rhetoric* (1456). The highly varied
and copious style produces energetic writing, and it's a feature
of Renaissance vernacular as well as Latin (you find it in
Rabelais and Montaigne in French, as well as Shakespeare and
Spenser in English).[69] Though today our preferred style is
more stripped down, the method of his *Copia* is still alive in
the way that Erasmus emphasizes a living practice: not only
'do as I say', but 'do as I do'.

For two years, from December 1508 to the summer of 1511,
we have no letters from Erasmus. In August 1511 he had just
recovered from the sweating sickness, a deadly viral epidemic

particular to the sixteenth century (the actual source and nature of which remain unknown). The illness usually began with violent chills, then sweats, then a final collapse that often resulted in death. But Erasmus was a survivor. He arrived in Cambridge inauspiciously, astride a lame horse that actually fell 'headlong to the ground' several times along the road.[70] He had come at the invitation of the bishop John Fisher, now chancellor of the university and until recently president of Queens' College (Fisher, a patron of Erasmus, was executed by Henry VIII in the same year as More, and like him later canonized).

Erasmus was housed, we are told, at the top of the 'I' staircase in the Old Court of Queens'. He is a lasting presence in the history of the college; one of the fellows still uses the 'desk of Erasmus' (apparently of eighteenth-century manufacture, at some point backdated to an earlier time).[71] He held no formal position, though he did offer classes in Greek. He began with the grammar of Manuel Chrysoloras, a hundred-year-old introductory textbook that was still popular in schools, but his class was poorly attended; he switched to a more recent and more advanced text by the well-known Theodore Gaza, teacher of an earlier generation of Italian humanists (a text Erasmus himself would edit and publish in 1516), though it is unlikely that this change of textbook made a difference. We do not hear much from him about his teaching after the first few classes. He wrote a lot about teaching, but was he himself a good teacher? Most of the time he worked on his edition of the letters of St Jerome or the Latin text of the New Testament, and added more proverbs for another edition of his *Adages*.

Hans Holbein the Younger, *John Fisher, Bishop of Rochester*, c. 1532–4, black and coloured chalks, brown wash, pen and ink, brush and ink on pale pink prepared paper.

Erasmus was bored living in Cambridge, and he was soon writing to his friend Andrea Ammonio, then resident in London, asking for news. Among his many ailments Erasmus suffered from gout, and, as those who have gout know all too well, beer must be avoided. So Erasmus begged Ammonio to find him some wine – 'But quite dry wine please.'[72] He was so pleased with what Ammonio sent him that he wrote to his friend a long, flattering poem, which was followed by a series of letters complaining about how further casks had been tampered with or delayed. Ammonio, always the good friend, was both patient and amused. It is entertaining to see such minutely personal concerns in the letters, enacted in the elaborate play of compliments and exchange of gifts.

Erasmus had come to England in search of the wealth proposed in that earlier letter from his patron Mountjoy, but little was forthcoming: 'I am, so far as promises of gold are concerned, unmistakably wealthy, apart from which I live in stark hunger!' He had spent 72 nobles so far living in Cambridge. This amount is more than the annual salary of the headmaster at any of the larger schools in the country, and one assumes that the money was used up in the move to Cambridge and his need to purchase books, and the services of copyists and couriers. He also often tried to help friends, and on their behalf he wrote to Colet and Fisher, both of whom claimed to have no 'special funds'. Colet mysteriously responds, 'poverty will, albeit poorly, come to poverty's aid.'[73] In response to Colet, Erasmus admits his shamelessness in requesting money – 'yet I am not so proud as to reject a gift.'[74]

Erasmus at this time was not able to attain any regular income and was entirely reliant on handouts, which depended

on the whims of his patrons; such was the cost of the freedom
he sought. There was a personal toll in all of this. As he said
to Ammonio: 'the embarrassment of my situation is now
heavier to bear than its discomforts.'[75] The irony of his situation is painful, given that he had some of the best patrons
in England, including the Archbishop of Canterbury. It was
only in March 1511 that he was made rector of Aldington par-
ish in Kent, which finally provided him with a living. But
rather than reside there, he gave up the appointment in July
of the next year, in exchange for a permanent pension paid to
him by the resident priest. This kind of skimming was common at the time, and given Erasmus's attacks on the greed of
churchmen, his acceptance of this necessary gift might well
strike us as hypocritical. After the publication of the *Copia* in
1512, he was not above writing to his friend Colet for the 15
angels (about £5) he had been promised for dedicating the
book to him.[76]

The problem of money also comes up in a long letter
Erasmus received from his former roommate in Venice, Girolamo Aleandro. Erasmus had encouraged him to move to
Paris, where he became a successful teacher of Greek. Despite
this success, Aleandro was in a similar position to Erasmus,
unhappy about both university bureaucracy and money: 'I am
living – but living day to day . . . if you look in my treasury
you will find there only spiders' webs.'[77] If he gave a free lecture the hall is packed, but if he was to charge a fee 'you can
see them all run off, "as do Chaonian doves when eagles stoop"'
(the learned allusion to Virgil's *Eclogue* 9 is the kind of thing
a scholar-humanist especially enjoyed). Of course in hindsight
the two men's complaints of poverty are ironic, for Erasmus

later prospered financially and Aleandro became a cardinal.
By the autumn of 1512 Erasmus was writing to Adolph of
Burgundy to offer to move back to the Low Countries so long
as he might obtain some kind of 'moderate competency', for
there had been no 'mountains of English gold'. Though the
panic over Erasmus's finances was soon to subside, worries
about money never left him.[78]

In February 1513, Pope Julius II died. This pope was
remembered both for his magnificence (he was the patron
of Bramante, Raphael and Michelangelo) and as *il papa terribile*
– the latter for his energetic political aggression, which
Machiavelli praised him for. For Erasmus, Julius epitomized
two of the core problems of the Church at Rome, greed and
war, and scholars are now mostly in agreement that Erasmus
was the author of the remarkable satirical dialogue *Julius
Locked Out from Heaven* (*Iulius exclusus e coelis*) – based on an
earlier dialogue by the Roman writer Seneca – which circulated in manuscript before it appeared anonymously in print
in 1518.[79] Julius, a noisy, brash, insistent character, has arrived
at the pearly gates and seeks entrance to heaven, but is refused
by St Peter because his violent life was entirely un-Christian;
Julius is accompanied by his Genius, here a kind of court fool
who adds an ironic commentary on the pope's claims that
because of his public displays, his buildings and his quest for
'towns belonging by right to the see of Rome', he 'served
Christ and the church so well'.[80] The work is closely related to
the anti-war and anti-wealth message that is found so strongly
delivered in Erasmus's *Adages* and *Folly*. Erasmus consistently,
if somewhat coyly, denied his authorship, and the work was
believed by some to have been written by Ulrich von Hutten,

Raphael, *Pope Julius II*, 1511, oil on poplar.

a warrior knight who was also a gifted satirist and a follower of Luther. Though there is no 'Erasmus' in this work or on the early title pages, there is an Erasmian presence that can be sensed very strongly, especially in the speech at the end by St Peter on the philosophy of Christ. It is no surprise that many contemporaries saw Erasmus as the author, nor is it

Julius II, fully armed, trying to get into Heaven, from *Von den Gewalt und Haupt der Kirchen*, a German translation of the *Iulius* (1521).

surprising that Erasmus should have felt the need to conceal his authorship.

BASEL AND FROBEN

During his time in Cambridge Erasmus had been working on three projects: a set of annotations on the New Testament; the letters of Jerome; and a fresh expanded edition of the *Adages*. All were now nearing completion. He needed the best possible printer, and for the revised *Adages* he planned to turn to Josse Bade in Paris, who had printed earlier works. He relied on an agent and bookseller named Franz Birckmann to get his material to Bade, but Birckmann sent it instead to Johann Froben in Basel. Erasmus had seen Froben's 1513 pirated version of the *Adages* and even though such an improper theft annoyed him he was so impressed with the quality of the production that he may already have decided to skip Bade and go to Froben (so that Birckmann's decision may have been privately approved by Erasmus beforehand). Going to Froben also made sense because a circle of scholars in Basel were preparing an edition of the works of St Jerome, and Erasmus's edition of Jerome's letters could be folded into that project. In autumn 1514 Erasmus headed up the Rhine to Basel.

On his way Erasmus stopped in Strasbourg, where he was given a rapturous welcome to the German lands by a small group of influential scholars who knew of his earlier writings, mainly the *Adages* and *The Praise of Folly*, and who were excited to have such a phenomenon move into their world. It was clear to them, and gratifying to Erasmus, that he was the 'prince of scholars', a reputation he had earned from his earlier work, chiefly the *Adages*. They were quick to claim this learned colleague from the Low Countries as a fellow German. When he arrived in Basel, Erasmus was also welcomed by a small circle of keen younger scholars: Beatus Rhenanus remained a devoted friend to the end and later wrote the first short biography of Erasmus after his death; Gerardus Listrius was to publish the learned commentary on *The Praise of Folly* just a year after meeting Erasmus; and Bruno Amerbach was one of the sons of the recently deceased scholar-printer Johann Amerbach, who had conceived of the Basel edition of Jerome.

In a long letter thanking the learned Jakob Wimpfeling for the greeting in Strasbourg, Erasmus described his unusual first meeting with Froben:

> I gave Johann Froben a letter from Erasmus, adding that I was very closely acquainted with him, that he had entrusted to me the whole business of publishing his work, and that whatever steps I took would have the same authority as if they had been taken by Erasmus himself; in fact, I said, Erasmus and I are so alike that if you have seen one, you have seen the other. He was delighted later on when he saw through the trick.[81]

What an odd little ruse, with the magic discovery of the *real* Erasmus at the end. And how strange that Erasmus should consider himself to be such a wonderful surprise. Now and then we get a glimpse of his odd humour. Nevertheless, Erasmus's happiness shows the comfort he felt right from the start. Basel, a small but prosperous city with an active community of scholars and printers, was the kind of place in which he could live happily. Indeed, Erasmus was to spend more years of his adult life there than anywhere else.

Hardly had Erasmus arrived than the presses began to print a first small project, a collection of essays translated from the Greek of Plutarch. This was completed by the end of February 1515. Immediately afterwards, the house turned to the revision of the *Adages*. The new edition contained many new proverbs, but also around a dozen essays that had been considerably expanded in line with *The Praise of Folly*. This collection of proverbs became the unlikely vehicle for some of Erasmus's most vocal social criticism (much along the lines of what Thomas More had begun to write in his *Utopia*). The commentary on the proverb *Dulce bellum inexpertis* ('War is a treat for those who have not tried it') was revised into a long, sustained and passionate essay on the condemnation of war and in praise of peace.[82] This tour de force was often published in a separate form (even into the nineteenth century).

Another essay of political reform was the revised account of the proverb 'the dung beetle pursues the eagle'.[83] Erasmus tells the ancient tale of the permanent war between the vicious 'people-devouring' eagle and the nasty, low-born dung beetle, who, in an act of revenge for the eagle's tyranny, pushes the eagle's eggs out of the bird's nest. The beetle is so crafty that it manages to destroy the eagle's eggs even after they have been given to the god Jupiter for protection. The dung beetle may be small and disgusting, but it has persistance and guile. Hence a warning: to use the words Erasmus wrote in his *Education of a Christian Prince* (1516), 'not even the most powerful prince can afford to provoke or disregard even the humblest enemy.'[84] The point is not, however, that the dung beetle is admirable in the way it seeks revenge. But the surprising power of the dungbeetle shows that the tension between the powerful and the apparently powerless is never resolved. Instead the essay is a warning about revolution from below. The only solution to this permanent class conflict is Christian community.

Another of the expanded essays was 'The Sileni of Alcibiades'.[85] We have already briefly touched in Chapter One on the memorable image of the statues of Silenus with the golden gods inside. In Plato, Alcibiades describes how Socrates is 'crazy about beautiful boys'.[86] Not surprisingly, Erasmus passes over the homoerotic implication of Alcibiades' praise of Socrates. For Erasmus, the image is all about the *anagnorisis*, the magic moment of revelation, when an unpretentious man is shown to be a great philosopher, or the reverse, when a great aristocrat or finely clothed bishop is revealed as a mediocrity. The point is the cognitive moment of shock when the truth is revealed. The essay then concentrates on the figure of Christ, notably the contrast between his simple humanity and his divine presence in our lives, following Erasmus's earlier observation in the *Enchiridion* that the Gospels are 'like those images of Silenus mentioned by Alcibiades [that] enclose unadulterated divinity under a lowly and almost ludicrous external appearance', an extraordinary union of the classical tradition and Christianity.[87] This talk of occultation or concealment and the opening up to revelation is also close to the central argument of his *Praise of Folly*, where the claim that even Christians are fools is another unexpected discovery. It is even rather like the way that Erasmus chose to present himself to

Froben on their first encounter, in which Erasmus offered himself up as a special surprise.

Soon after the *Adages* and the annotated *Praise of Folly* of 1515, Erasmus left Basel for a three-month trip back to England, in large part to complete work on the two major projects of the New Testament and St Jerome. He brought his manuscripts of Jerome and copies of the new *Adages* with him, but panicked when the box, entrusted to a friend, was temporarily waylaid. His edition of the works of Seneca had gone to press, but he received anxious correspondence from the press correctors regarding amendments. He returned to Basel in July 1515. By August the promised edition of Seneca had appeared (an edition that Erasmus later regretted because of its many errors), along with some educational work. Erasmus was busy.

THE NEW TESTAMENT

Now the printers turned to the most complex and demanding scholarly project of Erasmus's career. The discovery of Valla's work in 1505 had been transformative, and in 1511, during his time at Cambridge, Erasmus had been studying in detail the language of the Vulgate (or Latin) New Testament, working his way word by word through the text, consulting manuscripts in both Latin and the original Greek. The precise form of the presentation of his work only began to emerge as he approached publication. His principal effort had been in annotating the text (following the model of Valla), but it was only by the time of his arrival in Basel that he seems to have decided on adding to his own detailed scholarly notes a full

Latin text and also one in Greek, the latter addition encouraged
by Froben, who could see a financial advantage in producing
the first printed Greek text (in advance of scholars in Spain,
whose massive polyglot Bible was in production, but whose
edition of the New Testament had been delayed).[88]

The work went to press in autumn and the printing was
finished after an intense six-month period. The process was
demanding. The printers, we are told, used two presses and
printed 1,000 copies, twelve folio pages a day (requiring on
each of those days at least 6,000 pulls on the press, or maybe
double if the presses could not handle a full sheet). The
labour and the pace were brutal, and not just for the printers.
The compositors who set the type worked not only in Latin
but in ancient Greek, with its many accents and ligatures, and
some Hebrew as well. Erasmus and his small team of younger
scholars who worked as correctors not only had to have the
copy ready for printing, but they had to proofread the text as
the first sheets came off the press and recheck the print after
the corrections were made. The working conditions must have
been similar to what Erasmus had experienced in Venice with
the *Adages*.

The first edition Erasmus called the *Novum instrumentum*,
which means a 'new instrument' or apparatus, a 'new record'
or 'document' or, in a more medieval sense, a 'new instruction'. In later editions he changed the title to the familiar
Novum testamentum, the witnessing of Christ and the Christian
faith. To understand the need for a refreshed Bible, we have
to look back to Erasmus's *Enchiridion*, in which he had already
begun to outline his idea of Christianity. For Erasmus the
Christ of the Bible should be fully accessible. The words of

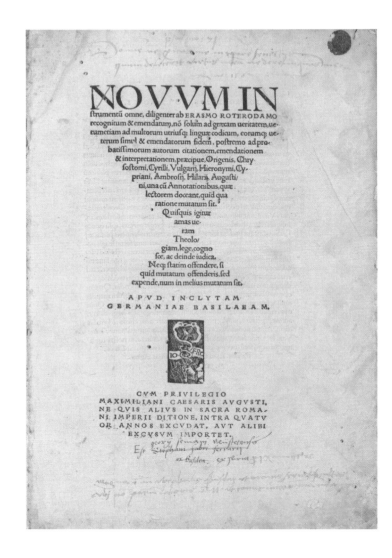

NOVVM IN

strumentũ omne, diligenter ab ERASMO ROTERODAMO
recognitum & emendatum, nõ folũm ad græcam ueritatem, ue-
rumetiam ad multorum utriufq; linguæ codicum, eorumq; ue-
terum fimvl & emendatorum fidem, poftremo ad pro-
batiffimorum autorum citationem, emendationem
& interpretationem, præcipue, Origenis, Chry-
foftomi, Cyrilli, Vulgarij, Hieronymi, Cy-
priani, Ambrofij, Hilarij, Augufti,
ni, una cũ Annotationibus, quæ
lectorem doceant, quid qua
ratione mutatum fit.
Quifquis igitur
amas ue-
ram
Theolo,
giam, lege, cogno
fce, ac deinde iudica.
Neq; ftatim offendere, fi
quid mutatum offenderis, fed
expende, num in melius mutatum fit.

APVD INCLYTAM
GERMANIAE BASILAEAM.

CVM PRIVILEGIO
MAXIMILIANI CAESARIS AVGVSTI,
NE QVIS ALIVS IN SACRA ROMA-
NI IMPERII DITIONE, INTRA QVATV
OR ANNOS EXCVDAT, AVT ALIBI
EXCVSVM IMPORTET.

Title page of *Novum instrumentum* (Basel, 1516).

the Bible show us Christ more clearly than any saint, scholastic commentator or simple priest can do via intercessional prayer, commentary or sermon. Erasmus's emphasis on a personal and direct faith can be traced in part to the communitarian and pietistic faith of the *devotio moderna*, the religious movement that he knew directly and indirectly via his early schooling and upbringing in the Netherlands, but also in part to his humanist idea, which came from his classical models, that a personal presence can be discovered in a written text. The Christ envisioned at the end of *The Praise of Folly* presents the rawest form of this personal religion that leads to a full reformation of one's spiritual life. Christ exists in the very words of the Bible, so the words in Latin need to be aligned as closely as possible with the Greek (Erasmus was aware that the actual language of Christ was not Greek, but because the four gospels were divinely inspired, the Greek provided direct access to Christ's meaning).[89]

To publish an edition of the Bible or even annotations to the Bible was hardly a novelty. The first major printed book in the West was a Bible magnificently produced by Gutenberg in Mainz some sixty years earlier, and there had been at least a hundred different Bible printings since. What Erasmus did, however, was extraordinarily ambitious and highly controversial – he maintained that the Latin Bible currently in circulation was flawed in many places. Even though such an opinion might now seem obvious to us, and was accepted by scholars then, the position verged on the heretical for many. How could the book of God be full of errors? Erasmus certainly saw the New Testament as divine in origin, however it had not, after all, been written in Latin originally, but in

Greek. For him it was no heresy to maintain that human translations are subject to error. In this position, he was following Lorenzo Valla. Furthermore, the actual copies in circulation compounded the errors already found in the mistranslation. Every copied text represented a step away from the original (a normal degradation found in all forms of copying). Because the Latin text was copied again and again, new errors were inevitably introduced. Erasmus proposed to clean up the text, to correct the Latin in relation to the original Greek, and to provide explanatory notes for places where there were errors or potential difficulties in the interpretation of the language. Of course, in doing this, Erasmus himself was capable of error, but the awareness of error, and a proposed method of correcting it, could result in a vastly improved text.

The printed text of the annotated *Novum instrumentum*, finished by February 1516 and on sale by March, is a splendid and substantial folio volume, 992 pages in length. It contains an impressive title page; a note from Froben, the publisher; and a lengthy introduction, containing a dedication to Pope Leo X, which briefly states the nature of the project:

> I perceived that that teaching which is our salvation was to be had in a much purer and more lively form if sought at the fountain-head and drawn from the actual sources than from pools and runnels. And so I have revised the whole New Testament (as they call it) against the standard of the Greek original . . . I have added annotations of my own, in order in the first place to show the reader what changes I have made, and why; second, to disentangle and explain anything

that may be complicated, ambiguous, or obscure; and
lastly as a protection, that it might be less easy in future
to corrupt what I have restored at the cost of scarcely
credible exertions.[90]

Then follows a *paraclesis* or supplication by Erasmus to the
reader, a *methodus*, or guide to interpretation (later expanded
into a *System of True Theology* or *Ratio verae theologiae*, an extraordinary book about how to read the text), and his *Apologia*, in which
he tried to forestall criticism of his project by seeking the
good will of the reader.[91] After 28 pages of this preliminary
material, the text follows in two columns, with the Greek on
the left and a corrected Vulgate Latin on the right. Annotations
on some thousand different passages follow directly after.
The volume ends with a short epistle from Johannes Oecolampadius (the Hebrew expert on the project) to the reader,
and two pages of errata, for errors began to be found even
before the text was released.

Scholars have often described the *Novum instrumentum* as
an edition of the Greek New Testament, as it was indeed the
first Greek version in print. Of course Froben could see the
financial advantage, but Erasmus was less concerned about
the Greek than about the Latin; the Greek was there mainly
to serve as evidence in the way that Valla before him had used
the Greek text. Indeed, Erasmus's Greek text was not prepared that well. Rather than compare many Greek manuscripts
(today we know there are some 5,400 Greek manuscripts of
the New Testament[92]) to see where errors occurred and to
figure out why, Erasmus merely reached for the best Greek
text he could find in the immediate region. Fortunately the

quality of his manuscript sources, which came from the local Dominicans in Basel, was good, though even these needed careful attention in transcription. The result is, however, by modern standards, a text with limited authority. Moreover, his text of Revelation was incomplete, so he back-translated from the Latin to the Greek to complete it (he had also done this here and there in his *Adages*, with proverbs he believed to be Greek in origin). Nevertheless, his work proved to be foundational.

Erasmus's principal task was in his scholarly annotations, which, proceeding by word and phrase, noted changes and explained them, sometimes in great detail, by lexicon, grammar, orthography and transmission of text. Some of the work was rushed. But Erasmus was not to be delayed by details. Indeed, as he admitted to a new friend, the great French scholar Guillaume Budé, shortly after he finished: 'Some things I even passed over of set purpose; to many I knowingly closed my eyes, and then changed my opinion soon after publication. And so I prepare the second edition.'[93]

Despite its problems, the *Novum instrumentum* immediately became an essential tool for believers who desired to return to the original source of the Christian faith. Of course, this technical study was not to everyone's taste, nor indeed was it intended for everyone. Erasmus envisioned that it would be used by scholars, although it is important to remember that the term 'scholar' at that time referred to the highly educated, not to professional academics. Initial sales were slow.[94] The work was highly praised and also strongly criticized, but Erasmus was ahead of his critics, having moved on to a second edition. In the end he did four revisions: in 1519,

1522, 1527 and 1535. The history of these editions makes a fascinating and complex story. Each new edition was produced to correct previous errors, to bring in new sources (including more from the Church Fathers), to offer more sophisticated interpretations of difficult passages, to bring his findings here and there into line with other editions that appeared, and to respond, sometimes with intensity, to the critics who were now attacking his work.

In the second edition, of 1519, Erasmus made hundreds of corrections and provided a more radically revised translation of the New Testament. The most famous change was his translation of the Greek at John 1:1: 'In the beginning was the word.' The Greek was *En archê ên ho logos*; Erasmus changed the traditional Latin *In principio erat verbum* to *In principio erat sermo* – the Greek *logos* was changed from *verbum* or 'single word' (often understood as 'law' or 'final decision') to *sermo*, 'spoken language' or 'speech' or even 'conversation'. The history behind the shifting translations of *logos* to *sermo* and *verbum* is complex, for both Latin words were often cited as synonyms, as Erasmus himself notes in his annotation. But he also observed that '*Sermo* more perfectly explains why the evangelist wrote *logos*, because among Latin-speaking men *verbum* does not express speech as a whole but one particular saying. But Christ is for this reason called *logos*: because whatsoever the Father speaks, he speaks through the Son.'[95] Yet, as we witness in his correspondence, Erasmus always strove to see language as an exchange among friends. *Sermo* is how he would describe the words being spoken by Jesus and the Evangelists, and in his translation he traces this kind of communication back to God. After all, we do not speak one word at a time, but in a flow, and *sermo* seems right if you see language as the words strung together contextually in a dynamic sequence, with each word given meaning in relation to others. He continued his argument for this translation in 1520, in *Apologia de 'In principio erat sermo'* (An Apology Regarding 'In the Beginning was the Word').

In addition to many very specific corrections Erasmus also began to mount a stronger defence for his work, which was soon attacked in waves. In the 1519 text he added *Capita argumentorum contra morosos quosdam ac indoctos* (Summary Arguments against Certain Contentious and Boorish People). Sometimes Erasmus would attack his critics (though never naming them directly) in the annotations themselves. At Matthew 6 in the Lord's Prayer, 'forgive us our trespasses', the Greek for 'forgive' is *aphes* (from *aphiêmi*, which has many different meanings: 'release, let go, suffer, permit' as well as 'forgive'). The Vulgate translates the Greek *aphes* as Latin *dimitte* (which can mean 'send away' or 'dismiss', as well as 'forgive'). Erasmus innocently asks, why not consider an alternative translation – 'why not rather *remitte*?' (*remitte* can mean 'forgive', but with a different emphasis, as it also means 'send back, relax, forego'). He goes on to show how the verb *remitto* is used elsewhere in the Vulgate (from where we have inherited the English phrase 'remission of sin'). For even raising this question he was attacked, so in a note on this passage in the 1519 edition, he let fly:

> Pray, what sort of people are these men? I write a modest note, saying in a few words what is correct, never uttering a single word that need disturb another who finds

dimitte more agreeable . . . and these people rail against me in sermons before unlearned folk, provoking them to attack; they rave at drinking parties, they rant in servant's quarters, on ships, on wagons, and who knows where else. Christian religion is done and over with, they say, they themselves studied theology in vain, for someone has appeared who does not shy away from corrupting the Lord's Prayer.[96]

Erasmus did not hesitate to take criticisms personally, and to use them as part of the dramatic presentation of his ideas, and to insist, as a scholar, on the correctness of his interpretation.

In the third edition, published in 1522, Erasmus made dramatic changes and shored up his positions with quotations from the Church Fathers. In the first two editions he had, according to his critics, left out a few words in the First Epistle of John 5:7–8, which appears towards the end of the New Testament (one of two letters believed to have been written by the Evangelist John when he lived in Ephesus). This verse in the Greek manuscripts reads, 'For there are three that bear record: the Spirit, and the water, and the blood, and these three agree in one.' But the Vulgate text had a longer text: '[7] For there are three that bear record *in heaven, the Father, the Word, and the Holy Ghost: and these three are one.* [8] *And there are three that bear witness in earth*, the Spirit, and the Water, and the Blood, and these three agree in one.' (The italicized text shows you the part Erasmus added, given here in the King James Version, and I have given the verse numbers, which did not regularly appear in any Bible editions until 1551, when the French printer Robert Estienne reprinted Erasmus's Latin translation.) The passage, known as the Johannine Comma (here 'comma' means 'clause', rather than a punctuation mark), was not in the Greek texts consulted by Erasmus, so he left out the words in his editions of 1516 and 1519. Omitting a direct reference to the Trinity suggested to his critics that he had slipped into the Arian heresy (a rejection of the Trinity); there was a rush of attacks, mostly from the Spanish scholar Diego López Zúñiga (also known as Stunica), who had participated in the production of the great Spanish Complutensian Bible.[97] A Greek manuscript was discovered that had the full text. So Erasmus decided to include the words of the Comma in 1522, even though he was convinced that this later Greek text had been revised in light of the Vulgate Latin. It seems his suspicions were entirely correct. But by adjusting the text, Erasmus managed to quiet his critics at least on this issue.[98]

The 1522 edition also now included his translation next to a Latin Vulgate and the Greek, in three columns. This edition is usually treated as the most authoritative, and was used by William Tyndale as a basis of his English translation in 1526. Erasmus's fourth (1527) and fifth (1535) editions offered many further refinements, demonstrating that the process of revision was never dropped over the years. In the 1516 edition the annotations had filled just under three hundred folio pages; by 1535 the number had more than doubled to 783, an extraordinary expansion but perhaps not so surprising, considering the seriousness of the debates and Erasmus's own tendency to expand his writing whenever he revised it (as he did so dramatically with the *Adages*).

With the publication of the New Testament, Erasmus had shown himself to be the master scholar of his time. He had moved beyond Valla in a few ways. He could now see that using the Greek as the basis for correcting the Latin text had problems, for the Greek Bible was obviously also subject to its own errors of transcription. Erasmus also saw that he could use other texts to correct the Bible; the early Church Fathers in their many writings often quoted from different versions of the Bible in Latin or Greek, and their use offered piecemeal hints to the way that the Bible had been known in late antiquity, before the medieval scribal tradition had introduced errors (though, of course, even the transcriptions of the Fathers were also likely in places to be corrupted). And unlike Valla, who had only provided a series of notes, Erasmus actually prepared a full translation.

Erasmus was able to show to a wider range of readers, who were drawn in to the debates, the importance of an educated and sensitive close reading of the specific words of the New Testament. He was hugely influential in drawing his readership away from the dialectical philosophy of the schools, to a more intimate encounter with the prime source of the Christian faith, both in the way he annotated the Bible and in his writings on how to read the biblical text. His enemies saw his approach as mere 'grammar', but Erasmus was able to connect the words on the page to the fraught theological debates of the time. The direct encounter with the biblical text became essential to Protestant sects, informing the rise of the Reformation, and his editions were used by scholars to create new translations. Even Luther, with whom Erasmus fought, used the 1519 edition of the New Testament for his famous translation into German, and he also carefully annotated his own copy of Erasmus's edition of 1527.[99]

Erasmus's commitment to an educated and sensitive close reading of the New Testament was apparent in his introductory documents and in the annotations themselves, and in the fierceness with which he defended this project. His edition was thus an extraordinary accomplishment, because it was not just an immense labour, it was also daring, morally committed, and the sign of a very particular kind of faith that was personal and which saw the words of Christ as the most immediate path to a fully realized faith. It swiftly gathered supporters as well as critics.

The new learning, with its intrusion of grammar into theology, was proving to be a most disruptive force to the theological faculties in the universities and some of the thinkers in the religious orders. The first serious salvo of the critics came after the second edition. Much of Erasmus's life for the next twenty years was spent fending off his critics, who now emerged in abundance, agitated not just by his criticism of scholastic philosophy, monastic life, the Church hierarchy and Catholic superstition, along with his annoying irony, but now also by his apparent tampering with the Divine Word. There was also something vaguely insolent about a single scholar completing a Greek text shortly before the publication by the immensely learned committee in the Complutensian university of Alcalà de Henares, near Madrid. These scholars had worked for years on their remarkable Complutensian Bible, with Old and New Testaments to be reproduced in all the relevant ancient languages. Their Greek New Testament had actually been printed in 1514, but they had to wait for the completion of their project and its papal approval before its distribution in the early 1520s. Yet Froben had already

secured a four-year monopoly on the Greek text as a form of
imperial decree. As was often the case, Erasmus got there
first. And he happily consulted the Complutensian Bible for
later editions of his own *Novum testamentum*.

ST JEROME

Erasmus had barely completed the exhausting labour on the
New Testament when he turned to his volumes of the collected works of St Jerome. From his very early years Erasmus
had been a reader of the great scholar and saint of late antiquity. In about 1489 he wrote from Steyn to his friend and
fellow Augustinian canon Cornelis Gerard about the letters
of Jerome: 'I have long ago not only read them, but copied
out all of them with my own hands.'[100] After he left England
on his first visit he announced his plans to prepare an edition
of Jerome,[101] and during his time in Cambridge in 1511–14,
he finally prepared an annotated edition of the letters. He
brought a draft of this work with him to Basel and continued
to work on it during his brief interlude in 1515 back in England.
Now he joined the Amerbach brothers to complete the nine-
volume edition of the complete works. His contribution filled
the first four volumes, mostly the letters and the expository
writings but also a section of works that had long circulated
under Jerome's name, but which he clearly identified as spurious. Erasmus's material was printed by June, and the
remaining five volumes of Jerome's biblical commentaries,
prepared by the Amerbachs, were finished in September.[102]

　　To make their edition, the editors had sought out many
extant manuscripts to find clues to the earliest and purest

text. They also relied on their own judgement of the language, to repair apparent errors in the Latin. It was slow work: 'like a modern Hercules I set out on my most laborious but most glorious campaign, taking the field almost unaided against all the monsters of error.'[103] Erasmus's manuscript notes for the edition are still extant in the University Library of Basel; as part of his work he used an interesting method for cutting and pasting the text. He used little drawings in the margin as markers to show the insertion of text from elsewhere in the manuscript; the cartoons of a face, perhaps because of the prominent nose, are now treated as self-portraits.

Despite his amusing methods, Erasmus claimed that 'the writing of his books cost Jerome less effort than I spent in the restoring of them.'[104] An edition of a text is more than an unthinking transcription of an earlier source. For a corrected edition, you have to weigh every word in the light of what is known about the language and also about the way the author is known to use the language. The quotations have to be identified, and odd uses explained. Sometimes there are strange and elusive problems. The scholar must be erudite, but must also exercise care and a moral commitment to the project:

> I only wish that all good scholars would devote all their forces to the task of restoring as far as possible to its original purity whatever in the way of good authors has somehow survived after such numerous shipwrecks! But I should not like to see anyone enter this field who is not as well equipped with honesty, accuracy, judgment, and readiness to take pains as he

Antonello da Messina, *St Jerome in His Study*, c. 1475, oil on limewood.

A Viam relinquere regiam. Regiam publicam ac
rectam vocat, alludens interim ad locum, q[ui]
est numeri Capi. xx. Moses missis nuncijs ad
Edom, petit transitum p[er] illius fines. Hortatur:
mandat frater tuus Israhel Ac post pauca
Navibimus q[ue] p[er] agros, nec p[er] vineas, nec bibemus
aquas de putris tuis, sed gradiemur via publica
nec ad dexteram, nec ad sinistram declinantes
donec transeamus terminos tuos.

Ex hac epistola et superioribus ad Heliodorum et Nepotianum
satis liquet, quæ sub divi Hieronymi ævi fuisse hic monachorum
genus, quod nunc passim videmus. Quittit possessionem vi
familiari, modo mediocrum, quittit uxorem cum matre
cum prole cum liberis, modo fugiat superbiam
ac periculosam consuetudinem, hortatur p[er] exigit, ut
si male poterit uiuere, in gubernio multorum, paucis
alijsue arbitrio uiuat potius q[uam] sibi suo, quod diserens
causa sanctoris aduersus exigentes laudat probat. De cucullo
de colore aut figura uestis nulla curatio, tantum ne
grave uestium et curiosa uult esse, ut nec sordibus
hypocrisim nec nitore fastum sapiat. Nec de reditibus
uotis, usq[ue] uerbum fit ullum. Vota hæc a nauribus
adiecta sunt, constructibus in dies uronachorum turmis.
Adde q[uod] Hieronymi temporibus, monachi cum ipso
pl[ur]i agebant, et clericorum munere fungebantur
sicut et cæteri. Foruisse ea uix magis expediret
republ[ic]æ christianæ, si pauciora forent monasteria.
et idem circa cultus, ordinum, uestratio, postremo
cerimoniarum ac statutorum.

Nihil christiano

Antidotum.

These cartoons of a face, often claimed to be a self-caricature of Erasmus,
began as part of a series of image place markers for inserted text in the
manuscript for the Jerome edition.

is with erudition; for there is no more cruel enemy of good literature than the man who sets out to correct it half-instructed, half-asleep, hasty, and of unsound judgment.[105]

The most important part of this work for the modern reader of Erasmus is his biography of Jerome, which appeared in the first volume right after the dedication to William Warham. It was here that Erasmus explained and defended the importance of Jerome for the contemporary Christian. Jerome was a bridge to the Bible and the old faith, someone of great learning who was able to merge classical culture and Christianity. He brought clarity and articulate style as well as understanding to his theological writing. But even more importantly, he was a model Christian, who was not perfect but who nonetheless sought purity in his life and work, an ideal for the Christian humanist.

Erasmus's short biography insists on a degree of accuracy not found in medieval accounts of the saint's life: 'I think that nothing is better than to portray the saints just as they actually were.'[106] Of course, as we have already shown in the first chapter of this book, the best way to find Jerome is in Jerome's own writings, so 'above all I have based my inquiry into Jerome's life on the works of Jerome himself. For who would have a better knowledge of Jerome than Jerome himself?' In doing so, Erasmus says, 'I invented nothing.'[107] He takes us from Jerome's birth through his education, his choice of the monastic life (which offered 'freedom', the 'power to come and to go as one wished', and 'the practice of the original, free, and purely Christian life'), his friendships, his travels to Rome, Syria, Egypt and Bethlehem, his 'fasting, vigils, and an unbelievable austerity', his studies. Erasmus does not neglect the famous dream of Jerome, in which 'he was carried off to the judgment seat of God and accused of being a Ciceronian and not being a Christian', and how he was chastened. There are his conflicts with those who envied him, for his writings 'clearly reveal his impetuous and fiery nature',[108] especially his conflict with Rufinus; yet these writings were necessary considering the attacks against him. All this study and writing was done in spite of 'frequent and prolonged illnesses even before he reached old age'.[109] Of course, Erasmus found it 'distasteful to say anything at all about his miracles', but focused instead on his 'blameless life',[110] for even if he was not a virgin (as Jerome clearly says in his writing), the saint was able to admire virginity. Erasmus concludes the life by reviewing opinions of Jerome and defending him from the critics, even including those moderns who have picked away at his learning:

> Let each sex and age study him, read him, drink him in. For there is no kind of teaching which cannot use his support, no way of life which may not be formed by his precepts. Let only the heretics abhor and hate Jerome. They were the only ones he always considered the bitterest of enemies.[111]

This biography is not just a clue to the life of Jerome. Erasmus clearly looks back on this great father of the Church, with his long life, his strenuous fending off of his critics, his love of literature and his piety, as a model. Many readers have noted that as you read Erasmus's biography of Jerome you are tempted to put the name 'Erasmus' in almost every place where Erasmus uses and praises the name 'Jerome'. As the scholars remind us, it is not that simple.

THREE

Affirmation, 1516–36

y 1516 Erasmus had published himself into fame. He had accomplished three huge projects and published numerous other books, and, in doing so, had also presented himself to a new public. Two years earlier, when he first ascended the Rhine to work with Froben, he was already seen, because of his *Adages*, as a triumphant 'prince of scholars'. Now, with his New Testament and its controversial set of annotations, he had shown his daring. He was also achieving financial independence. He even began to speak with some confidence about the intellectual and social world, in his own rather cautious words to Pope Leo X: 'This age of ours . . . has good hopes of becoming an age of gold, if such a thing there ever were.'[1] Yet the period that followed, with the sudden emergence of the Reformation, was certainly no age of gold for Erasmus. But his later years are not, as some have suggested, a time of decline or tragedy. Decline for Erasmus would be a cessation of publication, the end of his correspondence, a weakening of his wit or literary style, possibly accompanied by a permanent position in the Church or a court. In his final years he was immensely productive, and he managed, at great cost, to maintain his independence.

Despite increasing health problems and a grinding commitment to answering his adversaries, Erasmus engaged in a continuous affirmation of his ideas through a daunting programme of research and publication. It was the period of one of his most lively works, the *Colloquies*, as well as some of his best writing on pedagogy, stylistics and biblical interpretation. He also pressed on with a vast project of editing the early Church Fathers. Within the relatively small but widely situated elite culture of Latin readers, people continued to turn to him for inspiration. It is estimated that for a time his books represented as much as 5 per cent of all the books for sale in all of Europe, a performance surpassed only by Martin Luther.[2] He was seen as offering a model way of writing and an exemplary way of reading and interpreting older texts, of approaching Christ and possible salvation directly through the language of the Bible. He continued to use his own presence as a way for readers to engage with humanist ideas and Christian faith.

Writers, artists and scholars sometimes turn inwards with their visions and their gifts. Erasmus, as Luther shrewdly noted, was orientated towards the world. His particular vision of scholarship was devoted to an idea of the public good, which he saw represented by the moral reform of individuals and the possibility of a united Christian Church. So he pressed on, trying to win over those who disagreed with him, or at the least to prevent those who did agree with him from slipping into the fold of his opponents. Sometimes the resulting nuances were hard to follow – for his friends as well as his enemies. As we shall see, the debate with Luther was especially complex, for Erasmus initially approved of many aspects of the Lutheran challenge, and Luther initially admired Erasmus's scholarship and his critique of the contemporary Church. But this early mutual agreement did not last long or end well. And, related to his responses to Luther and other Lutherans, Erasmus also had to write many *apologiae* or 'defences' against his Catholic critics who resented a grammarian's intrusion into theology. His correspondence swelled as he laboured to maintain old ties and to establish new friendships with supporters and patrons. At the same time, he continued not just with new publications, but with revision of the old, sometimes just to correct errors but often to refresh the text with a new preface or new information. In part this work was necessitated by the conditions of publishing, for there were only very primitive forms of copyright (for instance local regulations by guilds, or sometimes a monopoly granted for a larger jurisdiction); revisions helped to keep revenues and his reputation intact.

All this attention and fame evoked new perspectives in the way Erasmus could be seen. Until this point in his life much of what we know about Erasmus comes from Erasmus himself. Now we begin to see him from many different perspectives – the way he is depicted by artists or written about by friends who admired him and by the many enemies who attacked him. In addition, the attacks and his responses show us different aspects of Erasmus through the way he presented himself in his letters and works. The attacks on him were relentless, and he did not hesitate to share his disappointment in the reception of his ideas about Christian community and ways to read the Bible; his anger would even spill over sometimes into paranoia – an unfortunate part of a life that is built on reputation. But his remarkable endurance, his work ethic, his need to be noticed and his commitment to his vision of Christianity carried him forward.

This last extended stage of his life began with a frenetic round of travel as he moved among cities in the Low Countries and back and forth to Basel. But it was during this time that Erasmus began to discover that he no longer had the physical energy of his early years. A difficult trip down the Rhine, which I shall turn to shortly, tells that story well. Travel was no longer so appealing, even though for the rest of his life he continued to propose (unrealized) plans for further travel, including to Italy. In this last period of his life he was finally ready to settle. In 1516 he was orientated towards the duchy of Brabant, the world he had first known, and he was urged to settle in Louvain by the emperor, whose councillor he had become; moreover, his pension as a councillor depended on his presence at court. But he found the hostility of the theologians so unpleasant that he left Louvain in 1521 with Italy as the intended destination. However, he stopped in Basel and settled there for more than eight years, initially surrounded by a small but loyal community of scholars. When the reform movement reached Basel, Erasmus felt forced to move to the nearby imperial Catholic city of Freiburg, and lived there from 1529 to 1535. He even bought a house. But when the reform movement died down a bit, Erasmus moved back to Basel to support the publication of his recent works. A year later, he died. Despite his incapacity for travel, he had continued to plan his return to Brabant.

SELF-PRESENTATION THROUGH LETTERS

Nowhere, as we have seen, is Erasmus's self-organizing presence felt more than in the letters, which he now began to
publish. He often kept copies of his letters, those received and
sent, from his earliest years. Many Italian humanists, from
Petrarch in the fourteenth century onwards, in imitation of
such ancients as Seneca and Cicero, had published collections
of their letters.[3] In 1515 Erasmus too began to publish his
correspondence. Unlike his predecessors, he brought out new
collections regularly, providing an ongoing narrative of his
life. The first of these collections, printed by Froben, included
only four of his letters, among them one to Pope Leo X, the
famous letter to Martin Dorp defending *The Praise of Folly*,
and a statement of his New Testament project. The next year
Erasmus expanded the project with a larger but still modest
collection of 21 letters, the *Epistolae aliquot illustrium virorum ad
Erasmum Roterodamum et huius ad illos* (Letters to Erasmus from
Certain Famous Men and His Letters to Them), edited by his
friend Pieter Gillis and published in Louvain (by the same
publisher as More's *Utopia*). After that, the collections poured
forth: in the years 1517, 1518, 1519 and 1521, followed by a pause
after he moved to Basel, then another collection in 1528,
topped off in 1529 by the massive retrospective *Opus epistolarum*
(Work of Letters), which included 1,025 letters, only 391 of
which were new.[4] The size of this later edition is rather
staggering.

For Erasmus, publication of the letters was one of the
ways of extending and affirming the kind of scholarly community that he had been, since his earliest years, so intent on
forming around himself, a community that contained the

powerful and the famous as well as learned persons of little
or no reputation. A published correspondence has the effect
of extending a private community into the public realm
because it invites the reader into private conversations, into
intimacies, and thus enlarges the circle of the community,
sometimes encouraging readers to listen in on the discussion
of obscure manuscripts or the minutiae of textual editing.
The timeliness of publication adds a dramatic dimension, for
it draws readers in to the ongoing narrative of a friendship
that is both professional and personal. Erasmus was often in a
hurry to get letters included in the latest published collection.
Indeed, we know of at least one correspondent who found
a letter in one of these collections before he had actually
received it.[5]

As time went on, Erasmus was increasingly intent on
controlling the publication of his letters and was on special

The expanded letters of 1529 compared with the modest collection of 1516.

lookout for those 'who take a private letter written to a friend and publish it', sometimes with alterations, as someone did to a letter he wrote to Luther.[6] Despite this high-mindedness, it is true that he too revised the letters he sent to print. Sometimes he would publish his letters and sometimes he would destroy them. In his *Catalogus lucubrationum* (1522), a long letter to Johann von Botzheim with a catalogue and account of his own writing, he says, not entirely exaggerating, that if he kept on with letter-writing he would end up with 'two wagons' of letters. He adds: 'I myself acquired many by chance and burned them, for I observed that they were preserved by many people.'[7] Others he had copied out, preserved and published himself. He especially seemed to like the letters from powerful people: 'I have boxes full of the most flattering letters from kings, cardinals, dukes, and bishops.'[8]

The full scale of the correspondence is also unknown, though we can infer, just from the number of letters that mention another letter sent or received but now lost, that it was at an absolute minimum twice as large as the 3,000-plus letters we now have, and must have been considerably larger. As mentioned above, we don't know what happened to letters written in the period from December 1508 to April 1511, and there is evidence in many surviving letters of other letters now lost. Most of the letters we now have came from Erasmus's own publications, though many, hidden away in archival collections, have since been unearthed by Percy Allen and other scholars. One effect of Erasmus's known correspondence is its imbalance: the first volume of Allen covers the correspondence for the first thirty years of his letter-writing (to the age of 48), and the next ten volumes cover the remaining 22 years.

The letters in Erasmus's collections tend to be recent exchanges, and despite his efforts to collect and maintain an orderly record of the correspondence, many of his dates have been shown to be incorrect or invented by him to serve the narrative that is presented in their publication. It is hard to see what his readers would have made of the way the letters were assembled. They were then not to be read as we read them now, in the meticulous order established by Percy Allen (with Helen Allen and Heathcote Garrod) in the twentieth-century edition, later adjusted here and there by the editors of the Toronto translation, as a continuous, evolving narrative. In the modern editions there is a deceptive tidiness to it all, because everything is organized according to the date of writing, not of receipt. Of course the timing of receipt and response is an essential part of any narrative that might be constructed from the letters. Much of the correspondence is really about the particular moment – when and how the letter was written (sometimes piecemeal over many days or suddenly at the demand of a waiting courier), when it was actually sent, how long it took to get delivered, when it was actually read, and by whom along the way.

A letter even before it appeared in print was often treated as an open and public document, a reminder that the division between print and handwritten manuscript was not nearly so absolute then as it is for us now. Letters were often read aloud to others or shown off to friends as objects of prestige or curiosity. People collected letters sent to others: Erasmus himself at one point held three letters written by Philipp Melanchthon, the reformer, to three different recipients.[9] And Erasmus could send variations of the same letter to different recipients, as we shall see with his famous description of his 1518 trip down the Rhine.[10]

Some letters were seen as too improper or illicit or even dangerous to be publicly circulated. Erasmus claimed in 1521 that a manuscript collection of his personal letters had been on sale in Pisa as early as 1509; a friend bought and sent him the material, which he then destroyed.[11] He cautioned Francesco Chierigati in 1520: 'Your letter reached me after being opened; so pray be careful when you write';[12] and he reminded Karel Uutenhove in 1530,[13] 'You know that today nothing can safely be put in a letter.'[14] It was not just servants or couriers who would open and peek at the letters as they were transported. Erasmus once caught a visitor from Poland attempting to make off with a letter that had come from Luther.[15] There was always the danger that a carelessly worded document (in print or in manuscript) could be used as evidence of heresy or social dissent.

Letters, especially those cleaned up by present-day scholars and set in an orderly record, provide us with an intimate sense of a life. We can read them almost as we would a journal, an account of a life written piecemeal as the life unfolds. Of course, such a narrative cannot be planned, but the writer of the letters will often hold to certain themes, and out of them a narrative can be constructed by the reader. The difference from a journal is that each letter is shaped not just by the sender, but by the sender's sense of his or her audience, which often shifts from recipient to recipient with the additional complication that the audience is also the reader of the letter as it is now found in a book. So the life story in a collected correspondence is complex; each letter must be calibrated,

so to speak, in terms of the recipient. Erasmus's letters change in topic, tone and style depending on the addressee: whether that be Erasmus Schets, his financial broker in Antwerp; Beatus Rhenanus, his younger colleague at the Froben press; his friend Thomas More; or Archbishop William Warham, his great English patron. One of the most remarkable exchanges was with the immensely learned Guillaume Budé, the leading humanist scholar in France; in the surviving 48 letters, the two men were constantly correcting one another in the most

Jean Clouet, *Guillaume Budé*, c. 1536, oil on wood.

arcane details of scholarship or writing style, then apologizing or explaining their criticism as a duty owed to a friend, while struggling to maintain a friendship that was on public display.

Scholars today have become very interested in the way Erasmus managed the publication and circulation of his correspondence, finding him to have an alert sense of how to create and maintain relationships and reputation, as well as creating a kind of institutional structure among the participants in this nascent Republic of Letters, with stylized forms of exchange such as expressions of mutual praise, thanks, advice, requested favours, and the giving and receiving of gifts. In part our interest in his correspondence also comes from the way it can be seen as a predecessor of today's fluid social media networks, which also operate as public/private communication systems.

Erasmus's letters were seen as exemplary, and early on were co-opted as stylistic models for young students.[16] Erasmus also finally published *De conscribendis epistolis* (On the Writing of Letters) in 1522, a work that he had actually drafted years before during his time as a tutor in Paris, and had revised in 1511 and 1515, but only officially published after the unauthorized *Conficiendarum epistolarum formula* (Formula for the Composing of Letters) had appeared in Erfurt, Leipzig and Mainz.[17] In his work he claimed his remarks are 'intended more for the teachers than the pupils', so it is not just about writing letters, but how teachers, by teaching how to write letters, can also offer moral instruction to the students. He argued that the form of a letter is fairly fluid, and, consistent with the new approach of the humanists, that there are few fixed rules. The most important thing is that 'the wording of a letter should resemble a conversation between friends.' Of course it matters how you address people in the salutation and the farewell of the letter, yet 'in the end it is better for letters which seem at times to have no order at all, even when they are in fact carefully constructed, to conceal rather than reveal their order.'[18]

This general rule is true for all letters, which Erasmus goes on to differentiate and discuss in detail – letters of thanks, the obliging letter, letters of friendship, of encouragement, of persuasion (with a famous lengthy example persuading a man to marry); letters of consolation, request, recommendation, advice, complaint, apology, information. Many of these types one can find in his own correspondence, where personal information, gossip, advice, requests for aid, political observations, displays of extremely particular esoteric learning, and moral truths are generously mixed, often in a flow of apparently free association that supports the idea of a mixed style recommended in his treatise. By his letters Erasmus created, maintained and expanded a network of friends and colleagues, laying the basis for what became in the seventeenth and eighteenth centuries a full-blown Republic of Letters and the rise of scientific communication.[19] Despite his solitary labours, Erasmus was always alert to the importance of intellectual community.

REVISION COMPOUNDED,
THE STRUGGLE WITH ERROR

This period of affirmation, as I am calling it, is characterized
by not only Erasmus's collection and publication of letters,
but his passionate revision of his own published writings.
One wonders, is there any writer in the history of Western
literature who revised as much as Erasmus? There is hardly
one of his books that he did not revise or an edition that was
not re-edited. We have already looked at the adjustments to
The Praise of Folly: first the text, then the revised text, then the
annotated text, then an index to the notes. His biggest projects, the *Adages* and the New Testament, as we have also seen,
each went through multiple expansions. And then there are
the books that rose up from the past once he became famous,
including *The Antibarbarians* (1520) and *On the Writing of Letters*
(1522), both drafted before 1500 but somehow saved by
friends, and reprinted in unauthorized versions, then redrafted
by Erasmus for more formal publication.

When Erasmus revised, it was always to correct and usually to expand. The letters are the most obvious and necessary
expansion. But the New Testament annotations doubled in
size. The *Colloquies* was another text that had its origins in the
late 1490s as a few short exercises in conversational Latin for
Erasmus's private students; after it first appeared in 1522,
Erasmus expanded it by 1533 to total some sixty dialogues. For
Erasmus, almost every new book seems to have been what
today in the digital age is called the beta version. It seems to
have been put out with the view not to be definitive, but
rather to get it out, to announce its initial presence, after which
it was to be revised or even substantially rewritten. This aspect

of his work challenges, in a striking manner, the traditional notion of scholarship which normally claims to be painstakingly 'definitive' and 'the last word'. In part the problem came from error, for, as he asks, 'what author was ever so perfect that no fault could be found in him at all?'[20] Many of Erasmus's works needed repair just from the proliferation of typographical errors, notably the New Testament of 1516 and the 1515 edition of Seneca (revised in 1529). But the revisions went beyond mere correction. Erasmus was always sensitive to the circumstances of publication, and thus there was no final, definitive text in his protean work life; every book, even his letters, was revised or was potentially subject to revision as circumstances (new information, new audiences, his own understanding) changed.

Mixed into this personal need for improvement of the texts, there was also the practical consideration. The book trade was only just beginning to be regulated, and even though in the Latin trade the book world was international, this regulation was local. Reprints were not controlled. Erasmus was extremely sensitive to the financial conditions of the printed book. A fresh edition was intended to displace the many reprints, keeping the printer's profits closer to home. New editions provided a chance to repackage the material; as we have seen, his early *Enchiridion* was revived by a fresh preface and republication in 1518, and with the repackaging became a bestseller. As one historian, Andrew Pettegree, has noted, Erasmus was both 'one of the most original minds of the century, and a truly commercial intellectual'.[21]

For the present-day reader of Erasmus these shifting texts are disorienting, a form of multidimensional chess, because we must consider not just *what* Erasmus wrote, but *when* this particular version appeared and *why* it has the form that it does. Even *where* becomes part of this puzzle, for Erasmus sometimes carefully shifts the publication of a book from one place to another; a new place will reframe or 'restage' the way the book is intended to be read.[22]

LOUVAIN

In May 1516, his two great projects of the New Testament and St Jerome now published, Erasmus was back on the road from Basel. He had been appointed as a councillor to the Burgundian court of Prince Charles, and for the next five years he settled in the Low Countries. First, however, he went to England. His renewed attempt to claim a broader dispensation in relation to his monastic vows, negotiated through the church in England, had been successful, though it took his friend Ammonio many months to track the ever-mobile Erasmus down to let him know.[23] Though he remained an Augustinian canon regular, he had never returned to his monastery, and in Italy he had dropped the clothing of the order; now he was allowed to travel freely, to own property, even to take up multiple church livings. Erasmus wished to remain free to pursue his scholarship and he continued to resist being tied down in any way – by family, monastic order, university position, state or residence. Nevertheless, he was always interested in pensioned positions that would provide him with income but would not require pastoral responsibilities or regular attendance at a court. Through gifts and pensions he had, at the age of fifty, finally attained the freedom he had sought since his youth. But just as this freedom came to him, other complications were appearing as a result of his increasingly public intellectual life.

A first recognition of trouble had already come to Erasmus in September 1514. He had received a letter from Martin Dorp, a Louvain theologian, who questioned him on the propriety of both his *Praise of Folly* and his ongoing work on the New Testament.[24] In *Folly* Erasmus seemed to spare no one in his critique of the social and intellectual life of his time; some readers were quite taken aback with the sharpness of his attacks. And the project of the New Testament was also upsetting to the status quo. What right did Erasmus, a mere grammarian, have to change the language of the Bible? Surely the Bible in the traditional form used by the theologians had proven itself over time to be sufficient.

As he was to do over and over again in the coming years, Erasmus wrote a response to this challenge.[25] In his letter to Dorp he defended both his social criticism and his role as grammarian whose linguistic expertise provided direct access to the words of Christ. By 1516 this letter, published in the first collection of his correspondence, was placed as a preface to the *Folly* and continues to the present day to be included in many editions. Dorp in response tried to hold his ground, but Thomas More wrote an even more substantial defence of Erasmus, in support not only of the *Folly*, but of the work on the New Testament.[26] Dorp dropped his objections and soon afterwards became a reliable supporter of Erasmus. This happened so easily that at least one sceptical scholar, Lisa Jardine, believed that the Dorp controversy may have been a managed 'performance'.[27] Nevertheless, Dorp's objections were symptomatic; the theologians of Louvain were to become increasingly insistent and annoying opponents, and Erasmus's sense of freedom gave way to a burdensome obligation to answer an increasing number of critics. His notion of friendship and community, his seeking of the good will of others, and his desire for the acceptance of his ideas insisted on a continuous explanation of his positions in the increasingly fractious world of the Reformation.

POLITICS, WAR, PEACE

Though Erasmus was caught up in his work on the Bible and Jerome, he was also very aware of the shifting politics of Europe. He was in the process of establishing relations with a variety of powerful patrons who were often at odds with one another: Henry VIII in England; Duke Charles (soon to become the Holy Roman Emperor); the newly crowned Francis I in France; Pope Leo X; as well as political leaders in Germany and other powerful figures in the Church. The political realm was unstable, with the French wars in Italy, the conflict between England and France, and the threat of Muslim invasion in the east, and in all this the shifting allegiances of the various players. The role of those counselling the great during these times was not an easy one.

Late in 1516 Erasmus managed the publication of Thomas More's *Utopia*, which he had brought with him to Antwerp. The work had been written in the same spirit as *The Praise of Folly*, but instead of a make-believe lecture, More's book was a make-believe travel tale to the land of the Utopians (the people of 'no-where'), written in the spirit of Lucian, the

Greek writer whom the two men had translated together ten
years earlier. *Utopia* is a powerful critique of the social polity
of the day. More was stimulated by news of the travels to the
New World (specifically those reported by Amerigo Vespucci);
he was able to perceive that the European ways of war, greed
and social disorder could be challenged by being set against
the imagined possibility of an alternative society (in the way
that a republic is proposed by Socrates in Plato's dialogue to
serve as an instructional device, an image of the ideal state).
The island of Utopia is described in the second part of the
book, but the first half, presented as a dialogue in the humanist style, is set in Europe. We are shown what it was like for
humanist advisors in the courts of prelates and monarchs, as
they tried to make common-sense arguments against war or
excessive punishment of the poor. Raphael Hythloday (whose
last name, in the ironic tradition of Lucian, comes from the
Greek word *huthlos* for 'talk, chatter') is a scholar in precisely
the situation that humanists such as More and Erasmus found
themselves in: highly educated councillors who were respected
by the prince yet who were ignored the moment they addressed
the pointlessness of war or the way the landed classes exer-
cised their power. More inserts himself as a character in his
own work, and this character seems at the end of the book to
doubt the very words of Hythloday, thus eluding the charge
of attacking the status quo, in much the same way that Erasmus
could hide behind his Folly.

Erasmus wrote his *Education of a Christian Prince* (1516) at
the same time that he was busily assisting in the publication
of *Utopia*. In his work, dedicated to sixteen-year-old Charles
(three years later elected Holy Roman Emperor), whom he

Bernard van Orley, *Charles V, Holy Roman Emperor*, c. 1515–16, oil on wood.

served as councillor, he proposed that the prince should be highly moral, well read, Christian and wise, and that he should coordinate his own ethical life with the needs of his people. This work should be read within the context of Erasmus's other political writings, all produced within a couple of years, arguing against the aggression of the powerful. As we have seen, the 1515 edition of the *Adages* contained a number of long political essays on social problems, the most famous of them being his lengthy anti-war essay 'War is a treat for those who have not tried it', which evolved out of a line from the ancient Greek poet Pindar.[28] Soon after the *Education of a Christian Prince* he wrote his *Complaint of Peace*, another speech like *The Praise of Folly*, but this time spoken in all seriousness by Peace, who advises the reader (and the powerful members of society) of the social cruelty and political dangers of war.

Erasmus and More wrote their two books just a short time after Machiavelli wrote his very different *Prince* (*c.* 1513, but posthumously published in 1532). All three humanist counsellors considered ethical norms in relation to the ruler and the people. Machiavelli examined the pragmatics of power through the harsh lens of Roman history, approving of such figures as the warmongering Pope Julius II. More also looked at social issues with a realist's eye, but proposed a quasi-Platonic ideal to allow the reader to see social failures; Erasmus, even more of a utopian than More, wrote against war and greed and outlined an ideal education for the prince, whom he praised for the very qualities he had yet to attain. Erasmus's approach was well known to his friends. As Wolfgang Capito shrewdly put it: 'you have a habit of seeming to intend to praise your friends and really giving them valuable though concealed advice. That is how you have now depicted not the man I am but the man you hope I shall be one day.'[29] One of the constantly appealing aspects of Erasmus is his optimistic belief in the possibility of personal and social improvement through education and self-regulation. These beliefs are tied to his idea of free will when he comes to argue with Luther. Of course, it was through education and self-regulation that Erasmus himself had attained his own place in society, and he in turn offers that possibility to others.

THE FIRST PORTRAITS

By 1517, with the papal dispensation and his new (but relatively short-lived) pension as a councillor of state, Erasmus's financial situation had improved. He undertook to send an unusual gift to his friend More, with whom he had been in active contact in the recent past. Erasmus hired Quentin Metsys, a leading artist, to make a double portrait of himself and his friend Pieter Gillis, clerk to the city of Antwerp. Both Erasmus and More had at times stayed at Gillis's house in Antwerp; it was there also that More had come up with the idea for *Utopia*. And not only is Gillis a character in *Utopia*, the book is dedicated to him. Indeed, it could be argued that the real utopia of *Utopia* is found in the small circle of friends who inhabit the tale and surround it in the prefaces and poems.

Today the portrait of Erasmus and Gillis is in two parts, cut in half some time after Charles I owned the work; the section of Erasmus is now in the British Royal Collection and the one of Gillis is in the collection of the Earl of Radnor.

Quentin Metsys, *Desiderius Erasmus*, 1517, oil on panel, half of diptych.

Quentin Metsys, *Pieter Gillis*, 1517, oil on panel, half of diptych.

Erasmus, depicted on the left, writes his *Paraphrase of Romans*, which appeared in November 1517, and Gillis, shown on the right, holds a letter from More with More's handwriting imitated perfectly (a feature that astonished More when he received the painting).[30] The painting represents an interesting shift in the iconography of the scholar, and seems to have been conceived by Erasmus and Gillis together with Metsys. Erasmus is not seated alone like a solitary St Jerome (a volume of 'Hieronymus' is conspicuous on the shelf behind him) but is with a companion, and the two are working in a cosy panelled library, which is not removed from the world so much as the centre of it: Gillis receives a letter from outside the study, Erasmus is writing a book to be sent forth, and the shelves are crowded with other identifiable books that have been edited or are being read by Erasmus and his circle.

Thomas More received the double portrait while he was in Calais in early October 1517, and sent an ecstatic and perceptive poem of thanks to Gillis. Having a portrait made by a well-known artist is another way we can tell that Erasmus had moved into a more prosperous way of living. He declares in the painting the relationship of humanist scholarship to intimate friendship. Though it is unclear how Metsys and Erasmus collaborated on the iconographical setting, the painting does effectively show Erasmus within the frame of friendship and a life of books and writing.

Two years later Erasmus commissioned a portrait coin from Metsys. Such coins, usually distributed as gifts, were based on coins from classical antiquity and were enormously popular in Italian humanist circles.[31] They usually had a portrait on one side and a clever device on the other. The Erasmus

coin is 107 mm (4 in.) in diameter. The obverse gives an impressive relief portrait of Erasmus, identified by the initials 'Er. Rot.', and around him is written *Imago ad vivam effigiem expressa* ('the image expressed according to life') and *Tēn kreittô ta syngrammata deixei* (in Greek, 'his writings show him better'). On the reverse is the picture of Terminus, the Roman god of boundaries, with *Concedo nulli* ('I yield to no one') written on either side of his sculpted bust; around the image is the Latin inscription *Mors ultima linea rerum* ('Death is the final limit of things') and, in Greek, *Hora telos makrou biou* ('Consider the end of a long life'). Terminus, the device Erasmus had adopted from the ring he received from Alexander Stewart (visible on his hand in the diptych for More), is now set indisputably forth as a god of death, a *memento mori*.[32] As we have seen, the claim that Erasmus's 'writings show him better' is a central theme throughout the work of Erasmus, and was later repeated in Albrecht Dürer's engraved portrait of 1526 mentioned in the Introduction. The coin is further evidence of his growing fame and the complex way in which he wished to be seen.

Quentin Metsys, coin of Erasmus, 16th century, bronze, showing a bust of Desiderius Erasmus on the obverse (left) and *The Terminus* on the reverse (right).

THE ENEMIES BEGIN TO GATHER

In mid-1517 Erasmus wrote to More: 'I have moved bodily to Louvain, intending to spend several months among the theology faculty, who have given me quite a kind welcome.'[33] After a short time rooming in the residence of a friend, he moved into the College of the Lily, where he lived until 1521. From Louvain he continued to travel to Brussels and Antwerp in his role as a councillor to the Burgundian court, and to Basel to attend to the publications from Froben's press. In the summer of 1518 he spent four months, May to September, in Basel as he prepared the second edition of the New Testament, to be published the following year. In 1520 he was away for another long period, as he went to Calais to see More at the meeting of Charles V and Henry VIII, and then travelled with the court.

When Erasmus arrived in Louvain (treated as a regular member of the faculty but never fully voted in), his greatest concern, other than his own research, was to help in the establishment of a new Collegium Trilingue, a College of Three Languages, which was established in September 1518. This was a residential college for students who could also enrol at the University of Louvain, which retained more of the medieval curriculum. The three languages of the college were those of the Bible: Hebrew, Greek and Latin. The college was a tiny institution, with a professor for each of the three languages and a handful of students. Erasmus, as a friend of the founder's family, was actively involved in the early years of this novel institution.[34]

Despite his initial reception at Louvain, the short debate with Martin Dorp was a warning. Erasmus's New Testament and the distinctly humanist project of the Collegium Trilingue were soon to gain him enemies in the conservative faculty of theology, which taught the kind of scholastic philosophy that Erasmus had so detested in Paris and had mocked in *The Praise of Folly*.

The battle engaged a number of figures, but it initially focused on a single individual named Edward Lee.[35] Lee had studied at both Oxford and Cambridge and had begun a career in the Catholic Church and in the court of Henry VIII. He decided, in his mid-thirties, that he wanted to learn Greek, so he moved abroad to Louvain. Erasmus met him and in July 1517 wrote approvingly to Cuthbert Tunstall, at that time an English envoy in Bruges, that 'Lee is working very hard at his Greek.'[36] Soon afterwards, however, Lee fell in with the scholastic theologians in Louvain and began to assemble a series of critical notes on Erasmus's recently published New Testament. Erasmus was eager to improve his work and was naturally interested in what any fellow scholar might have found for correction in a close reading of his annotations. He consulted Lee, who offered a few of his notes for the second edition, but Erasmus distrusted the source because of Lee's association with the hostile members of the Louvain faculty, who were opposed to a mere grammarian of pagan literature seeking to correct the words of the Holy Book. By May 1518 Erasmus had written a long letter to a friend, rejecting, in 95 detailed points, the work of Lee (whom he calls the 'man whose pamphlet you have sent me').[37]

Lee took Erasmus's rejection personally. He felt that Erasmus considered him insignificant, and went on to claim that one day he actually saw Erasmus in a tavern laughing about him and his notes. Lee doubled down on his annotations on Erasmus's annotations, and soon claimed to have found hundreds of errors in the first edition. Erasmus, hypersensitive to the accusation of error, now insisted on seeing these notes, and increased his efforts to obtain them, as he said, 'by every method, even underhanded'.[38] But Lee would not deliver. This wilful retention of the notes provoked Erasmus to distraction. By 1519, even after Erasmus's second edition had gone to press, the claims and counter-claims had been circulating in the small world of Louvain and beyond. Erasmus was now seized by a kind of paranoia that also appears in his later writings. Here he is seen in a lengthy letter to Thomas Lupset (a former pupil of John Colet), complaining bitterly about Lee and a few others in Louvain:

> There are gangs of conspirators who have consigned themselves on oath to the infernal powers if they do not utterly destroy the humanities and classical theology; and they have sworn to hold forth against Erasmus everywhere: at drinking-parties, in markets, in committees, in druggists' shops, in carriages, at the barber's, in the brothels, in public and private classrooms, in university lectures and in sermons, in confidential conversations, in the privacy of the confessional, in bookshops, in the taverns of the poor, in the courts of the rich and in kings' palaces, among superstitious old men and blockheads rich as Midas, to the ignorant public, and to foolish women – through whom like the serpent of old they find a way to deceive their husbands. There is no place they cannot penetrate, no lie

they will not tell, to make me, a general benefactor,
into an object of general hatred.[39]

The reference to himself in the third person is indicative:
'Erasmus' is more than just his name; it is an idea that is in
circulation in the world. For Erasmus, these ineffectual notes
by a novice scholar of Greek, and supported by a couple of
others in the theology faculty at Louvain, had now grown
into a massive general threat to not only himself (whom he
styles the 'benefactor'), but his entire scholarly enterprise
and the very disciplines themselves. This outburst can be read
as either amusing hyperbole, or a sign that he was losing
control.

Possibly the most telling document was by Lee. He finally
published his *Annotations* in early 1520, and to this work he
attached a long letter, set in the form of an imagined dialogue
he was having with Erasmus. Lee's list of grievances was
extensive. In the letter, he accuses Erasmus of spiteful and
obscene attacks, and in one instance, to prove his point, he
quotes a passage taken right out of Erasmus's recent *Colloquies*
in which two young men discuss a persistent theme: what it
means to receive letters unaccompanied by money:

AUGUSTINE What useful purpose do these inane
letters serve?
CHRISTIAN They can be used for wiping the
buttocks, and are fit for wrapping mackerel and
the like.
AUGUSTINE For my part, I know a man whose
tongue I would rather divert to such a task.

CHRISTIAN I on the other hand know someone by whose tongue it would be as risky to be wiped as by aconite leaves.

AUGUSTINE He really deserves then to eat aconite, the busybody [*ardeleo*].[40]

Aconite, also called monkshood or wolf's-bane, a well-known plant in homeopathy, is poisonous if taken in unregulated quantity. After quoting the passage, Lee asks a good question: 'Erasmus, are these words worthy of you? Are they worthy of a man who wishes, like you, to be thought a theologian and the world's greatest critic? Could anyone say anything filthier, more revolting, more poisonous?' In this passage, accurately quoted by Lee and no doubt rightly understood by him to refer in some way to himself (as the unnamed *ardeleo* or 'busybody'), we get a brief glimpse into the scatological imagination that was sometimes called upon to insult an enemy.

Erasmus, who soon cleaned up the passage, nevertheless felt called upon to defend himself from Lee's attack. Within weeks he responded with the magnificently titled *Apologia by Erasmus of Rotterdam Which Is neither Arrogant nor Biting nor Angry nor Aggressive in Which He Responds to the Two Invectives of Edward Lee – I Shall Not Add What Kind of Invectives: Let the Reader Judge for Himself.* In this, he tried to make light of Lee's concerns. For instance, his response to Lee's shock over his obscenity:

First of all, I ask you, dear reader, what is obscene about someone who teaches the Latin language giving this example: 'This book is good for nothing except wiping behinds.' Is it so obscene to name that part of

the body when a part popularly considered more
obscene is named in the Bible: 'vagina'? Tell me, if a
schoolteacher threatens his boys with the rod, is he
considered to speak obscenely because he names that
part of the body which is usually struck? . . . I should
like to ask Lee: Has he never heard the male member
mentioned frivolously at social gatherings with his
friends, or the word for hinder parts that is used even
by respectable people? And how does this agree with
his quotation from Jerome in Annotation 31? Jerome
says that it is not dishonourable to mention any part
of the human body . . . In this passage I certainly cannot see anything obscene. It is spoken passionately
rather than obscenely against a virulent tongue that
deserves to be cut out with the sword and given over
to the most abject uses.

Erasmus continues with an anecdote that could have been
plucked from the notorious *Facetiae*, a jest book written by the
fifteenth-century scholar Poggio Bracciolini:

As a young man, I remember, I once travelled aboard
a ship carrying the usual mixed crowd. Among them
was a theologian who had made a great name for himself, a member of the Dominican order, whose sermons
were popular with the people. He was a corpulent
man. A sailor began joking about him for obviously
leading a soft life. When he had said many ridiculous
things – the kind of jokes common people usually
make about prefects of nunneries – the theologian

replied that he lacked only one comfort in life, which
had not yet been mentioned. When the sailor asked
right away what that was, he said: 'Your tongue, to
wipe my backside.' Loud laughter ensued, and no one
thought that it was spoken indecently, because it was
spoken against a slanderous tongue. For this reason I
cannot sufficiently express my surprise at Lee, whose
eyes would discern a detestable obscenity in my words
even though they are not spoken in my own person
and are uttered during a drinking bout.[41]

This 'merry tale' that ends the response is clearly devised to
deflect all criticism of obscenity, even while it confirms that
Erasmus is capable of writing such lewdness. Or perhaps it
means that if Erasmus, accused of obscenity, is now so willing to tell this tale, perhaps there is nothing obscene in what
he is doing. Either way, that the speaker of the obscene
response in this joke is a fat Dominican friar is a nice shot at
the hostile theologians. I have chosen this fairly minor part
of the exchange because it presents an extreme in the way
that the arguments could flow. Even in this one small point
of dispute, one can see Erasmus's need to engage his reader
with a shared sense of humour, an invitation to join him in
complicit friendship in a kind of after-dinner joke, told among
good (male) friends, in the humanist manner.

Soon after his response, Erasmus prepared his own reprint
of Lee's annotations. In the reprint, he did not include any
of Lee's personal attacks, 'since I supposed that he must by
now regret such a display of ill temper'. He prepared to
reprint 'all the more readily because, though some good is to

be derived from his annotations and my answer, squabbling of this kind brings the reader no profit at all'.[42] Erasmus is now back to the high ground where he seems more naturally to belong. The controversy was suddenly over. The notes were there for all to see, Erasmus even expressing some gratitude (even though they had minimal impact on his own work). Lee moved back to England. Despite this broadside attack on him by Europe's greatest scholar, and by the other eminent scholars who joined Erasmus, he had a remarkably successful career in church and court, finally becoming Archbishop of York in 1531.

This argument with Lee is a minor episode, compared with some of the later debates. Yet it shows how what may have started as an honest attempt to spot errors in the 1516 text and commentary was easily co-opted into a broader conspiracy. Erasmus's concern is personal, but it is also tied to a higher principle, the obligation in the learned community to share one's learning loyally as is expected among friends. Yet, as we can see, the controversy was carried far beyond the usual academic manners. There is an imbalance on the part of the two participants. The debate is personal yet public.

There was certainly a spirit of contention in the world of scholarship, which Erasmus described in his *Complaint of Peace*:

> Scholar argues with scholar . . . indeed in the same seat of learning logicians war with rhetoricians and theologians argue with lawyers. Even in the same profession, Scotist battles with Thomist, Nominalist with Realist, Platonist with Peripatetic, so fiercely that there is no agreement amongst them even on the smallest points,

and often enough they fight with the utmost fury on the subject of goat's wool. Then the heat of the debate mounts from argument to insult, from insults to fisti-cuffs, and if they don't settle the matter by daggers or spears they take to stabbing with poisoned pens, tear one another with barbed wit, and attack each other's reputation with the deadly darts of their tongues.[43]

In such debates, the specifics seem to become secondary. Yet the stakes are high because 'truth' – the ideas that must be known; the way they must be known and discussed; the canon of essential texts, and so on[44] – is under social contestation. Moreover, disagreements could lead to the charge of heresy: in 1529 Louis de Berquin, a lawyer and translator of Erasmus into French, was burned alive for his heretical reformist beliefs. There was thus a significant danger in these accusa-tions of heretical learning. The truth mattered. On a lesser level, to a scholar committed to the well-edited text, even a misspelled word or misplaced comma was an abomination; but on a greater level, a wrong word could be a sign of heresy. Accuracy and truthfulness in textual editing attained a moral dimension by being tied to religious conformity.

Added to this moral dimension was the issue of competi-tion and hierarchy in the intellectual community. The scholar's sense of moral superiority could be exacerbated by profes-sional envy: 'Potter envies potter, and smith envies smith' is the appropriate proverb from Erasmus's *Adages*.[45] The result was the cruel disdain of one scholar towards another, the *odium philologicum*, often arising from the extreme contempt for error.[46] So, along with the issue of error, there was also the aspect of friendship, an essential bond for the humanist scholar. For Erasmus, Lee broke the rule of friendship that all work must be shared among friends; and for Lee, Erasmus too broke the rule of friendship, that the work of others must be received gratefully even if it is then kindly brushed aside. Friendship, especially when it is really a performance of friendship, has trouble surviving the demands of philological truth.

THE BODY OF THE SCHOLAR

The scholar is traditionally a brain without a body. If there is a body, it is always distracted, uncoordinated and tripping into ditches. The image of the hapless, physically incompetent scholar is still with us today. Perhaps the scholar might console him- or herself with this observation by Erasmus, who comments (with wishful thinking) on the 'frail body' of Augustine: 'Men with special gifts are rarely blessed with strong bodies, for nature takes from the strength of the body what she has added to that of the mind.'[47]

In part schools have helped to maintain this image of the scholar, for it is only fairly recently in Western history that physical education was made part of the regular academic curriculum. In the Renaissance, schools trained students to sit and study for long hours, for the real focus of school, then as now, was on physical stillness – early modern schooling was a form of education that taught the student how *not* to move. The schoolmaster in Erasmus's *Colloquies* disapproved of games when the boys in his class asked him if they could go outdoors to play. Movement was limited to the fine motor skill of writing. The most strenuous classroom activity for both master and pupil was the beating of students. Outside school there were of course many sports for the poor and the rich. Humanist writers on education would often encourage physical activity, but it was slow to be adopted into any school curriculum. For instance, Richard Mulcaster, the Elizabethan schoolmaster, born just a few years before Erasmus died and who lived into the seventeenth century, wrote extensively about the importance of physical exercise in schooling, yet no formal sports were played at Merchant Taylors' or at St Paul's, the two schools in which he taught.

A *corpus* is a body, a *corpusculum* a 'little body'. Erasmus in his letters had a great deal to say about his *corpusculum*. He presented himself as weak, his body a kind of enemy to himself. But this little enemy does not go unnoticed. Erasmus obsesses about diet, clothing, the rooms he lives in, his bowel movements, the state of his urine, and his ailments – colds, problems with sleep, severe reactions to certain foods (mostly fish), his horror of being in a room with stoves (he preferred the circulation of air that you get with a fireplace), dysentery, sweating sickness (that strange and often deadly infection of the sixteenth century that he once caught in England and survived), kidney stones, abscesses and other infections (such as the extreme infection in his abdomen that he caught when he was 64 years old[48]), gout and other forms of arthralgia and arthritis. The failure of his body affected the quality and production of his work, and as soon as he was healed from a disease, he would be back at his studies. And because the work was so sedentary, so passive, yet with the requirement of constant attention to minute detail, it also took a toll on his nervous energy. He complained about exhaustion a lot of the time. He did learn certain techniques that allowed him to remain focused, and for many years he did all of his writing standing up (the manner in which he is shown in many of his portraits). We know he enjoyed walking or relaxing in gardens like that of Froben or, later in Freiburg, that of Johannes Brisgoicus.[49] We have already seen how Erasmus took to riding during his first visit to England; in a letter written when he was in his sixties, he said, 'I confess that I was once captivated by a passion for riding and the raising of horses cost me a good sum of money.'[50] The English scholar Roger Ascham (tutor to the intellectually gifted Elizabeth Tudor before her coronation as Elizabeth I) wrote in his book on archery that while Erasmus was in Cambridge, he 'wolde take his horse, and ryde about the markette hill, and come agayne'.[51]

In Erasmus's letters readers discover a lot of information about his health, sometimes in remarkable detail. In early September 1518, Erasmus had left Basel, where he had been since May, with work remaining to be done on the New Testament, and was heading down the Rhine to Louvain, accompanied by a servant. We can follow his Rhine journey day by day in a letter written to Beatus Rhenanus, his young colleague back in Basel.[52] In it we find out about Erasmus's dislike of the ordinary conditions of travel, his joy at being recognized, and his remarkable stamina (considering how much he loathed the dangers and discomforts of travelling).

The first day on the boat heading down the Rhine was pleasant enough, but when the passengers disembarked for dinner and overnight accommodation, Erasmus began to complain:

At nightfall we were cast ashore at some dreary village whose name I did not choose to inquire, nor would I willingly write it if I knew. That place was nearly the death of me. We had supper in a parlour of no great size with a stove, more than sixty of us I should think, the dregs of the human race, and that at ten o'clock. The smell! The noise! Especially when they were already heated with wine. But I had to sit there and take my timing from them.

From there the next day they moved on to Speyer, though Erasmus's horse was badly shod and limping. After that, they travelled by carriage to Worms and on again to Mainz, where they arrived after six days. While on the carriage, Erasmus happened to meet a well-connected government official named Ulrich Varnbüler (there exists a drawing of Varnbüler by Dürer), who found better rooms for Erasmus for a couple of nights. Then they took the boat via Boppard to Cologne.

In Boppard Erasmus was recognized by a customs official:

I cannot tell you how delighted the man was. He carried me off to his house. On his desk all among the customs forms lay the works of Erasmus! He cried out his good fortune, called for his children, his wife and all his friends. Meanwhile, as the shipmen were loudly protesting, he sent them two flagons of wine.

Erasmus never forgot this official, named Christoph Eschenfelder, and later they corresponded; Erasmus even dedicated a book to him.[53]

From Boppard they were accompanied by a few fellow travelling Church officials, and in the morning they arrived in Cologne, where Erasmus heard rumours of the plague. The weather had turned, and he headed off on his lame horse to Bedburg to stay with the Count of Neuenahr in his castle. Erasmus enjoyed spending time with the young count, who, 'as Homer remarks of Menelaus, speaks right fluently' (a remembered allusion to *Iliad* 3.214). There he spent 'five delightful days, in such tranquillity and comfort' that he was able to finish his revisions to another section of the New Testament that he was carrying with him.

At this point the story takes a sudden shift. When it was time to leave, the count, concerned by the poor weather, attempted to convince Erasmus to stay. But, as Erasmus said, 'some evil genius' robbed him of his senses, and he set out. 'I climbed into an open carriage, with a wind blowing "such as upon the lofty mountain-tops / splinters the swaying oaks"' (quoting now from Horace's *Epodes*, 10). He proceeded through the wind and rain, 'exhausted by the shaking of the carriage' on the rocky road. When he arrived in Aachen he was taken to a residence of canons; the only dinner on offer was a dish of carp. The next day he was fed stockfish, some of it raw. He began to feel ill, and 'retired to the latrine for a good riddance'; to make sure he had purged himself, 'I put my finger down my throat once or twice and up came that raw fish.' This habit may have started when he was young, when he first complained about eating fish. The weather and the bad diet were bearing down on him. Even so, the group set out, despite there being rumours of bandits along the road. By now, riding the horse was excruciating for

Erasmus, apparently because of a skin lesion caused by his recent custom of scratching his groin in order 'to provoke a movement of the bowels'. The area of his groin became inflamed and a lump emerged as he was riding. They stopped in Maastricht, had a light meal, and proceeded to Tongeren, where he became extremely unwell.

The next day, Erasmus pressed on to St Truiden, where he demanded that the carriage stop so that he could relieve his bowels. The evening air afflicted him again, and he continued, in pain, to Tienen. There he found a carriage that was travelling to Louvain, and he flung himself aboard. When he arrived in Louvain, rather than going to his rooms in the College of the Lily, he stayed with Dirk Martens, the printer. He was now confined to bed. One new swelling appeared, perhaps, he says, contracted from when his servant had been massaging his back a couple of nights earlier. He called for the doctors. The first surgeon suspected the plague. Then, Erasmus says, 'I sent for the Jew. "To judge by your urine," he said, "I wish I was as fit as you."' But now the surgeon and the surgeon's father, who had also been called in for consultation, both argued that Erasmus had contracted the plague. Another surgeon arrived, and jocularly exclaimed, 'I shouldn't be frightened to share a bed with you . . . [and] have intercourse with you too, if you were a woman.' He continued his examination, until he discovered the sores that had developed; at this point 'his nerve was shaken.' Instead of returning later that evening as he had promised, the now fearful doctor sent his servant. Erasmus had not considered the plague, but the swellings were indicative: 'I . . . commended my fate to Christ the great physician.'

With the doctors now banished, and after days of a diet of diced chicken and wine from Beaune, Erasmus began to recover. 'Seventeen days later black dead flesh came away from my sores'; the groin continued to have swellings, and he drove off the flies with his hand. After four weeks he was able to move about: 'If indeed it was the plague, I drove the plague away at the cost of great effort and discomfort and determination; for often a great part of any disease is our fancy that we have it.' The letter concludes that he found he was no longer afraid of death: 'When I was a young man, I remember how I used to tremble even at the mere name of death'; now 'I fear death very little.' He had passed his fiftieth year (he was almost 52), and claimed, 'I have already built a monument to bear witness to posterity that I existed.' As he tells it, his faith in Christ and his faith in himself seem to have carried him through.

This letter, well known for describing Erasmus's experience of travel, turns out to be about an illness, a voyage around the body of Erasmus as much as down the Rhine. He had in fact, according to modern analysis of his symptoms, contracted the plague; swellings in the lymph areas of the groin and the blackened gangrenous flesh arising from the swellings are telltale marks. Erasmus, as well educated as anyone might be at that time, and very intent on self-diagnosis, could only hopelessly search about for the causes or nature of his ailment. According to him, his suffering may have come from the weather, his diet or a self-inflicted infection in his groin. For Erasmus, if it was the plague wreaking havoc with his body, he had no sense of how it arrived or why it went. It was all a mystery.

Erasmus might be seen as pathetic in the way he fusses over his diet and his ailments in his correspondence. Yet his Rhine letter, though obsessive in its details, shows no shame or delicacy whatsoever about his bodily functions. Indeed, what is almost as extraordinary as the content of this letter was Erasmus's effort to have it widely distributed. His courier, as he left Louvain with letters for persons scattered all the way back to Beatus in Basel, was told to read the Rhine letter aloud to all recipients. It became well known. Soon afterwards, it was reprinted in his New Collection of Letters published by Froben in October 1519. The assumption is that his bowel movements and rotting flesh are as interesting to his readers as any other aspect of his life and thought. Erasmus seems to have been less squeamish than many of his present-day readers. Certainly his survival of the plague was to him a matter of pride.

Erasmus lived in an uncertain demographic environment. If you survived the precarious stage of early childhood, when nearly half of infants died, you might well live as long as Titian or Michelangelo (that is, into your eighties), or you might die of dysentery, cholera, smallpox, measles, the plague, typhoid or other terrifying, poorly understood diseases that swept through cities. Syphilis was a horrific new affliction that appeared in Naples during the French invasion of Italy in 1494–5. Even from its early rise in Europe it was known to be sexually transmitted; Erasmus wrote a colloquy expressing with disgust and sorrow the situation of a young woman about to be forcefully wedded to an older syphilitic man.[54] For a few decades in the twentieth century, following a post-mortem conducted in 1928, scholars thought that Erasmus too had contracted syphilis, but by 1974 it turned out that the wrong body had been exhumed from Basel's cathedral.[55] Erasmus was careful about the plague, whose causes remained mysterious, though he knew to leave a city as soon as he heard that the disease was proliferating there. Even so, he still contracted it, and to his surprise survived it (he had no idea that the survival rate for bubonic plague was about 50 per cent, though for more virulent forms, such as pneumonic plague, the survival rate was closer to 0 per cent).

Erasmus constantly expressed contempt for or disappointment with his own body, yet he seems to have been remarkably resilient; he survived several deadly diseases as well as the recurrent and excruciating pain of kidney stones and crippling gout. For most of his life he was remarkably energetic and at times even buoyant in illness, qualities that can be sensed in his written work, such as when he recounts his most recent 'birth' of a kidney stone in a 1523 letter to Marcus Laurinus, a younger friend and learned churchman then in Louvain, in which he described himself 'as far gone in pregnancy as any old sow'.[56] The gender transposition is fascinating (rather like that of the physician who jestingly proposed the possibility of intercourse with Erasmus).

Finally, a word on Erasmus and his doctors. There must be an irony that he published a *Declamation in Praise of Medicine* in March 1518, just a few months before his Rhine voyage and the varied assessments he received from the doctors. He had written this years earlier, for Ghysbertus, one of his physicians in Paris, and now published it with a dedication to Henricus Afinius, the town physician of Antwerp. It is a lavish praise of medicine and doctors. Not only as a master

of herbal remedies, with the power to bring the sick back from
apparent death, the doctor is considered a moral force who
advises 'abstinence and sobriety'.[57] Erasmus even admits that
'It is the task of the theologian to see that men are saved from
sin, but without the physician there would be no men to be
saved.' Erasmus consulted doctors throughout his life, and
never seems to have entirely given up on them. He greatly
admired Dr Cop, another Paris physician, to whom he wrote
that famous poem on old age. In 1527 he met Paracelsus, who
had been called to Basel to treat the ailing Johann Froben
(who nevertheless died later that year). Paracelsus was a controversial and innovative physician who rejected the traditional
humoural medicine of Galen in favour of alchemical medicine.
Erasmus was drawn to him and they corresponded briefly. But
as one reads the various letters that refer to health, it becomes
clear that Erasmus's favourite physician was himself. He
self-diagnosed and he was an enthusiastic experimenter with
cures. For instance, he remained convinced that there were
certain wines that could drive away his kidney stones and gout,
and he actually considered moving to wine-growing areas of
northeastern France so that he could have an uninterrupted
supply of this fine medicine. Now and then a professional
intervention was effective, for instance in 1530, when he had a
stomach abscess lanced and drained.[58]

    Erasmus and his body are of considerable interest to us
today. In the present-day culture of professional life, a principal
argument for health is that the body must be cared for in
order to achieve greater production. In this way of thinking,
education of the body is undertaken in order to promote the
health of the mind. The health of both mind and body is seen

in terms of its productive energy. Erasmus subscribes to this proposition: he often writes about illness interrupting his work, and in his Rhine letter, the only reason death was no longer to be feared is that Erasmus had already made his 'monument to bear witness to posterity'. I think this emphasis on production is one more way we can see how the humanist project has carried on into our own culture today. Though many now would reject this separation of mind and body, it seems that the problem of the bothersome *corpusculum* is still with us.

THE SCHOLAR'S HOUSEHOLD (BASEL AND FREIBURG)

By 1521 Erasmus had had enough of Louvain and the hostility of the theologians, even though the previous year saw the College of the Three Languages enter a new building and join formally with the University of Louvain. The situation had intensified with the controversy over Luther, a battle to which we will turn shortly. Erasmus's immediate requirement was to find a place where he could continue his scholarly work effectively and recover his balance, as it were.

In May 1521 he was invited by Pieter Wickmans, a cleric known to many of Erasmus's friends, to stay at his new house in Anderlecht, now a suburb of Brussels. Today you can visit the 'Erasmus-house' if you take a brief Metro ride from downtown (on the Erasmus line, of course). After a short walk through the small commercial centre, you come to an ample brick manor house and lovely garden surrounded by a high wall. The original house has been renovated over the years, but you can still sense the Erasmian aura provided by many of his publications in the old editions, pictures, prints and

medal displays. One can feel the presence of Erasmus moving from room to room or imagine him seated at what is called his desk, which still carries an unlikely quill pen (Erasmus preferred reeds). This delightful place is today the only museum dedicated entirely to Erasmus (the Rotterdam Public Library and the Historical Museum of Basel contain more modest shrines). Erasmus enjoyed his stay in Anderlecht: 'Scarcely had I spent two days here and my fever had departed to the devil and my digestion was sound again. I really seemed in this country to grow young again.' In another letter, he claimed 'never was anything a greater success.'[59] With his time now finished in the Low Countries, Erasmus pondered a trip to Italy, and as a first step he headed back to Basel to work on his projects currently in press.

We have seen how difficult travel had become for Erasmus. Thomas More summed up the challenges in his 1520 'Letter

Exterior view of the house at Anderlecht.

to a Monk' (this unnamed monk having attacked Erasmus's writings and mocked his style of living):

> What a fine sort of fun, to get seasick from being on a ship, to be battered around by its tossing, to be threatened by storms, and to have death and ship-wreck continually before one's eyes! When he crawls so often through rugged forests and wild groves, over rough slopes and precipitous mountains, along roads beset with bandits, when he is buffeted by the wind, splashed with mud, drenched with rain, worn out by his travels, and exhausted by overwork, when he fre-quently lodges in a miserable inn ... what a hedonist's life he appears to be leading! ... [A]ll these hardships, which could easily wear down a vigorous and sturdy young man, are confronted and borne by Erasmus' old body [*corpusculum*], which is already breaking down with the strain of his study and work.[60]

It comes as no surprise that Erasmus was finding his travels a burden.

Erasmus arrived at Basel in mid-November 1521 after an exhausting twenty-day trip on horseback through the Rhine cities. After this, he never travelled great distances again, though in his second year at Basel he did make a couple of short trips to Constance and to Besançon. Even after he moved to nearby Freiburg, Basel remained the centre of his work because of Froben and the regular correspondence and visits of his friend Bonifacius Amerbach. And when the reform perturbations of Basel calmed sufficiently, he moved

Hans Holbein the Younger, *Johann Froben*, c. 1522–3, oil on panel.

back in 1535 in order to publish his longest book, *Ecclesiastes*, a guide to preaching that is also an introduction to the reading and interpretation of Scripture.

Even though he was getting old, during this time Erasmus redoubled his efforts in writing and publication. He had become subject to his own ambitious trajectory. He had established the kind of reputation that demanded his continuous attention; his correspondence and his programme of publication are in this sense contiguous, with, as we have seen, constant updates, revisions, responses and defences mixed in with entirely new productions, themselves subject to revision. To do all this work he now needed more stability and assistance. As he was living outside institutions, he now had to create his own workshop that combined household management with the business of visitors, couriers coming and going, and all the work that goes into production for the press. This life was busy, but because it was more settled in one place and now less interrupted by sudden travels, it was more orderly. Erasmus often complained about his continuing workload, and underwent periods of painful physical illness and exhaustion, but he never succumbed to the offers that came to him with regularity to become a resident scholar or a church official in some place other than Basel, even though he often fantasized about leaving for Italy or returning to Brabant.

Working with Johann Froben was an extremely congenial and highly productive experience for Erasmus, though the relationship went through some serious challenges.[61] Froben was a fine craftsman but (unlike Aldus) he was not learned. The small group of scholars that worked with the press as correctors were, however, outstanding. The advantages of working with Froben were a press that gave priority to his publication, financial stability and access to Froben's far-reaching network of booksellers and agents who could help with financial transfers and the successful distribution of his works. During the years between the first arrival of Erasmus in Basel in 1514 and Froben's death in 1527, Froben's four presses, expanding to six in 1522, produced something like three hundred different titles, almost half of them written or edited by Erasmus.[62] Half of these Erasmus books were produced after Erasmus arrived in 1521. Froben's was a small but highly efficient operation; it was influential, but not nearly as large as Anton Koberger's in late fifteenth-century Nuremberg, which had 24 presses, or Christophe Plantin's

Unknown Basel master, *Hieronymus Froben*, capsule portrait with lid, 16th century, oil on wood.

in sixteenth-century Antwerp, which had 22. After Froben
died the press was taken over by his eldest son, Hieronymus,
and new partners, who also worked closely with Erasmus.

When Erasmus first arrived in Basel, he lived for a short
while in a large apartment on property owned by Froben,
then he moved into a house that Froben may have bought
for him, and was supported in part by an allowance of 200
florins from Froben.[63] In September 1522 he declared 'I have
. . . set up as an apprentice housekeeper.'[64] He had servants
of two kinds. One was the personal servant to look after
domestic life, like Syrus who works for the cranky master
Rabinus in the colloquy 'The Master's Bidding'.[65] This servant, often referred to as a *puer*, Latin for 'boy', looked after
things such as minding the fires, fetching groceries and

delivering messages. During the Basel and Freiburg years this domestic labour was undertaken and supervised by a housekeeper, Margarete Büsslein. She was made memorable in Erasmus's unkind description: he called her 'a thieving, grasping, drunken, lying gossip' (*furax, rapax, bibax, mendax, loquax*).[66] This ironic description was made to one of his former servant-pupils who would have known her well, so it was apparently made light-heartedly. She also appears, in her own name, as a comical servant in another of the colloquies ('The Poetic Feast'). She clearly was a forceful presence. She seems to have been a loyal servant, considering that she put up with Erasmus's dirty underwear, dietary demands and medical complaints from 1522 to 1535, for she even moved with him to Freiburg. Surprisingly, when he returned to Basel in 1535, he did not bring her back, perhaps because initially he had intended to move back to Freiburg after his work with the printers was finished. Amerbach and a couple of others had to arrange her termination with a reasonable payment. For a present-day reader, it is always interesting to see what Erasmus has to say about women and his relations with them. Despite the early delight he showed in English kisses, later he never showed any interest in female beauty or sexual attraction. Sometimes, as with Margaret (More) Roper or Charitas, the learned sister of his friend Willibald Pirckheimer, he speaks admiringly of female learning; at other times, as with the unlearned Büsslein, he prefers a knowing laugh. It would be most interesting to know what she had to say about Erasmus.

There was another kind of servant who helped with Erasmus's scholarly work, as a paid intern or research assistant, called a *famulus* (Latin for 'servant', a term that Erasmus even applied to himself when he served as an imperial councillor).[67] There was an established tradition in pre-industrial Europe of sending the young away from home for school or apprenticeship, or for schooling in households (Thomas More, for instance, in his early teens served as a page in the household of Cardinal Morton). The young men who worked for Erasmus, who were aged anywhere from their late teens to their mid-twenties, were often talented scholars and were in fact paid apprentices. There was little sense that there was any class difference between these servant-pupils and their master. Serving as a *famulus* was a good option for young men of any social standing, especially when the work was with a famous scholar such as Erasmus. During the final twenty years of his life, Erasmus relied more and more on these well-educated academic apprentices as amanuenses to copy manuscripts, to deal with correspondence, to help with publications and sometimes to act as couriers, and they are often even named in his letters, sometimes in his actual books: Lieven Algoet, Gilbert Cousin, Franz van der Dilft, Karl Harst, Joannes Hovius, Nicolaas Kan, Felix Rex (whom Erasmus nicknamed Polyphemus), Quirinus Talesius and some thirty others.[68] Polyphemus and Kan (as Cannius) are two characters in 'Cyclops', one of the *Colloquies*; they exchange elaborate witticisms, talk about their religion and the importance of the Bible, and defend the New Testament of Erasmus. Some of these apprentices went on to have distinguished careers, often outside the academic world. A well-educated *famulus* could even help with the work in Greek. Erasmus's first known *famulus* was John Smith in Cambridge, some time after 1509; before he left Louvain in 1521 the formal presence of these *famuli* in his life was already established; in 1521 he wrote to Warham, his English patron, saying that 'I feel a regular grandee, keeping as I do two horses who are better cared for than their own master, and two servants better turned out than he is.'[69]

The position of *famulus* was a fluid and complicated mix of domestic and scholarly tasks. Some of the work was to entertain the master. In March 1527 Erasmus wrote to John Longland, Bishop of Lincoln: 'Some of Clement's writings and several letters of the early popes had just been published. I asked my servant to read them to me, for I find this a pleasant way in which to beguile the interval between dinner and sleep.'[70] In March 1531, when there was no 'agreeable companion to keep me in a good frame of mind', another *famulus* was reading the published letters of his friend Guillaume Budé during Erasmus's walk after supper.[71] The servant-pupils might have to copy out letters or an old manuscript. They might be called upon to help with an index or in the collation of a manuscript (one person would read aloud and the other would follow with his own reading, to compare each and look for inconsistencies). At the same time, the *famulus* would be listening to the master, learning a better colloquial Latin, perhaps with their Latin or their manners being corrected (for Erasmus, good Latin and good manners were directly connected).

In the Rhine letter where Erasmus describes his bout of the plague, he mentions getting a massage from a servant. Was the masseur an uneducated manservant like the one with him on the Rhine trip, or was it one of his learned *famuli*? In 1511 Stephen Gardiner, a future bishop and lord chancellor of England, at the age of fourteen was dutifully preparing

Erasmus's daily meal of lettuce cooked in butter and vinegar.[72]
Quirinus Talesius, later a burgomaster of Haarlem, was allowed
to write letters on behalf of Erasmus, helped with accounts
and went on lengthy trips as his courier.[73] The job must have
had its unexpected and unusual moments, with instruction
and advice from the master. This extra-curricular learning is
what Erasmus liked most. Indeed, much of his pedagogical
theory is an attempt to turn the classroom inside out, to install
in formal education a mixture of the unexpected and personal
along with high intellectual standards. Thus, as one would
expect, the *famulus* not only earned a salary but had the oppor-
tunity to be close to the great Erasmus – that is, not simply
to see up close how the scholar actually went about his work,
but to be drawn in to the powerful network of the learned.
Once the *famulus* proved himself, Erasmus would look after
him, placing him with another scholar, helping him to get
into university or obtain a place in the Church.

   One of the last of the *famuli*, and also one of his favourites,
was Gilbert Cousin (he was known by his Latin surname
Cognatus), a well-born and well-educated young Frenchman
who at the age of 24 came to work for Erasmus as an aman-
uensis, and who stayed with him on and off from 1530 to 1535.
He later moved back to the region he had come from,
Franche-Comté, and even though he published widely, he
found himself on a difficult path as a defender of the Erasmian
Catholicism; in his last years he was under permanent house
arrest for his anti-Roman sentiments.[74] There is a well-known
illustration of Cousin working with Erasmus in a study, printed
in one of his books in 1553. The print is based on a painting
that had been commissioned by Cousin and that he kept near

him as a keepsake, so it is likely that the image gives us a picture that in some ways reflects the reality: the facing desks, with Erasmus on the right, dictating; Cousin on the left, writing away at a raised lectern, a standing bookshelf behind him, and a pot of flowers (like the mysterious lilies of the valley in the Dürer print) on the desk between.

Cousin also wrote a short how-to book on servants (the Latin book had the Greek title *Oíketês*, 'household slave' or 'servant'), written and published during the time that Cousin served Erasmus. This book (translated into English in 1543 as *The Office of Servauntes*) shows the reader how to hire and care for, and what to expect from, a good servant. Cousin takes what was probably the Erasmian view – the servant was to be judged in the larger context of his personal development and loyalty, not by the fussy demands made by a master like Rabinus in

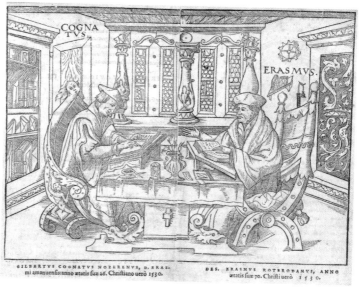

Cousin and Erasmus working together, print based on a painting, published in *Effigies Des. Erasmi Roterodami . . . et Gilberti Cognati* (Basel, 1553).

the *Colloquies*. Cousin himself had managed to make the leap from servant of Erasmus to colleague and even friend, though never an equal, for Cousin was always in awe of the master.

Erasmus was never, despite his reputation, a sole mover and maker; as we can see so clearly, he depended on institutions, networks of friends and patrons, publishers and servants. The presence of the *famuli* reminds us that his intellectual labour was not solitary and depended on a social framework, a point elaborated on recently by the historian Ann Blair.[75] For Erasmus this framework is found not only with his famous friends, but with the servants, the printers and publishers and the couriers, some of them highly educated, who were engaged with him and his vision. This was a kind of miniature network that was tied together by loyalty, social convention, shared intellectual formation and interests. Though the *famuli* were rarely raised to the dignity of a colleague, they sometimes did the work of a colleague, and they are referred to everywhere in Erasmus's correspondence as they wander in and out of his life. The life of Erasmus appears as a series of concentric circles gathered around him – the immediate *familia* or household, the *amici* or core friends and patrons, the admirers who were more at a distance, and, forming another kind of outer circle, the enemies. It was within the *familia*, however, that Erasmus did his daily work.

A good working library is essential for a scholar, especially one who is not working within an institutional context.[76] We know from an inventory made at his death that Erasmus had a collection of some 413 books (sometimes several were bound together, so he actually owned more than five hundred separate titles). This is a substantial working library, but not exceptionally large; some of his contemporaries owned thousands of books. Erasmus had, however, most of the major printed texts of ancient and modern authors that he needed for his scholarship. He started to build a library as a young man, and tried to move it when he changed residence, but his constant movement meant that he was separated for long periods from his books. When he moved to Louvain, then Basel, then Freiburg, then back to Basel, the library, usually packed in barrels, was a major concern in his travel plans.

The survival of a personal library offers us the possibility to look behind the scenes at the scholar's research methods, sources and other aspects in what might be called the factory of production. Ownership is of course not the most reliable guide to actual intellectual influences; a book is in a library for many different reasons (it may once have been read carefully or it was meant to be read in the future or perhaps was there merely to be consulted, or it was a gift and was never read at all; and so forth). Books were often stored in chests, but it seems likely that Erasmus kept many of them displayed on shelves (as in the portrait by Metsys or the picture of Erasmus and Cousin working together in Freiburg). Historians of the book are interested in the way a personal library might have been organized for the swift recovery of knowledge, though a library of 413 volumes is not overwhelmingly large; one suspects Erasmus knew how to find each book simply from its shape and binding, and would not have needed any form of labelling or system of filing, once the book was placed in a regular relation to the others.

Erasmus's library was gathered as a response to the needs of work. It included a lot of major standard editions, such as

Plato, Aristotle and Augustine. However, we do not know in detail how he used these books, which he clearly regarded as essential to his practice of scholarship. Early on in his career, Erasmus encouraged others to annotate their books heavily. There is a letter (dated 1489 by Percy Allen) which Erasmus sent to an unknown recipient with his own transcription of the plays of Terence. He encouraged the friend to use this precious handmade book energetically:

> I consider as lovers of books not those who keep their books hidden in their store-chests and never handle them, but those who, by nightly as well as daily use, thumb them, batter them, wear them out, who fill out all the margins with annotations of many kinds, and who prefer the marks of a fault they have erased to a neat copy full of faults.[77]

Of course, if a book has been marked up, the marginal notes can tell us a lot about the way the scholar engaged with it during the act (or acts) of reading. Some people indexed their books, some marked off an interesting passage with the stroke of a pen or even a dirty fingernail, or drew an engaging picture in the margin (as you can see from the illustration by a contemporary reader of the *Adages* featured on p. 92), some wrote insulting comments or even crossed out offensive passages. Luther's extant copy of Erasmus's *New Testament* (1527 edn) gives us over two hundred marginal notes on Erasmus's commentary (we do not have the 1519 edition that he used for his translation of the Bible).[78] Now, if only we had Erasmus's marked-up copy of Luther's *On the Bonded Will*, for that book is listed in the inventory. It may be that in his lengthy *Hyperaspistes*, Erasmus's response to Luther's book, he said all that he was thinking. But maybe there is more. Another thing that would be of great interest is whether Erasmus prepared indexes of the books that he was reading, the same way that he prepared indexes for his books in print (like the *Adages*, the St Jerome edition and his *Praise of Folly*). We know that Erasmus himself appreciated the marginal annotations of earlier readers: the early humanist scholar Rudolph Agricola (a great hero to Erasmus) had annotated his copy of a 1478 edition of Seneca before his death in 1485; Erasmus borrowed this precious book to consult extensively for his own revised edition of Seneca in 1529.[79] His instruction for the shipping of Agricola's old book indicates his reverence for the material object: 'You need have no apprehensions about it; no one will touch it besides me. Cover it with paper wrapping with a outer covering of a waxed linen cloth. It will be sent back with the same care.'[80]

The fate of Erasmus's library is unusual. In 1524 he had a visitor who stayed with him for a while (not as a *famulus*, but rather as a *convictor* or companion, in the role of what might be called a disciple). This companion was a 25-year-old Polish scholar named Jan Łaski, who had studied in Bologna and Padua; as nephew of the Archbishop of Gniezno, he was destined for higher things.[81] The two got along well. Before he left, Łaski offered to buy Erasmus's library, with the condition that Erasmus could retain the books until his death. The deal was signed in June 1526. Łaski later ran into financial problems, and Erasmus offered to cancel the arrangement, but Łaski hung on. When Erasmus died in 1536 the payments were still not complete, and Łaski had to settle up before he could collect the books. The books were shipped to him, including many that Erasmus had purchased in the ten years since the deal was signed. But Łaski by this point had been disinherited and was travelling from place to place, and he began to sell the books. Some were lost during a Channel crossing (Łaski had moved to London for a while), and the library, whose contents had been inventoried in 1536, was ultimately scattered. Only a handful of the original books have been located, so we do not have the materials that are needed to uncover in detail the way Erasmus read his books, though several of his manuscripts (now in the Vatican Library, and at Copenhagen and Basel) do provide fascinating insights into his methods as a writer: how he built up his texts cumulatively, how he revised them and how he built his indexes.

WHEN SCHOLARS GO TO BATTLE

'But oh, the slanders which many madmen now pour upon my defenceless head.'[82] For the last twenty years of his life, Erasmus was not only famous as a great humanist scholar and a thoughtful voice in religion. In many circles he was notorious. His humanist ideas offended the teachers of scholastic theology; his religious ideas offended dogmatic Roman Catholics and committed Protestants. And his wit generated envy and distrust among his enemies. His debates are lengthy and complex. We are interested in what these controversies have to tell us about his work as a scholar and the way his belief in the value of friendship and intimacy as well as his religious faith were shaken by these attacks, and also, perhaps, how they forced him now and then into becoming someone other than the persona he had conceived.

Because of the varied way we subjectively read and interpret texts, with individual interpretation an inevitable feature of every reading of a text, there is always disagreement in the humanities. Arguments over meaning are expressed in private exchanges or in the classroom or in specialized publications, but now and then they explode into outright public controversy, sometimes highly personal and vicious, with refined and outrageous attempts to wound. We have touched on this already. It is often said, in the political or professional arena, that a disagreement 'is not personal' – perhaps because the debate is over the truth. But in the world of humanist discourse, it is personal, because interpretation is tied to the interior mind and a point of view that is shaped by the particular intellectual history of the individual reader (as Erasmus himself helps us to understand). Often enough the disputes begin with petty insults or minor misunderstandings. Fortunately, such petty disputes are often laid aside, if only through exhaustion. But some are taken right to the limit.

Misinterpretation or losing a battle over meaning can have serious consequences. We can see the perception of extreme risk at play in the way interpretive decisions are made today in a court of law or in the political arena. In Erasmus's time, a new interpretation of a line or two in the Bible might be seen as heretical and threatening to the social order; the heretic could be excommunicated, sent to prison or even burned at the stake (we have already mentioned Erasmus's admirer Louis de Berquin, who was executed in 1529).[83] The very nature of human belief, social order and the idea of self was determined by a relationship to God. The risks of misunderstanding or of preaching error regarding that relationship were great.

Erasmus saw his time of strife as a version of the Trojan War, but his twenty-year war was twice as long as the one at Troy, and, unlike Achilles, he engaged two armies at once: the Catholics and the Protestants.[84] We have already seen two of the first controversies, one that was set off in the letter from Martin Dorp regarding *The Praise of Folly* and another in Louvain, with Edward Lee. There are some forty different such battles, some quickly settled or safely ignored, others dangerous to Erasmus's reputation and at times, he felt, possibly to his life.[85] Some of the debates continued long after his death. His best-known enemy was Martin Luther, but the most relentless were his fellow Roman Catholics, who attacked him as a friend of Luther. His responses fill up more than one-tenth of his collected works.

Erasmus found the constant need to answer his critics exhausting: 'How much better it would be to agree together, and pass our time in the garden of the Muses,' he said to his French correspondent Étienne Poncher, who was appointed Bishop of Paris in 1503.[86] And yet, as his biographer James Tracy has said, 'This self-described lover of peace will never be properly understood unless we recognize that he also loved a good fight.'[87] Erasmus was articulate, tenacious and often responded quickly. He also had a streak of paranoia that added urgency and an unusual nastiness to some of his writings. His need to maintain his reputation, his livelihood, his friends, his independence, his *amour propre*, the rightness of his scholarship as well as his higher vision of Christian humanism – these mixed motives all contributed to the energy of his response.

He had already attracted critics for his comments on scholastic philosophy and the monastic orders, mostly in his *Praise of Folly*, but with the publication of the text and annotations of the New Testament he proved to be an even more unsettling presence. For Erasmus the New Testament was a sacred text, the living words of Christ and the Apostles now preserved in written form. In Erasmus's view, it is through the written words that we make our approach to the divine. Yet even though the Scripture was divine in origin, it remained in the human world by being written down and transmitted through copying, translation and interpretation. Even St Jerome acknowledged that translators were capable of human error.[88] All these processes are distinctly human, not at all divine, and are thus open to fault. Nevertheless, to many of Erasmus's contemporaries, even scholars, the Vulgate Bible was *the* Bible, much as the King James Bible later came to be considered in English to be the direct word of God. To meddle with its language was improper, even when there were very obvious technical errors in its transmission or translation. By raising the possibility of change, and then, in 1519, by proposing his own corrected Vulgate, Erasmus raised the ire of those theologians who already disliked him.

We have seen what happened with Edward Lee in the dispute over the text of the New Testament. Indeed, even the reading of a single line could affect a friendship. For instance, Jacques Lefèvre d'Étaples, an enormously learned French scholar then known for his work on Aristotle, had met Erasmus, and they were naturally drawn to one another by their shared love of the humanist *bonae litterae*.[89] Lefèvre had studied in Italy and was now well known in the small world

of international scholarship. He was turning to biblical scholarship, in part influenced by Erasmus's edition of Valla's book
on the text of the New Testament. However, these men, who
shared so much, were to have a falling out. In Hebrews 2, the
biblical author (unknown, but often said to be St Paul)
describes the place of man and Christ in relation to God. It
is a difficult passage. Lefèvre argued that the correct reading
of Hebrews 2:7 (which I give here in English) was 'you made
him [that is, man] a little lower than God', whereas Erasmus
had argued that the passage actually said 'a little lower than
the angels'. The problem is that 'man' in an earlier verse
refers to both man *and* the Son of Man (Jesus in his human
condition), and Lefèvre's interpretation attempts to give Jesus
a direct relation to God. Erasmus followed the text more literally, and thereby stressed Christ's humanity (today's
standard translations follow Erasmus). In the second edition
of his text of St Paul's letters, published in 1515, Lefèvre
referred to Erasmus's version as *impius* or heretical. Erasmus
was always concerned to be seen as orthodox in his opinions,
even if his opponents considered him anything but. However,
for a major scholar such as Lefèvre to call him *impius* was too
much. Erasmus immediately wrote an *Apologia* to explain his
own position more clearly, and had the published book
respectfully hand-delivered to Lefèvre by a mutual friend. In
his book, Erasmus argued that his interpretation and Lefèvre's,
while different, were both doctrinally acceptable. As Erasmus
correctly understood, aligning the two scholars was important, for humanists had to stick together to repel the
accusations of heresy against humanist scholars. Even after
the *Apologia*, Lefèvre maintained a disconcerting silence. Later

Erasmus was able to do a favour for Lefèvre; the two met again in Basel in 1526 and appear to have been reconciled. But for several years the threat of a reputational wound by a fellow scholar, a scholar of such rank as to be considered in some quarters his equal, weighed on Erasmus.

In this debate, resolved over time, we can see how academic debate, though it originates in a passionate search for truth, is also fuelled by challenges to reputation and hierarchical standing that extend beyond the immediate relations of the two men. At any one time there may be many geniuses at work, many middling scholars, and many who engage and then choose to retire, but at the very top there is what has been termed a 'limited field of attention' that allows for only a few competing ideological leaders.[90] This limited space opens up in times of educational, religious or technological change. Erasmus was writing in a time of deep contestation. His modifications to philological research, theology and education had successfully challenged long-standing ideas of truth, and he came to occupy that limited room for attention. A challenge even by a like-minded scholar could affect this reputation. The attack by Lee was less serious than that of Lefèvre, but because Lee was low in status and in the party of known adversaries, he was potentially more dangerous. The battle with Lee became personal and cruel. The battle with Lefèvre was partially resolved, but there was a lingering distrust. These varied outcomes are typical in the complex world of humanist friendship.

The greatest public challenge to Erasmus came from Martin Luther.[91] Luther was born in 1483 and grew up in relative comfort in a mining town in Germany. He went to university intending to study law, but was more drawn to theology and philosophy. In a transitional moment in his life, at the age of 22, he was almost struck by a lightning bolt and he made an immediate vow to St Anne to join a monastery. Soon afterwards, he became an Augustinian monk (Erasmus was an Augustinian canon regular, a different order). Luther was ordained in 1507, and by 1512 had become a doctor of theology. In 1515, a sign of his competence, he became administrator of the eleven monasteries in his region. Yet he was not a passive servant of the Church. Like Erasmus and many others, he was engaged in a personal search for religious salvation and was deeply disappointed by the lack of piety in both monastic life and the Church generally. During his continuing studies, he began to reject the scholastic philosophy and to formulate an idea of faith outside the usual church structure.

In 1517 a call went forth in Luther's region offering indulgences (in this case, a payment accompanied by prayer that was believed to reduce the punishment in this life or the afterlife for committed sins). The funds were to pay for the ongoing construction of St Peter's Basilica in Rome. So, on 31 October, as part of his questioning of the ways of the Church and as normal academic practice, Luther proposed in his current university at Wittenberg a list of 95 theses (short statements to be disputed) that he was willing to debate publicly. The nature of these theses, which challenged the whole idea of an indulgence, was however highly contentious, and caught the eyes of many people. His scandalous text was quickly published. Church authorities were nervous and annoyed, and, as they called Luther to task, his private thoughts began to harden into public opinion. He defended his theses in April 1518 in

Heidelberg before other Augustinian monks. His public position was in turn strengthened by a conversion he experienced in 1519. In three short years, a large community of followers formed in support of him (many Germans were tired of being pushed around by the Roman Church and were drawn to a more personal piety of the kind that Erasmus had also witnessed in the *devotio moderna* of the Brothers of the Common Life and written about in his *Enchiridion*). Soon afterwards, Luther, who continued to speak out, was facing excommunication. Already well educated, he turned out to be a highly articulate communicator and effective leader. Through the adversity he faced, he gained in reputation, power and confidence. The engraved portrait of him by Lucas Cranach the Elder shows him in 1520, still a member of his order.

Luther could not help but see Erasmus as having headed down the road before him. Erasmus was scathing on the subject of monasteries, the behaviour of monks, the warlike and avaricious Church. And in his 1516 edition of the New Testament, he showed himself to be a close and devoted reader of the Bible. But Luther did not warm to a certain quality he found in Erasmus. As he said in March 1517 in a letter to one of his colleagues: 'The human prevails in him more than the divine.'[92] Readers who sense a strong piety in Erasmus might find this assessment unfair. There is no doubt about Erasmus's piety, about his acknowledgement of the powerful mystery of the Bible – his willingness, for instance, to read the Bible allegorically in order to seek out its divine and hidden truth (the *Enchiridion* early on encourages attention to the allegorical meaning). Yet Erasmus also seems to live in and for the world, and for some readers that is his greatest strength. As I

Lucas Cranach the Elder, *Martin Luther as an Augustinian Monk*, 1520, engraving.

said at the start of this book, Luther called Erasmus an eel. By now we can see that the 'fig-leaf' by which we seize the Erasmian eel appears to be a constellation of qualities: his love of humanity, his friends, the ancient texts of the pagan and Christian worlds, and a welcoming Christ whom he finds to be a living presence in the words of the biblical text. From the early *Enchiridion* to the late *Preparation for Death*, Erasmus is concerned with the way religion travels through language and is lived in this world. Unlike Luther, he does not seem to suffer personally for his faith. Looked at this way, Luther's assessment seems correct.

Despite his initial reservation, Luther tried to connect with Erasmus. First it was through friends, such as Philipp Melanchthon, a gifted younger scholar (and one of the great figures of the Reformation movement). Erasmus ingenuously claimed not to know much about Luther: 'Martin Luther's way of life wins all men's approval here, but opinions vary about his teaching. I myself have not yet read his books.'[93] Earlier in the same month, April 1519, Erasmus had written to Frederick the Wise, Elector of Saxony, a protector of Luther, that 'I know as little of Luther as I know of any man . . . His life, at least, is highly spoken of by all who know him.'[94] Soon afterwards he received a letter from Luther praising Erasmus; Erasmus answered cautiously, giving the advice that Luther should deal with his enemies by 'courtesy and moderation'.[95] The letter was circulated, and Erasmus had to defend his generous response, which was seen by some Catholic theologians as too conciliatory, a sign of weakness or perhaps even a willingness to join Luther. Later in the year he wrote to Cardinal Albert of Brandenburg, repeating that 'Of Luther

I know as little as I do of anyone; his books I have not yet found time to read, except for dipping into some of them here and there.'[96] But any attempts to distance himself from Luther were unimportant to his enemies, who could see the interests Luther shared with Erasmus. And Erasmus, who had acknowledged Luther's learning, saw that the humanities, not just theology, were under attack. This confusing position was not improved by Erasmus's response to the papal bull *Exsurge Domine*, of June 1520, which laid out the 41 heresies of Luther. He continued to defend Luther, even arguing that the papal bull was not really the informed doing of Pope Leo X. Erasmus's position was complex, and while it was clear enough to him, it was not so to his enemies or indeed to his followers.

Despite his training in theology, Luther early on saw himself and was seen by many as a humanist scholar, an association he shared with Erasmus. Because the humanities were being threatened, Erasmus continued to support Luther and pushed for a possible conciliation with the papal authorities, even though he did stop Froben from publishing a collection of Luther's writings. He did this both openly and occasionally in secret.[97] In one anonymous work (now fully accepted by scholars as his), he attacked the papal delegate Girolamo Aleandro, whom he saw as a destructive force against any conciliation. Aleandro, that old friend with whom he had roomed in Aldus's household in Venice, and whom he described as 'unquestionably the best scholar of our age in the three tongues',[98] he now described as a Jew, hence (in his terms) a betrayer of the Gospel – 'his conceit is uncontrollable, his greed insatiable, his lust as unspeakable as it is unbounded.' Indeed, he never shook this new fantasy that Aleandro (who became an archbishop and a cardinal) was Jewish, and the 'blood-brother of Judas'.[99]

His attitude towards Jews has for many readers been a black mark against Erasmus; clearly he had fully accepted the conventional anti-Semitism of the time, though there is no sign that his attitude was as poisonous as that found in the later writings and the table-talk or transcribed conversations of Luther.[100] As we saw with the obscene attack on Lee, Erasmus sometimes reached out for blunt weapons and, in doing so, exposed what we now see as a failure in his own ideal of tolerance. Such things happened when he was at war. He was complicated in his responses. After his attack on Aleandro, he prepared a set of notes for Frederick of Saxony, who was being pressured by the papal legates, and here he argued – and it is a compelling and profound observation – that Luther was not the enemy so much as a symptom of a great social longing: 'the world is thirsting for the gospel truth, and seems to be borne on its way by some supernatural desire.'[101]

Erasmus was arguing for some kind of compromise, but this was impossible. By January 1521 Leo X had excommunicated Luther, and by April Luther was at the Diet (imperial assembly) at Worms before a secular tribunal, the famous scene of his final claim, 'Here I stand' (words that scholars now believe he never spoke, however well they sum up his position).[102] Now under the threat of death by the imperial faction, Luther was whisked away under the protection of Frederick of Saxony to the castle at Wartburg; during this period of captivity, he translated the Bible into German (for the New Testament relying on the Greek in Erasmus's 1519 edition).

Agostino Veneziano, *Girolamo Aleandro, Archbishop of Brindisi, c.* 1536, engraving.

In April, at this crucial moment in the developing crisis, Erasmus was in Brussels. We get an interesting glimpse of how he was seen by an observer at this time. The painter Albrecht Dürer had been in the area a few months earlier and had dropped in on Erasmus (a rough sketch shown opposite, now in the Louvre, was the result). When he heard of the disappearance of Luther, whom he thought had been taken by the enemy instead of a friend, Dürer was deeply shaken. In his journal he exclaimed,

> O Erasmus Roterodamus, why do you hold back? See, what the unjust tyranny of worldly might and the powers of darkness are capable of! Hear us, soldier of Christ! Ride forth with the Lord Christ, defend the truth, win the martyr's crown. Else you are nothing but a feeble old *Manneken*.[103]

Yet Erasmus was no Luther. He was a great influencer, not a great leader. He really disliked Luther's aggressive position, yet he continued to fight for him. He struggled to get a better deal for Luther from Leo X's successor, Pope Adrian VI, but none was forthcoming. For all this work, and more, history has decided that he will be the *Manneken*, the weakling in this battle. Calling him that certainly makes for a clearer narrative. Yet Erasmus was extraordinarily tenacious and high-minded, as he fought for, and successfully maintained, his independence, and at the same time argued for what he felt was right in the work of Luther.

During the next couple of years, Erasmus was hard-pressed to join one side or the other. Finally he figured out an approach

Albrecht Dürer, *Erasmus*, 1520, black chalk on paper.

that would satisfy the many requests to respond to Luther. He did not challenge him on the evolving doctrines regarding the sacraments, the nature of the body and blood of Christ in the Eucharist, marriage of priests, confession or Church government. Instead he chose a topic that seemed slightly off to the side, the idea of free will, discussed by Luther in his *Assertion* (1520) as one of 41 items named as heretical in the papal bull that led to his excommunication.[104] Erasmus's *Diatribe de libero arbitrio* (Discussion of Free Will) came out in 1524.[105]

The *Diatribe* (which in both Latin and Greek meant 'discussion', not the searing indictment that it has come to mean in English) was a daring move for Erasmus. Though he had studied theology and was widely read in philosophy, the issue of free will is not easy and philosophical argument was not his forte. The problem is that though the initial questions are relatively simple, the answers are difficult and really cannot be resolved without a bold move. If God is fully prescient and knows who will be saved and who will not be saved from our state of sin, how free are we in our own efforts to be saved? Aren't our choices already known by God and part of His plan? If they are already known, how can these choices by made by us? Are they not strictly speaking already made? And yet, for Erasmus, who was committed to teaching, moral improvement and self control, there had to be some allowance for agency.

We might get around our obvious lack of free will by redefining or qualifying our understanding of God's power to predict and command, or by restating what we consider to be the conditions of freedom. Erasmus instead attempted to resolve the issue using three principal arguments. First, the Bible is obscure, and it may well be that we do not understand what God wants us to understand, because the mind of God is essentially unknowable, so we do not know if he refuses our will. Second, there are in the Bible, from the Ten Commandments onwards, many exhortations for us to act in ways that clearly imply that we can and should make choices; why are these exhortations in the Bible if they are not intended to be followed by an exercise of our agency? Third, Erasmus argued that we are misinterpreting those places in the Bible, such as in St Paul, that appear to refuse free will. He ends his lengthy citation of passages and commentary with this question: 'Why, you may ask, attribute anything at all to free will?' His answer is that we need free will in order 'To allow the ungodly, who have deliberately fallen short of the grace of God, to be deservedly condemned; to clear God of the false accusation of cruelty and injustice; to free us from despair, protect us from complacency, and spur us on to moral endeavour.'[106] Of course, Erasmus concludes, our salvation depends on the grace of God, but there is room for human agency. In the end, however, this subject of free will is not something that should be discussed more than necessary, 'especially in front of the unlearned'. He ends by claiming that if he is wrong, so are all the commentators on this subject over the past 1,300 years.

After finishing the work, Erasmus waited for Luther's response. He was wary, even though those close to Luther were optimistic. He heard from Melanchthon:

As for your *Diatribe* on the freedom of the will, it had a very mild reception here . . . Your moderate attitude

gave great satisfaction, though you do slip in a barbed
remark now and then . . . I personally am quite clear
about Luther's good will towards you, and this gives
me hope that he will make a straightforward reply. In
return it is your duty, my dear Erasmus, to make sure
that this discussion is not embittered by any greater
ill will on your side.[107]

Erasmus responded:

But as for Luther's intentions, there is much which
makes me hesitate; and if I do not dare to trust my own
judgment absolutely, I think, nevertheless, that I can
plumb a man's mind as well from his writings as from
his company. Luther has a fiery and tempestuous temperament. In everything he does you can recognize
'the anger of the son of Peleus [Achilles] who knows
not how to yield'.[108]

In other words, Luther's writings show him better. It is interesting to see how this idea of reading a personality through
a written text is now applied by Erasmus to this battle with
Luther. And one cannot help but note that if this really were
a Trojan War, and Luther were Achilles, Erasmus had unwit-
tingly placed himself on the losing side.

Luther's response, *De servo arbitrio* (The Enslaved Will),
appeared at the end of 1524. It was a long and carefully prepared rebuke, as brutal and as fiery as Erasmus had anticipated.
Luther begins his book by expressing his sorrow that so great
a scholar should have made such a fool of himself: 'your book

struck me as so cheap and paltry that I feel profoundly sorry for you, defiling as you were your very elegant and ingenious style with such trash . . . like refuse or ordure being carried in gold and silver vases.'[109] After this wonderfully condescending start, he goes on, 'I owe you no small thanks, for you have made me far more sure of my own position by letting me see the case for free choice.' Erasmus's treatment was 'plain evidence that free choice is a pure fiction.'[110] These words, 'that free choice is a pure fiction', directly repeat the claim Luther had made in his earlier *Assertion*.[111] In other words, Erasmus's studied attempt to correct Luther's thinking had only confirmed his position.

Luther proceeds to march through Erasmus's arguments, laying waste to them as he goes. He dismisses the idea that the Bible is too difficult to understand. The Bible is only obscure to those who do not read it carefully. If you cannot read the Bible well, it means that you are not open to the Bible, that you have a 'darkened heart' and 'truly understand nothing of it'.[112] For Luther, it is 'fundamentally necessary and salutary for a Christian to know that God foreknows nothing contingently, but that he foresees and purposes and does all things by his immutable, eternal, and infallible will'.[113] His response was long and revisited all Erasmus's claims in detail, including the key passages in the Old and New Testaments, and thoroughly rejected his reading of St Paul. At the end Luther does pay an unusual compliment, that Erasmus was right about one thing: the issue of free will is essential to Luther's faith:

> You and you alone have seen the question on which everything hinges, and have aimed at the vital spot; for

which I sincerely thank you, since I am only too glad to give as much attention to this subject as time and leisure permit. If those who have attacked me hitherto had done the same, and if those who now boast of new spirits and new revelations would still do it, we should have less of sedition and sects and more of peace and concord. But God has in this way through Satan punished our ingratitude.[114]

Erasmus received Luther's book at the very end of 1525 or the beginning of 1526. He knew the book was destined for the Frankfurt book fair in the spring, and that once released it would have a tremendous impact in the world of learning. He immediately got to work on a response. The speed of writing and publication was impressive: his detailed response (twice the length of his *Diatribe*) was ready in a few weeks, and all six presses of Froben had it printed by February. The work was called the *Hyperaspistes* or 'shield bearer, defender' (the word is Greek; *aspis* in Greek means 'shield' but also 'viper' or 'asp', a sense that Luther later applied to Erasmus).

Early on in this work Erasmus strikes a theme that we have by now determined to be crucial to the underlying world of humanities scholarship, and that is friendship. Erasmus's *Diatribe* was written as a 'discussion' from one friend to another, but Luther has written as an enemy who pretends to be a friend. Erasmus accuses Luther of breaking this unspoken bond, by writing with poisoned words:

But since in this so very unfriendly response you want to appear to be a friend, and (heavens spare us!) a

fair-minded one at that, I want you and your adherents
to know that I am not so stupid as to be taken in by such
tricks or so faint-hearted as to be disturbed by your
insults. It would have been simpler if you had openly
raged against me in your accustomed way. For you ordinarily put on the lion's skin and conduct your business
with a club . . . I know the force of your style, which is
like a torrent rushing down a mountain with a great
roar and sweeping rocks and tree trunks with it.[115]

In his *Hyperaspistes*, Erasmus gives a response to Luther's attack
by following the same point-by-point refutation. Here he
again principally stresses the difficulty of Scripture, the need
for interpreters, and the way that the Church has provided
a continuous tradition of interpretation. Luther has improp-
erly stepped outside that tradition, for only Luther in his own
mind knows best. Erasmus, faced with a tradition of con-
flicting interpretations, is less sure. This is not scepticism,
but an acknowledgement of the role of the Church and its
many theologians. Who, he asks, is right? He concludes with
the theme that opened the book, the need for balanced, reciprocal friendship:

you still have leisure to write such large books, such
elaborately abusive books, against a person whose mind
is completely unknown to you, at least it is so if you
judge it to be only like what you make it out to be. If
you had ranted and raved with free and open insults,
we could praise your frankness and put it down to
your temperament; but as it is you carry on with crafty

malice. If you had been content with two or three insults, they might seem to have just slipped out; as it is your whole book swarms everywhere with abuse. You begin with it, you proceed with it, you end with it. If you had glutted yourself with only one kind of insult, calling me a blockhead, an ass, or a mushroom, one after the other, I would have given no answer except that line from the comedy: 'I am a human being and I consider nothing human foreign to me.' But such things could not satiate your hatred; you had to go on to make me into a Lucian or an Epicurus, disbelieving Holy Scripture to the extent that I think there is not even a God, an enemy of Christianity, finally a blasphemer against God and the Christian religion. Such are the charms scattered throughout your book, which is set over against my *Discussion*, which contains no insults.[116]

The second part of the *Hyperaspistes*, which responded to the second half of Luther's *De servo arbitrio*, appeared in the middle of 1527. It revisits the passages on free will in the Old and New Testaments and looks again at the passages that seem to propose the bonded will, thus completing the material in the first part. Erasmus asks again, does God's foreknowledge impose absolute necessity? In this analysis he more carefully looks at the power of grace, but still sees room for human agency, which Luther has resolutely denied. When you read the book, you get a sense of the effort that went into it, but also of a repetitive quality, an obsessive return to a rereading of the older argument. The *Hyperaspistes 2* was reprinted only twice in Erasmus's lifetime. And Luther claimed never to have read either part of Erasmus's lengthy response.

This debate over free will is still alive today, though in a very different form, with God and salvation often left out of the discussion. Luther was deeply spiritual and could sense ways in which his own background, his context (which was a Christian faith), compelled him to act in his life. According to him, we are already set on our spiritual path in life and God has determined the final outcome. Though we can act well in our daily lives, we cannot ourselves achieve a final salvation. This kind of thinking persists today in the way that some argue that our larger context (now in terms of evolution, genetic inheritance, family history, psychological trauma, social conditions of birth and so on) sets a path forwards for us that we are forced to follow, locked into a powerful logic, not even shaken now and then by chance events. By contrast, while Erasmus acknowledges the power of the mysterious force that seems to drive us forwards or draw us onwards (for him it is Christ), he also allows for moments of individual agency – our right to remake ourselves as best we can, to make choices for the good, to improve not only ourselves but our social world. For a teacher and believer in our ability to make ourselves (as he indeed had made himself), his position is consistent. Salvation comes from God – he never suggests otherwise – but our decisions in life can lead to a moral purity that will be seen favourably when judgement comes. There are many today who would agree with his position given our present-day emphasis on self-help, individual agency and the importance of education in effecting social and personal change.

Though Luther claimed never to have read the *Hyperaspistes*, he remained obsessed with Erasmus. His *Table Talk*, random comments written down by those close to him, is full of Erasmus the eel, Erasmus the Epicurean, Erasmus the Momus (a scoffing critic), Erasmus the Caiaphas (the Jewish high priest who helped to kill Jesus), Erasmus the lover of Satan, Erasmus the rogue, Erasmus the inflaming teacher of young boys, Erasmus the king of ambiguity, Erasmus the starling, Erasmus the bedbug, Erasmus 'more harmful than Lucian', Erasmus the hater of religion, Erasmus who treats life as comedy and tragedy, Erasmus the fallen man:

> The expression of his face indicates shrewdness [*calliditatem*], but he only scoffs at God and religion. He uses, to be sure, the greatest words, Holy Christ, the holy Word, the holy sacraments, but in truth he is very indifferent to these things. He has a gift for biting satire, and his writing is very clever, as in his *Praise of Folly* and his *Julius*; but in teaching he is most cold [*frigidissime*].[117]

Luther and Erasmus never met. Here Luther is commenting on a portrait (Lucas Cranach, close to Luther, did a portrait modelled on one by Holbein). Nevertheless, the personal aspect of the quarrel seemed just as real for Luther as for Erasmus. To Luther, there was something so profoundly disturbing about Erasmus that he was aroused to a visceral hatred.

The public debate between the two had a final eruption in 1534. Luther wrote a letter dated March to Nikolaus von

Amsdorf, a Lutheran in Magdeburg. It was soon published.
In it, he railed at length against Erasmus — against his scepticism, his unreliability as an interpreter of the Bible, his
danger as an educator, and his 'indirect, ambiguous, insidious,
indecent, Satanic' language.[118] It comes across as an obsessive
rant. Erasmus was encouraged to return the attack, but he
was exhausted: 'I have no desire to contend with Luther. As
for me, every day I prepare for my last day — I am an old man
terribly afflicted by illness, broken down by labours, over-
whelmed by rabid and raging books.'[119] Soon enough,
however, he rallied, with a spirited response to Luther's
'absurd and deranged' accusations,[120] and it was published in
April 1534. 'Luther the brawler', he says, 'is trying to convince
the world that Erasmus not only is an unbeliever as regards
divine matters, but that for a long time now he has been using
tricks, stratagems, and everything in his power to unsettle
the whole Christian religion, then dash it down entirely and
in its place bring paganism back into the world.'[121] He defends
his *Catechism* (a work accused by Luther of poisoning the
mind of the young) and his theory of language, his own and
the Bible's, including ambiguity: 'As if Holy Scripture and the
orthodox Fathers' writings as well were not full of ambiguous
words! For anything metaphorical is ambiguous, and there
are no plain human words in which we can speak adequately
of divine things', a striking insight.[122] He admits, 'I am by natural inclination rather given to jesting, both in my writings
and in my conversations with friends,' but Luther is a 'tyrant
of hyperbole' who contradicts himself and twists the meaning
of the Bible to fit his own doctrine.[123] Even though it is common to claim that Erasmus was broken by the controversies,

Workshop of Lucas Cranach the Elder, *Martin Luther*, c. 1532, oil on wood.

Lucas Cranach the Elder, *Desiderius Erasmus*, c. 1530–36, oil on panel.

this lively response to Luther is a late display of that kind of 'affirmation' that I believe carried him through his final years.

The Luther debate must have been extraordinarily stressful, but even more exhausting were the continued attacks on Erasmus by Roman Catholic scholars. The enemies from Louvain and Paris were joined by others from Italy and Spain. Erasmus's ideas regarding pagan literature, historical consciousness, methods of improving ancient texts (not least the Bible), criticism of monastic behaviour, superstitions and Church greed (especially in his *Colloquies*), and his pietist theology of Christ, altogether formed an extremely potent threat to the conservative elements in the Catholic Church. Many believers – today we might term them 'progressives' – were drawn to Erasmus's philosophy of Christ and its idea of a tolerant world of friendship and moral harmony, in part the ideal of ancient moral philosophy, but tied to a faith that favoured the individual in a direct relation to Christ. The reaction of the conservative Church to Erasmus was of course also a reaction to Luther (after all, by 1524 he had learned that he had laid an egg that Luther had hatched, even though his was a hen's egg, 'and Luther', he went on to say 'has hatched a chick of very, very different feather'[124]). Erasmus's interpretations of the New Testament, his attitude towards monasticism and the sacrament of marriage, his satirical writings, his independent spirit and life, even his marvellous literary style – all these came under sustained fire from different quarters. He wrote responses, explanations, castigations and *apologiae* to keep these enemies at bay. For someone deemed by his enemies to be cautious, changeable, sneaky or too clever by half, he never let up on this earnest labour of explanation and defence. There is a nobility in his willingness to stand up for his positions even when they could alienate his friends and further provoke his enemies. The constant attacks on Erasmus and the constant need for vigilance and response took their toll on mind and body. As he said a letter of March 1529 to Ludwig Baer, the Basel theologian and a loyal friend, if it were not for his Christian faith,

> how could this little body, this feeble spirit, have borne up under the assaults of so many ills? To say nothing of the burdens of old age, which are weighty enough in themselves, or the much weightier burdens of ill health, what could be harder for the human heart to bear than to be attacked on every side by men with the instincts of a gladiator, and that without cease or res-pite. It is said that Hercules never faced two monsters at once.[125]

BASEL AND THE MOVE TO FREIBURG

Basel, with its location on the Rhine river, was a prosperous trading town with some 10,000 inhabitants. The town was a late joiner to the Swiss Confederacy, only doing so in 1501, yet the cantons reacted differently to the Reformation, with Zurich, Berne, Basel and Geneva accepting different versions of reform, and other cantons rejecting it, resulting in two centuries of internal conflict in Switzerland. The Reformation came to Basel as it did to so many other places: through the energetic representations by particular individuals who early on accepted the revolutionary project of Luther. In Basel one of these individuals was Johannes Oecolampadius, the scholar of Greek and Hebrew who had worked closely with Erasmus on the New Testament. Initially a Roman Catholic cleric, he celebrated the first Protestant communion in the city in 1525, and within a couple of years he had married. Oecolampadius' trajectory was typical of many humanist-trained Germans who had moved away from Erasmus's nuanced Catholic position. He was one of the figures who had accelerated the reformation in Basel that culminated in 1529 with a mob attack on the churches, which were stripped of all Catholic images. About the same time the city fathers banned the Catholic mass. By 1529, Erasmus had had enough.

In April of that year Erasmus made his reluctant move to Freiburg am Breisgau, the German imperial city, 70 kilometres (45 mi.) away, where other Catholics had also relocated. He took rooms in an impressive building called 'Zum Walfisch', or 'House of the Whale', that had been recently built by the emperor's treasurer, and after a year and a half he bought a house a few streets away.[126] The house, including its renovations, cost Erasmus 800 florins, a sign that he really had reached material prosperity (800 Rhenish gold florins were enough to pay the wages for an Antwerp master mason for twenty years).[127] Freiburg was not the happiest change for him, however. The town had a university and there was a community of Basel expatriates, but it lacked the intellectual stimulation of Basel, as well as proximity to old friends. In Freiburg Erasmus continued with his scholarly writing and maintained his relations with both the printers and old friends in Basel. In this sense the Basel and Freiburg years can be seen as continuous.

JOAN. OECOLAMPADIVS
IN DOMINI QVONDAM FVLSI LVX SPLENDIDA TEMPLO
CVM TALI VVLTV CONSPICIENDVS ERAM
SI VELVTI VVLTVS POTVISSENT PECTORA PINGI
STAREM DOCTRINA CVM PIETATE TYPVS.

During these fifteen years in Basel and Freiburg Erasmus was enormously productive. We have looked at his controversies during this period, but at the same time he was also engaged in a massive project to publish, after the 1516 St Jerome edition, many different works of the early theologians: Cyprian (1519), Hilary (1523), John Chrysostom (1525), Irenaeus (1526), Arnobius (1527), Ambrose (1527, in four volumes), Athanasius (1527), Augustine (1529, a major undertaking,

Hans Asper, *Johannes Oecolampadius, c.* 1531–50, oil on limewood.

in ten volumes), Lactantius (*c.* 250–*c.* 325), Gregory of Nazianzus (1531, translated by his friend Willibald Pirckheimer just before the latter's death in 1530) and Basil (1532). A work on Origen, published in 1536, a few months after Erasmus's death, was a final addition to that vast project.

For Erasmus, reprinting the works of these writers – sometimes rather hastily assembled – and getting them into circulation was an urgent need, in order to provide some historical depth and greater sophistication to the theological debates of the time.[128] He did not accept the Protestant idea of *sola scriptura*, of a simple reading of the Bible. For Erasmus these authors in their interpretation of the New Testament provided an authentic and exemplary merging of the moral philosophy of antiquity with a fresh spiritual revelation of Christianity, a model of the way the old readings could guide modern readers. Along with these texts in theology, Erasmus also continued to produce editions of ancient literature: there were texts of Seneca (we have already mentioned his corrected edition of 1529, in which he now rejected as spurious some of the works he had accepted as Senecan in his edition of 1515), Xenophon, Aristotle, Terence, Demosthenes and Ptolemy.

During this later period Erasmus also pressed on with his extensive publication of books on education, self-betterment and social harmony, all closely tied to his philosophy of Christ. His educational principles were based on the ancient three-part principle of nature, art and practice, in which the ability of the young student is meant to be enhanced, not crushed, by the rational programme (or 'art') of learning, which must attend to the psychology of the learner (his or her 'nature').

And the notion of practice allows the student to absorb over time the skills that are presented in the programme. These ideas from Plato, Aristotle and the Roman Quintilian are still very much alive, even if now much refined by contemporary cognitive psychology.

Erasmus was principally a teacher of rhetoric (as in his works on style and letter-writing), but the principles of his programme can be extended to all forms of teaching, from technical education to the teaching of gymnastics (as was to happen in the decades that followed). In his ideal programme the young are to be educated to enter into a community of conversation with each other and with both the ancient texts and the Christian faith. His earlier works on writing and his last major book, the *Ecclesiastes* on preaching, all work to achieve this goal. They were supported by such collections as the *Adages* and by the later collection of wise sayings called the *Apophthegmata* (1531), dedicated to the fifteen-year-old William of Cleves (1516–1592, for a short time brother-in-law of Henry VIII), yet meant to be read by all. Even the modest book *Civility of Children* (*De civilitate morum puerilium*), published in 1530, treats day-to-day manners as part of this educational programme, with a focus on bringing children into an ordered world of cleanliness and engagement, the work being a remarkable 'symptom' of what the sociologist Norbert Elias calls (with close reading of this work by Erasmus) the 'civilizing process'. This tiny work provides an unexpected look into the way the body – from proper clothing and eating of food to how to share a bed with a companion, with prohibitions on nose-picking, farting and improper exposure of the genitals – is to be absorbed into humanist education.[129]

'ERASMUS WRITES COLLOQUIES'

One work in particular stands out in Erasmus's educational programme, in the way it evolved from the simple instruction of Latin phrases into a fictional practice of looking at and making sense of the social world. This work is his *Colloquies* (*Colloquia*):

> Kings make war, priests are zealous to increase their wealth, theologians invent syllogisms, monks roam through the world, the commons riot, Erasmus writes colloquies. In short, no calamity is lacking: hunger, thirst, robbery, war, plague, sedition, poverty. Doesn't this prove human affairs are at an end?[130]

The term 'colloquy' comes from the Latin *colloquium* and means simply 'a conversation'. Erasmus's colloquies began as model conversational exchanges for classroom use, offering correct forms of and variations on greetings, requests and the like. He had apparently prepared such a text in the late 1490s, along with some of the other school texts, such as the *Adages*. In 1518 a version of his old formulaic colloquies was printed by Froben – much to the surprise of Erasmus, who was still in Louvain. He immediately revised the work and got his Louvain publisher Dirk Martens to print the new one. The *Formulas of Familiar Conversations* thus began as a standard set of everyday Latin questions and answers with multiple variations meant to be studied and imitated by younger students at Latin school. Similar modelling exercises using repetition and a developing vocabulary had long been in use by medieval teachers and indeed are still used in contemporary language instruction.

In 1522 Erasmus, now in Basel, expanded the work and dedicated it to his seven-year-old godson Erasmius, the youngest child of Johann Froben. By 1533 there were some sixty of these conversations. With the revisions, language instruction gave way to conversational sketches about problems in the everyday world, each one organized around an emerging moral question, modelled to some extent on the Greek satirist Lucian, who had had such an influence on *The Praise of Folly*. Thus a general discussion of funerals leads to the question 'how should a man die?' The curious behaviour of animals leads us to ask if soulless animals can have feelings towards one another. A conversation between two youngsters playing a game called knucklebones asks what one learns by gambling. Charon, the mythical boatman across the river Lethe, is suddenly about to be swamped by a vast number of people dead from the battlefield; the surprising question that emerges is: 'How do rulers dupe their subjects into waging war?'[131]

These dialogues give a glimpse into the everyday and not-so-everyday life of the age, and at the same time offer remarkable challenges to conventional thinking. It is the cornucopian and comic world of Bruegel, but a Bruegel without the peasants, situated in the urban and educated world known to Erasmus. In addition to schoolboys speaking to their masters and each other in the day-to-day world of the classroom, you get to overhear a man telling his friend how horse dealers can cheat you and how to cheat them back; the story of a learned scholar who is fooled into believing in the alchemical manufacture of gold; advice from an older woman on how to survive a marriage; two men discussing sexually transmitted diseases; a description of a pilgrimage with the travails of travel and a strange encounter with a snot-filled rag from a minor saint. The variety is marvellous. Through the voices of many different characters, or through their interaction, you get Erasmus's way of thinking through a problem, whether it is how to survive a night in a German inn or how to interpret the Greek of the New Testament, always tied to a leading moral question embedded in a Christian way of thinking. The *Colloquies* are thus not just language exercises, they are commentaries by Erasmus on the world around him. A few old men speaking about their lives since they last met becomes a reflection on how one is to live a life of charity. There are conversations on dishonesty, impiety, hypocrisy and social fears. As in a fairy tale or other short narrative, the moral question is quickly foregrounded and the process of its resolution becomes the 'action' of the dialogue; the aim of the conversation is to offer moral clarity.

These dialogues are an ideal vehicle for Erasmus's ironic free style, now enacted by a range of characters from across society, all speaking Latin. They expand his earlier experiments in presenting Latin oral discourse in his *Antibarbarians*, *Praise of Folly* and *Julius Exclusus*. The colloquies allowed Erasmus the freedom of fiction, what a modern philosopher would call 'world making', and what was seen in the Renaissance as verisimilitude – an imitation of the real world enhanced by art.

The colloquies can be read as commentaries by Erasmus on his own ideas. This approach is tricky, as his readers must have recognized. Is Erasmus the butcher or the fishmonger in a conversation that addresses the dietary rules of his time in 'The Fish Diet'? We already know from his time as a student in Paris how much he hated fish. But in his colloquy, it is the fishmonger, not the butcher, who claims to have attended, some 'thirty years ago', the Collège de Montaigu, where he experienced the unintended cruelty of the rector Jan Standonck at first hand, which he describes vividly ('cubicle with rotten plaster, near stinking latrines', 'astonishingly savage floggings' – 'how many rotten eggs used to be eaten there! how much bad wine drunk!'[132]). These two members of the uneducated class converse in Latin about regulations for dress and prayer. Their basic problem with the Church is its distracting attention towards petty details (the fear felt by 'a Franciscan girded with an unknotted cord, or an Augustinian girded with wool instead of leather'[133]), as though such minutiae of dress determine what makes a good Christian. The butcher and the fishmonger agree that 'it might be useful for Christian people to be bound by fewer minor regulations, especially if these contribute little or nothing to godliness.'[134] Of course this is Erasmus speaking, and in this colloquy both speakers are Erasmus. He clearly expects us to find him in his own text, not just as a character named 'Erasmus' or as the well-known Erasmus whose work is cited here and there by characters, but as a not-so-shadowy figure hovering behind every one of the conversations that he presents in direct discourse.

In 'The Abbot and the Learned Lady', Antronius the abbot objects to the many furnishings in the room of the young Magdalia, and by 'furnishings' he means her many books. Magdalia, according to the abbot, reads too much, especially too much Latin and Greek. We know Antronius is in trouble when Magdalia asks him, 'How do you measure good times?'

and the lazy abbot answers, 'By sleep, dinner parties, doing as one likes, money, honours.'[135] Bad answer. By the end this young woman has carved up the churchman with her wit and her commitment to learning and the moral life. The heart of the colloquy is in the way the debate or discussion is pursued. Antronius is an imagined type – the kind of ignorant, time-wasting, self-indulgent priest that Erasmus detested, the kind of priest that will spell the end of priesthood as it was known at that time. Magdalia is the ideal young woman of human-ism, perhaps a composite of Charitas Pirckheimer, sister of Erasmus's friend Willibald Pirckheimer and abbess of a con-vent of St Clare in Nuremberg, and Margaret Roper, Thomas More's daughter (a portrait by Holbein shows her with book in hand).[136] Magdalia is strikingly bold: 'If you're not careful,' she says to the abbot, 'the net result will be that we'll preside in the theological schools, preach in the churches, and wear your mitres.'[137]

Erasmus is able to find moral and theological significance in all kinds of encounter. This is one of the great strengths of the Colloquies, the way that everyday life is directly related to significant questions. So, in 'Shipwreck' Adolf tells Antony a terrifying tale of a storm at sea, the kind of storm Erasmus may well have experienced himself when crossing the English Channel. In the colloquy only five out of a total of 58 passen-gers and crew survive the storm and the resultant wreck. After an appearance on the mast of St Elmo's fire, the wind comes up quickly and the storm is unleashed and intensified. 'Ever seen the Alps?' asks Adolf. 'Yes, I've seen them,' says Antony. 'Those mountains', Adolf continues, 'are warts compared with the waves of the sea. Whenever we were borne on the

crest, we could have touched the moon with a finger; whenever we dipped, we seemed to plunge through the gaping earth straight down to hell.'[138] The first concern with the oncoming storm was property; yet, to keep the vessel afloat, precious goods were soon surrendered to the waves. Then the passengers began to pray, and this is where Erasmus really takes focus, on the behaviour and prayers of those who fear they are near death. They prayed to the Virgin Mary; they prayed to the sea; they pledged their lives to a religious order; they offered to go on a pilgrimage; one man pledged a massive wax candle if he could be saved (though when asked if he has the funds to pay for such a gift for his saint, he responds, 'Do you suppose

Hans Holbein the Younger, *Margaret More, Wife of William Roper*, 1535–6, vellum laid on playing card.

I am serious? If I once touch land, I won't give him a tallow candle'[139]).

Through all this the narrator, Adolf (who had clearly read his Erasmus), did not make vows to any saint, but prayed directly to God the Father. The only other quiet passenger was a young woman with a baby. The ship was at the moment of breaking up when land was seen. The first one to shore was the woman and her baby, who, by the charity of the passengers, had been placed upon a plank and who calmly floated to shore (perhaps Erasmus wishes us to see them as a type of the Blessed Virgin Mary with her Child). After mother and child had been looked after, chaos ensued. The crew and passengers overcrowded the lifeboat or dove straight in. Adolf shared a broken mast with a priest who knew how to handle himself in the surf near shore (he would turn away from each wave with his head in the water and not try to fight the surf); they were two of the very few who made it to land, where they were cared for by the kindest of all people (Hollanders, of course). Antony, who has been listening to this tale, ends by saying that he 'would rather hear such tales than experience at first hand', which is certainly the Erasmian position. The point of it all is, of course, to examine how we behave near death, how easily we are afflicted with hypocrisy, how we ought to seek salvation, and why the intercession of the saints is less powerful than prayer to God and to the Son of God. And it also helps, as we learned from the priest, to know some basics of swimming. The drama of the piece is helped by a realism in the scene, no doubt from Erasmus's own experience of a bad Channel crossing. The scene is not presented directly but instead in the words of Adolf, allowing it to be in Latin and not in the vernacular language that one would assume even a scholar might use in the moments before his death.

Of the 62 dialogues and formulae in the *Colloquies*, the one with the most rounded and complex statement of the Erasmian ethic and theology is 'The Religious Banquet'. It is a picture of Renaissance *otium* or 'retirement', but not the conventional idea of an individual living in relaxation apart from the world, as in Andrew Marvell's mid-seventeenth-century poem 'The Garden'.[140] Instead, this colloquy, a Christianized version of Plato's *Symposium*, presents us with a community of philosophical Christians engaged in generous hospitality and thoughtful and difficult conversation, even more fully realized than the get-together in *The Antibarbarians*. As they discuss the problem of death, one of the characters reflects on the death of Socrates, who even without a Christian faith 'endeavoured to live righteously'. Another character responds to the truth of that claim, for even though the ancient philosopher did not know Christ, 'when I read such things of such men, I can hardly help exclaiming, "Saint Socrates, pray for us!"'[141] We see the way that Erasmus is able to connect the ethics of pagan antiquity with Christian faith in a way that astonished his contemporaries. It was this kind of radical thinking that Luther acknowledged when he said: 'On my deathbed I shall forbid my sons to read Erasmus' *Colloquies*, where, under the guise of false and foreign characters he speaks of the most impious things and teaches that the church and Christian faith are to be rejected.'[142] Erasmus does indeed challenge traditional pieties, and the book is powerful and highly engaging because of it. Rather than retreat from his enemies, he confronts them with fictional conversations that are in places even more irritating to his enemies than his *Praise of Folly*.

An important spin-off from the *Colloquies* was another dialogue that was published in 1528, and its reception shows how controversial Erasmus had become towards the end of his career. It is a satire of a humanist scholar who is hopelessly devoted to the works of the ancient writer Cicero. The dialogue is called *The Ciceronian* (*Ciceronianus*). It is a comical investigation of a serious problem faced by the humanists of Erasmus's time. If we are to imitate the classical authors, who provide us with the best Latin style as well as the clearest pagan guide for ethical behaviour, what form should this imitation take? How far should we go? The Ciceronian, whose name is Nosoponus (from the Greek approximate of 'the workaholic'), tries to explain his crazy *zelodulea* or 'addiction to style' to his friends Hypologus ('loss of words') and Bulephorus ('bearer of counsel'). He is so far gone that while he can use the word *amabam* ('I used to love') he cannot use *amabatis* ('you used to love') because the latter form is not found in Cicero. He knows this because he has indexed all the words in Cicero, an activity he pursued in solitary study, for (a predecessor of Marcel Proust) he has created 'a shrine of the Muses in the innermost part of the house, with thick walls and double doors and windows, and all the cracks carefully sealed up with plaster and pitch, so that hardly any light or sound can penetrate even by day.'[143] In order to assess the nature of his condition, the three characters try to identify an equivalent devotee to Cicero in all of Europe. The roll-call of scholars is enormous. The only name that seems to fit well is the French scholar Christophe de Longueil, though Bulephorus admits that even he did not restrict himself to Cicero alone.

By the end, Nosoponus realizes that he needs to solve his problem with the guidance of Bulephorus. 'What do you advise me to do then? Throw Cicero away?' 'No, no. Any young candidate for eloquence must always have Cicero in his pocket – and his heart.'[144] Imitation is good, that is, 'imitation which assists nature and does not violate it'.[145] The idea is to imitate, but to do so 'in accord with . . . your own native genius'.[146] Cicero is a great model, and if Cicero himself had studied the philosophy of Christ he would now be remembered as a saint (a daring claim, as we have already seen with Socrates). He should be modelled but not 'blindly followed, but taken as a pattern and even challenged'.[147] But the end of study is really for Christ: 'This is the purpose of studying the basic disciplines, of studying philosophy, of studying eloquence, to know Christ, to celebrate the glory of Christ.'[148]

To us, such a work seems innocent enough. But criticism followed swiftly. Some were offended that Josse Bade the Paris printer was said to be more of a Ciceronian than Guillaume Budé the scholar; apparently the readers did not understand that to be called a failed Ciceronian was a compliment, and the rift in this complex friendship was never really repaired. But the most bitter attack came from Julius Caesar Scaliger (1484–1558), a gifted scholar from Italy who had moved to France. After reading *Ciceronianus*, he was overcome with a violent detestation of Erasmus and in 1531 published an *Oration Against Erasmus in Favour of Cicero*, followed by an even more intemperate *Second Oration*, which came out in 1537, a year after the death of Erasmus. In the first *Oration* he attacked Erasmus's

scholarship and his Lutheran sympathies, along the way
including hearsay such as that Erasmus was known as a drunk
when he worked for Aldus all those years ago in Venice.[149]
Erasmus, who had not heard of Scaliger, assumed that the
author was his old enemy Aleandro, until he was corrected by
friends (including François Rabelais, who had become a correspondent). The controversy was only resolved three years
after the death of Erasmus. By 1539 Scaliger seems mysteriously
to have utterly reversed his opinion. He published a surprising
epitaph: 'Ah, why do you leave me, Erasmus / before my love
has united us?'[150]

'I DEPART FROM LIFE AS FROM AN INN,
NOT FROM A HOME'

Just before Erasmus moved back to Basel he wrote a book
called *De praeparatione ad mortem* (Preparing for Death). He was
asked to do this at the insistence of Anne Boleyn's father, and
he completed the work very quickly. It was published in Basel
in 1535. 'Of all terrifying things the most terrifying is death:
so says a philosopher of great repute,' is how Erasmus starts
his treatise, quoting Aristotle.[151] But he quickly shifts the discussion from the pagan philosopher to Christ and the New
Testament. There are people who do not have faith in Christ
and 'who bewail the death of others and even shudder at
the thought of their own death and curse it'. This book is
for them. Yet, he goes on, 'What is more surprising is that
there are so many people like me [*similes mei*]; although they
have learned and profess the complete Christian philosophy,
they are nevertheless terrified of death.'[152] The 'like me' is a

striking admission. It is the only reference to himself in the
work, yet it comes at the beginning and thus anchors the text
in Erasmus's own experience. The emphasis of the book is less
on dying than on how one should live before death, and thus
takes us back to the *Enchiridion* of some thirty years earlier. We
should prepare for death not by relying on last-minute gestures, but by exercising a lifetime of thoughtful behaviour: for
the Christian, this means a sustained faith in Christ and his
goodness. We should be permanently aware of our fragility
and know that some day, perhaps soon, we will leave the life
of family, friends and possessions. Fear is good, if it engenders

Hans Holbein the Younger, *Bonifacius Amerbach*, 1519, oil and tempera
on spruce.

righteousness: for the believer, 'the fear of God . . . is the beginning of wisdom', as Erasmus says, quoting Psalm 111.[153]

At the end of life the Catholic will seek confession, but if a priest is not nearby, there is no need for despair. 'To wish for faith and love' is more important; the 'visible rites' are comforting, but the real test is the personal faith of the dying person: 'The most effective solace . . . is never to move the eyes of faith from Christ.' It even helps to have an image of Christ or a saint before the eyes of the dying person, and passages of Holy Scripture read aloud. The very end is the moment that Satan can become active; it is then that 'he distorts everything.'[154] 'The words of the New Testament are more suited than those of the Old to drive away despair and to raise our hopes. It is not surprising: Moses terrified the Jews with the Commandments, Christ gave consolation to all peoples through faith and grace.'[155]

Preparing for Death proved to be timely. During his time in Catholic Freiburg, from 1529 to 1535, Erasmus had been enormously busy, but by the end of it he was ill and exhausted. His output had been breathtaking but now, at 68, he was slowing down. He could sense his own end. He wished to see through the press in Basel his major work on rhetoric, the *Ecclesiastes* on how to read and preach the word of God, and an edition of the works of Origen, the ancient Christian theologian who had so influenced him from the time of the *Enchiridion*.[156] Because the religious conflicts in Basel had settled down now that the reformers were clearly in ascendance, he was able in 1535, even while retaining his Catholic faith, to pay a visit to the city he preferred to all others he had lived in and visited.

To make this trip of some 70 kilometres (45 mi.), now suffering from arthritic pain and kidney failure, he had to be carried in a cart. When he arrived in Basel he settled in an apartment on the second floor of a house called 'Zum Luft', which was owned by Hieronymus Froben.[157] He continued to work when he could, and did see the publication of the *Ecclesiastes*. But most of the time in Basel he was bedridden, and it was soon clear that he would not be moving back to Freiburg. Erasmus celebrated the Easter of 1535 with a mass in his own chambers. By the following spring of 1536 he was very sick, and on 11 July that year, among a small circle that included his devoted friend Bonifacius Amerbach and Hieronymus Froben, he died. The scene of the death is described by his younger friend Beatus Rhenanus:

> At last, his strength gradually failing – for he suffered from dysentery for about a month – when he sensed his life's end was near, he displayed as always clear signs of Christian patience and a devout mind in affirming that his whole hope was fixed upon Christ, exclaiming earnestly 'O Jesus, mercy; Lord, set me free; Lord, make an end; Lord, have mercy upon me'; and in the German tongue 'Liever Got' (that is, 'Dear God') . . . No other words did he utter.[158]

Despite the specificity of this scene, Beatus was not at the deathbed. Whether or not Erasmus did say his last words in Dutch (which Beatus called 'Germanica lingua') is open to dispute. If he really did speak these vernacular words, the claim has a kind of poignancy. His cry 'Liever Got' presents him as having a religious belief tied to a vernacular self. And even if he did not speak the words in Dutch, it tells us that the people around him wanted to see him return to his vernacular roots, perhaps as someone secretly sympathetic to the Lutheran reform. After all, at his end he had no priest beside him. There is an alternative, Catholic end to his life that was circulated in the seventeenth century – that he died in the arms of a priest, calling out O mater Dei, memento mei! ('O Mother of God, remember me!') – an unlikely version of his death that was said to have come from one of his servants present at the time.[159] Erasmus had a character in one of his *Colloquies* declare 'I depart from this life as from an inn, not from a home.'[160] This may be his most effective observation on his own death.

The day after he died, Erasmus was buried in the minster, by now the principal church for the reform in Basel. A eulogy was pronounced by Oswald Myconius, the schoolmaster who long ago had the Holbein brothers illustrate the *Folly* and who was now a leading Lutheran pastor (and rather disliked by Erasmus because of that). The final engraved portrait by Holbein gives us the memorial image of Erasmus, standing next to his Terminus.

Despite his early panics over money and his later obsessive communications with his Antwerp banker Erasmus Schets, Erasmus's substantial estate was valued at 8,000 florins (enough, to use our comparator, to hire a master mason in Antwerp for two hundred years of work; thus, in today's terms, several million euros, British pounds or U.S. dollars).[161] His library was sent off, as arranged eleven years earlier, to Jan Łaski, once the final payment was made. Most of the funds

Hans Holbein the Younger, *Erasmus with Terminus*, 1520–25,
woodcut on ivory laid paper.

in the estate financed the charitable support of students in Basel and Louvain, with small specific gifts for friends. He had in one of his earlier wills outlined a plan for his collected works, and Amerbach, Hieronymus Froben and others then undertook the project. The nine volumes appeared from 1538 to 1540, an impressive monument that, when we remember his thoughts after his brush with death from the plague, would have been quite sufficient in his eyes 'to bear witness to posterity'.

Erasmus had been involved in the great religious conflict of his time, with the rise of Luther and the Roman Catholic response. Nevertheless, he left behind him a large community of readers, both Catholic and Protestant, who had been deeply influenced by his vision of a humanist 'philosophy of Christ'. His impact continued on long after his death.[162] He may have lived much of his life in a study surrounded by books, but we have seen how he became a transformative figure across Europe. His controversial books were some of the first to be placed on the Roman Catholic index of banned books when it was instituted in 1559, yet his way of engaging with the Greek and Roman classics through a humanist practice was imported into the Western tradition through Catholic and Protestant schools, and aspects are found even today in certain areas of curriculum and classroom practice. Even though he was, by our standards, racist in relation to Jewish people and Turks (or Muslims), he emphasized tolerance and a rejection of war among Christian nations and sects, and thus provided a framework for later acceptance of religious and ethnic diversity. Though he wrote mostly about and for men, he encouraged the new learning and piety for women.

And though he wrote only in Latin, he encouraged translation into the vernacular languages. His unflagging critical intelligence and alert style are still accessible to readers in hundreds of translations of his works in many different languages, and his reputation (a thing he claimed not to cherish) is kept alive by a community of scholars in many different countries.

Hans Holbein the Younger, *Erasmus*, 1523, oil on wood.

FOUR

The Spirit of a Scholar

n the National Gallery in London the famous Holbein portrait of Erasmus hangs just to the side of the much larger and even more famous *Ambassadors*, painted some ten years later. The portrait had been painted in 1523 as a gift from Erasmus in Basel for Archbishop Warham back in England. Erasmus is depicted standing at a balustrade, his hands resting on a red folio that has a Greek and Latin title written on the fore-edge – *Heraklioi ponoi Erasmi Rotero[dami]* ... (The Herculean Labours of Erasmus of Rotterdam) – placed in such a way as to serve not just as a title to the book but as title to the picture. The face captures your attention with its specificity and apparent accuracy: the hooded, downcast eyes beneath slightly raised eyebrows, a guardedly expressionless expression. The delicate hands resting on the book seem anything but Herculean. Is this a picture of 'ironic man'? As I looked at the portrait, I also looked at the other lookers, hoping to pick up a few hints from their conversation, but they stopped for the standard seventeen seconds before moving on.[1] No one paused to reflect on this great scholar, his extraordinary presence in his own time, his many friends and enemies, on his encyclopaedic learning, his irony, his fierce attacks on hypocrisy and narrow thinking, his belief in the possibility of independence, his charity, his longing for concord and social harmony, his hatred of war and greed. Nor was there anyone to explain his narrowness, his distrust of Jewish people and Turks, his unabashed love of fame, his fondness for the attention of the rich and powerful.

After half an hour I had grown tired of looking. The picture had become a static mask, not a living presence. I walked around the room. Then I turned to William Heckscher's old and famous article 'Reflections on Seeing Holbein's Portrait of Erasmus at Longford Castle', which I had loaded on my iPad.[2] I now reread the article with the painting directly before me. What a masterful scholarly performance, called forth by a masterful painting. Holbein's static image began to hum with meaning, as the work was loaded up with the refined details of Heckscher's learning.

As I followed the patient examination of the column (actually two columns) to the left, the contents of the shelf on the top right, even the colour of the strangely positioned curtain, the clothing of Erasmus (the fur is sable, but for Heckscher the source of the fur must be named more precisely as *Mustela zibellina*), the small adjustments one can still see to the hands on the book, the tranquil gaze (with the stoic implications), this painting, which had begun to exhaust me, suddenly sprang back to life. I was now looking at Erasmus in a particular place and time, his hands perhaps on a volume of the very edition of St Jerome that he had dedicated to Warham. It is not as though the painting contained this textual information, but it seemed to demand it in order to become energized.

This energy came from the power of the individual details to each of which Heckscher had given the closest scholarly attention (much as Erasmus had done with the New Testament).

Indeed, Heckscher's particular account of each motif was more interesting than his general thesis that the theme of the painting is 'envy'. This theme he derived from Latin written by Holbein, barely visible on the fore-edge of another book on the shelf high up to the right: 'I am Johannes Holbein – no one will be my imitator [*mímus*] as easily as my critic [*momus*].' Such a claim by the artist fits with Erasmus's own idea of the labours of Hercules: 'tasks of the kind that bring very great blessings to other people, but almost no return to the man who undertakes them, except a little reputation and a great deal of ill will.'[3] Yet even with his several rings and the richness of his fur collar, one could feel no envy or ill will towards Erasmus. If one were a portrait painter, one might well feel envy towards the remarkable skill of Holbein. I did however feel envy towards the scholarly Heckscher, who had such extraordinary learning at his disposal. Even Erasmus would have been impressed.

'There's no art to find the mind's construction in the face.' This statement, offered wisely by King Duncan early in *Macbeth*, poses a simple fact: one cannot read the mind of another by looking at their face. What do the pressed lips, hooded eyes and slightly raised eyebrows tell us about Erasmus? Is his expression coded in some way? The eighteenth-century physiognomist Johann Caspar Lavater tried to analyse Erasmus's face and called it 'one of the most expressive, most important faces that I know'. Yet he was able to identify only '(a) The fearful, cautious, thoughtful position,

b) the laughter in the mouth, c) the subtlety in the glance.'[4] Lavater seems to have been reading parts of the correspondence or *The Praise of Folly* back into the face, supporting Erasmus's claim that his writings show him better. His face is opaque, a mask. His writings, not his facial features, have to serve as the clue to his accomplishments and to his spirit or inner life as well.

Scholars have argued that the portraits of Erasmus were part of his continuing plan of 'self-fashioning', of creating and broadcasting an iconic image of himself that was consistent with the letters, the many prefaces, the controversies that project a very specific kind of personality (learned, authoritative, yet peace-loving, seeking of friendship). Certainly this painting, a gift to his great patron, is part of an iconographical attention to the community that he had built around himself. The idea of exhausted self-sacrifice, indicated by the generalized title 'Labours of Hercules' on the fore-edge of the proffered volume, as well as by a slightly drained expression on Erasmus's face, is also a nod to his self-described role within his circle. It is as though the painting insists that we read back into it aspects of a life that are not in the painting, but in our knowledge of its subject.[5]

As I have tried to show, there is some truth to the idea of Erasmus's 'self-fashioning'. Erasmus wanted to be famous, and he worked hard to maintain his centrality to the humanist project, especially in his later years, overtly using the networks of his correspondence and the printing press. He certainly 'managed' his reputation. His repeated responses to attacks on his writings are part of this affirmation of reputation as well as a battle for truth. But the concept of 'self-fashioning' makes Erasmus into a very modern type, a predecessor of our own secular age of constructed celebrity. Erasmus himself would reject this idea of a reputation; for, as he says in the letter to Dorp appended to *The Praise of Folly*, 'in heaven's name, what is all this that men call reputation except a perfectly empty name left over from paganism?'[6] Of course there is a special pleading here. Yet there is something about Erasmus that escapes this model of a self-fashioner and that finds its way into the self-portrait of his writings. For one thing, his friendships arise out of a strange mixture of obvious convenience and well-demonstrated affection. His protean quality, his love of abundance in his language, his style (what the poet Wallace Stevens once called 'a certain chic'[7]), his independence, his evasiveness, his restlessness, his many errors (textual errors, but also errors about people and events), his constant need to revise (a recognition of both his failure to get it right the first time and the circumstantial nature of his writing) are all too complex to have a single-minded motivation. There is something in his writing and his life that lacks the control that a fully managed life might ordinarily show. He may be a self-fashioner, but his self, like his *corpusculum* or 'little body', is not entirely under his own control. He is responsive to changes in circumstance, his longings, his critics, continuous movement and his yearning faith in Christ, who in his writings is an essential yet often rather indistinct presence. These qualities, abundantly apparent in his writings, are difficult to find in this portrait, which is calm, except for those delicate fingers that rest nervously on the cover of his book.

A year after the portrait was painted, Erasmus wrote to Warham: 'A painting by a distinguished artist becomes more and more admirable the more often and more attentively you look at it.'[8] Curiously, Erasmus said this to Warham not about the Holbein portrait, but about his experience of rereading the writings of Jerome in preparation for the revised edition of the works that came from the Froben press from 1524 to 1526. He is telling us that reading a text is like looking at a portrait – that Jerome, in this case, may be 'seen' in his writing. That is what I have been arguing for in this book: as we read Erasmus, a presence, a living presence, what can be called his 'spirit', is formed in our minds. He produced many kinds of writing, but in each of them you can find evidence for a life. Sometimes, as in his letters, the life is directly there in front of you; other times, he can catch you by surprise with a simple turn of phrase, even in an obscure annotation on a biblical passage, or a sudden reference to himself in his short book on how to prepare for death. You become aware of his presence in his stylistic gestures. So perhaps it really is true that 'his writings show him better.'

We know that a *persona* in writing is a mask that both reveals and conceals. But a further complication in our reading of Erasmus is our own modern sense that a person can be seen in several ways. This sense is borne out in *Erasmus Variations*, an artwork from 1958 by the Anglo-American artist R. B. Kitaj, now in the collection of the Tate Modern. In it, Kitaj depicted nine Erasmuses, roughly based on the doodles in the Jerome manuscript (known to Kitaj by their reproduction in the English translation of Johan Huizinga's widely circulated biography). Holbein need not worry, Kitaj is neither *mimus* nor *momus*. The painting says less about Erasmus than it does about our own realization that there are many Erasmuses, that

different formulations of Erasmus can all be posited at once, and how a composite image can tell us about the fluid way we perceive the other. Kitaj's *Erasmus* shifts about, and the faces, some of them unrecognizable, some possibly female, are in tension with each other. Erasmus, despite his self-described willingness to set himself before us in his own work, has been read in many different ways over time. Today we see a life in

R. B. Kitaj, *Erasmus Variations*, 1958, oil on canvas.

a more fragmentary way, more aware of our own unstable relation to the object of our interest. We seem to have accepted our distrust of finality or totality. Yet we are always aware of an essence, even if it is of our own individual distillation.

One new face of Erasmus has, for instance, been emerging in recent years. For centuries Erasmus has been seen as the promoter of tolerance. Yet despite his violent rejection of war, he was openly willing to go to war with the Turks during the frightening years of the late 1520s when the Ottoman troops finally reached the outskirts of Vienna. And we have already noted his inflammatory words that described his old friend Aleandro as a Jew. Biographers have all noted these inconsistencies, and most have let them slide.[9] After all, did he not give his support to Johann Reuchlin, the scholar of Hebrew?[10] Did he not enthusiastically praise the Jew Matthaeus Adrianus for taking the Hebrew professorship at the Collegium Trilingue in Louvain?[11] He was certainly never a Luther, with a string of offensive pamphlets in his later years. Yet Erasmus, as we have seen, does indeed often aggressively divide the world into us and them, and by our present-day standards, he does not come across well. Does his tribalism mean there is a fatal flaw in the humanist enterprise? Or are we using Erasmus's own proposed manner of humanist critique to criticize Erasmus in ways that we might have expected him to apply to himself?

This problem of reading Erasmus, of finding the spirit of Erasmus in his own works, is the mark of a slow but persistent shift in humanist discourse. In the opening lines of a controversial essay by the German philosopher Peter Sloterdijk, a response, after more than fifty years, to Martin Heidegger's 1946 'Letter on Humanism', we read:

Books, as the poet Jean Paul once remarked, are thick letters to friends. With this phrase, he aptly articulated the quintessential nature and function of humanism: It is telecommunication in the medium of print to underwrite friendship. That which has been known since the days of Cicero as *humanism* is in the narrowest and widest senses a consequence of literacy. Ever since philosophy began as a literary genre, it has recruited adherents by writing in an infectious way about love and friendship. Not only is it about love of wisdom: it is also an attempt to move others to this love.[12]

Sloterdijk goes on to explain what has happened to the once-powerful tradition of humanist writing in our era. For him, the shift is explained by the impact of the non-literary media. Radio, television and the Internet have created in our culture what he calls 'new foundations' that are 'clearly postliterary, postepistolary, and thus posthumanistic'. The consequence has been that

> modern societies can produce their political and cultural synthesis only marginally through literary, letter-writing, humanistic media. Of course, that does not mean that literature has come to an end, but it has split itself off and become a sui generis subculture, and the days of its value as bearer of the national spirit have passed.

Thus what might be called the project of Erasmus has undergone a remarkable transformation: 'The period when modern humanism was the model for schooling and education has passed, because it is no longer possible to retain the illusion that political and economic structures could be organized on the amiable model of literary societies.' Though Sloterdijk has been criticized for his lack of clarity and his fondness for overstatement, this particular analysis has merit. Something has happened to the humanities and the old discourse of humanism in our time. The ideal of Erasmian humanism – a cosmopolitan, well-educated Republic of Letters – has moved to the margins of our cultural life. A shift in political, ethnic, gender and ecological values has led to a change in the cultural hierarchy.

Despite our hesitations and the new trajectories in our literary culture, there are aspects of Erasmus that still survive for us, that take him outside his historical moment and the programmatic frame of humanist education. We can still turn to him for his irony, laughter, and the free exercise of social criticism. He is a gifted writer in many strange genres: the academic lecture, the edited text, the translation, the commentary, the treatise, the reference book, the textbook. All are written forms that today we see in service to literature rather than being literature themselves. Yet his lecture in *The Praise of Folly*, his technical commentaries on the Bible, his massive reference book the *Adages*, the textbooks on writing and education and the ethical and religious life, and his re-visioning of the language manual in the *Colloquies* are full of spontaneous energy and moral urgency that scholarly writers of today can learn from. He does not wall up ancient texts with the kind of professional scholarship that culminated in the nineteenth-century academy. And because he

offers his contemporaries a scholarly moral guide, he takes on
the role of what we call the public intellectual.[13] Erasmus is
repelled by ignorance. He offers critiques of bad government
and bad living, as well as badly edited texts. Despite his continuous fussing over money and his objects, we find in him a
residual distrust of greed. He has a profound commitment to
charity and community. And even if in the West we have been
turning away from the formal institutions of the Church, we
can learn from Erasmus about the necessary personal disrup-
tion and reformation that come with a fully realized spiritual
faith grounded in tradition. There is also his independence.
Erasmus says: 'I belong to no man's party,' and 'My own wish

Hans Holbein the Younger, *Terminus, the Device of Erasmus*, c. 1532,
oil on wood.

is to be a citizen of the world."[14] Yet in his letters and allegiances he shows how scholarly independence relies on a
community of friends, including patrons, servants, fellow
scholars, printers and, of course, readers – friends who are
there not only to support the work but to be challenged by it.

Chronology

27–28 October 1466?	Because of his father's status as a celibate priest, Erasmus's birth is illegitimate. Soon after he is born in Rotterdam the family moves to nearby Gouda, where his father serves as a priest and Erasmus spends his early years at home and at school
1478–83	School at St Lebuin's in Deventer
1483–4	Death of his parents, both from the plague
1484–7	Sent with his brother to study in 's-Hertogenbosch, southeast of Gouda, at a school associated with the Brothers of the Common Life
1487	Joins the Augustinian Canons Regular in the monastery at Steyn near Gouda, and takes his vows the next year
1493	Begins service in court of Henry of Bergen, Bishop of Cambrai
1495	Ordained a priest in Utrecht (his ordination allowed by episcopal licence in light of his illegitimate status)
1495–9	In Paris, first while attending Collège de Montaigu, then as a sometime student at university lectures and as a tutor to foreign students. He begins to publish short pieces of writing

1499	Arrives in England at the invitation of Lord Mountjoy, one of his students; friendship with Thomas More and John Colet
1500–1502	Moves about in France and the Low Countries, where he studies and writes; his first scholarly book is the *Adages* (shorter version)
1502–4	Lives in Louvain and the Low Countries, undertaking further studies in Greek; publishes his spiritual guidebook, the *Enchiridion*, and a long speech in honour of Philip of Burgundy, the *Panegyric*
1504–5	Resides in Paris and the Low Countries. Publication of the manuscript of Valla's commentary on the New Testament
1505–6	In England with Thomas More. His *Epigrams* are published in 1506
1506–9	Travels to Italy as companion to two young students; receives a doctoral degree from Turin; works in Venice in the printing shop of Aldus Manutius on a revised *Adages* (longer version) published in 1508; travels to Rome and Naples
1509–14	In England, with a visit to Paris to publish *Praise of Folly* in 1511; lectures in Cambridge, 1511–14. (Henry VII dies and is succeeded by Henry VIII, who reigns until 1547; Pope Julius II dies in 1513, and is succeeded by Leo X.)
1514–16	In Basel at the workshop of Johann Froben for revised *Adages* (1515), the first edition of his New Testament with Annotations (1516), and four of nine volumes of an edition of St Jerome (1516); travels to England and the Low Countries; is appointed councillor to Charles, Duke of Burgundy; arranges the publication of More's *Utopia* in Louvain in 1516. The regular publication of his correspondence begins in 1515. (Francis I becomes king of France until his death in 1547.)

1517	In Antwerp with Pieter Gillis; receives a dispensation from some of his monastic vows from Pope Leo X; portrait for More
1517–21	In Louvain, involved with the College of the Three Languages; travels to Calais, Basel and Cologne and in 1521 stays in Anderlecht near Brussels. Continues his work on the revision of the New Testament and in 1517 begins the serial publication of his *Paraphrases* on the New Testament, each part dedicated to a major European ruler or prelate. (Luther presents his 95 Theses in Wittenberg in 1517 and is excommunicated in 1520; Charles V becomes emperor in 1519; Pope Leo X dies in 1521, is succeeded by Pope Adrian VI, soon succeeded by Clement VII in 1523.)
1521–9	In Basel, with short trips to nearby Besançon and Constance. Continues to revise many of his earlier works, edits many texts of ancient authors and early Church Fathers, publishes educational and moral writings, such as his *Colloquies*, *Ciceronianus*, *On the Early Liberal Education of Children* and *The Right Way of Speaking Latin and Greek*, and produces controversial writings against Catholic and Protestant critics across Europe. His principal theological opponent is Martin Luther (1483–1546): Erasmus's *Discussion of Free Will* (1524) is answered by Luther's *The Bondage of the Will* (1525), and Erasmus counter-responds with his *Hyperaspistes* 1 and 2 (1526 and 1527). During this time, several portraits are painted by Hans Holbein the Younger (1497–1543) and an engraving is made by Albrecht Dürer (1471–1528)
1529–34	Moves to Catholic Freiburg after Basel turns Protestant; continues his programme of editing older texts and publishing further answers to his critics. Following the siege of Vienna by the Ottoman Turks, writes *The Necessity of War against the Turks* (1530). Continues to produce works on education (*On Good*

	Manners for Boys, 1530). His *On Restoring the Unity of the Church* appears in 1533; *On Preparing for Death* in 1535. (Pope Clement VII dies in 1534, and is succeeded by Paul III)
1535–6	Returns to work with Hieronymus Froben in Basel for the printing of his *Ecclesiastes* (1535) a treatise on teaching and preaching, and an edition of Origen (published posthumously)
12 July 1536	Dies a Catholic. He is buried in the Protestant church in Basel. His collected works are published between 1538 and 1540

REFERENCES

For abbreviations given in the following reference notes,
see the list of abbreviations in the Select Bibliography.

Introduction: Fame and the Humanist Scholar

1 Ep and Epp refer to the numbered letters in volumes I–XXI
 of the CWE, and, except when indicated otherwise, to the Latin
 letters in the *Opus epistolarum*, ed. P. S. Allen et al., 12 vols (Oxford,
 1906–58); this comes from the dedication of the works of Jerome
 to Archbishop William Warham, Ep 396, lines 50–53.

2 Ep 999.

3 Niccolò Machiavelli, 10 December 1513, in *The Chief Works*, trans.
 Allan Gilbert (Durham and London, 1989), vol. II, p. 929.

4 Alan Dundes rightly points out that the 'monomyth' is not a 'myth'
 but a *legend* or a *tale* of the hero, in 'Folkloristics in the Twenty-first
 Century', *Journal of American Folklore*, CXVIII/470 (Autumn 2005),
 p. 395.

5 Marie Barral-Baron, *L'Enfer d'Érasme: L'humaniste chrétien face à l'histoire*
 (Geneva, 2014); Stefan Zweig, *Triumph und Tragik des Erasmus von
 Rotterdam* (Vienna, 1934).

6 Joseph Coppens, 'Où en est le portrait d'Érasme théologien?', in
 Scrinium Erasmianum, ed. Joseph Coppens (Leiden, 1969), pp. 573–5.

7 Galen Strawson, 'Against Narrativity', *Ratio*, XVII/4 (2004),
 pp. 428–52; a more accessible version of the argument appears
 in 'Unstoried Life', in his *Things that Bother Me: Death, Freedom, the Self,
 etc.* (New York, 2018), pp. 177–201.

8 Martin Luther, 'Erasmus est anguilla', no. 131 in *Tischreden* (1531–
 46), 6 vols, in *Werke kritische Gesamtausgabe* (Weimar, 1912–21).
 To wrap an eel in a fig-leaf is explained in Erasmus's *Adages* I iv 95
 (*Folio ficulno tenes anguilla*), in CWE XXXI, p. 380. Alciato's '*In*

Deprehensum' first appeared in 1531 and translates as 'For a long time wherever you fled, I pursued you: but now here you are, trapped in my snare. No longer will you be able to elude my power. I've caught the eel in a fig-leaf' (Emblem 21, trans. William Barker and Jean Guthrie in *Alciato's Book of Emblems*, at www.mun.ca/alciato).

1 Preparation, 1466–1500

1 The letters were collected first by Erasmus, then reprinted by his early editors. Finally in the early twentieth century Percy Allen and several associates published all the letters that could be found in *Opus epistolarum*, 12 vols (Oxford, –58). Most of these letters have now been translated into English for the *Collected Works of Erasmus*, which is how they will be cited here.

2 Erasmus's father, Gerard Heyle, was sometimes known as 'Gerard of Rotterdam'; see Koen Goudriaan, 'New Evidence on Erasmus' Youth', *Erasmus Studies*, XXXIX (2019), pp. 184–216 for recently discovered facts about the early years. Erasmus began to call himself 'Desyderius Herasmus Roterodami' on the title page of the 1500 *Adagiorum collectanea* (see p. 63). *Desiderius* is Latin for 'the desired one', and Greek *erasmios* has a similar meaning; the choice of Rotterdam stresses his origins in the Low Countries (see Marjorie O'Rourke Boyle, 'The Eponyms of "Desiderius Erasmus"', *Renaissance Quarterly*, XXX/1 (1977), pp. 12–33).

3 Beatus Rhenanus, who was a younger colleague of Erasmus and knew him well, wrote a short biography just after his death, in which he claimed that Erasmus had been a chorister in Utrecht Cathedral before he went to Deventer; *Opus epistolarum*, ed. Allen (1912), vol. I, pp. 56–7.

4 Ep 1341A, CWE IX, p. 294; *Opus epistolarum*, ed. Allen, vol. I, p. 2. Most of what we know about the early years comes from this letter and from the *Compendium vitae* (see note 6 below), now with some details added from the archival research of Goudriaan, 'New Evidence'.

5 Erasmus plays freely with the dates regarding his youth, and even later he adjusts dates in his letters, hence some of the confusion, but most of the time he holds to 1466 according to a thorough

examination by Harry Vredeveld, 'The Ages of Erasmus and the Year of His Birth', *Renaissance Quarterly*, XLVI/4 (1993), pp. 754–809.

6   The *Compendium vitae* is found in *Opus epistolarum*, ed. Allen, vol. I, pp. 46–52, and is translated in CWE IV, pp. 403–10; there is a good note on its contested authenticity by James McConica at the head of the CWE text.

7   Ep 447; the name 'Grunnius' came to Erasmus via St Jerome, explained in CWE LXVIII, p. 740, n. 60.

8   The now extinct monastery is listed in M. Carasso-Kok, *Repertorium van verhalende historische bronnen uit de Middeleeuwen: heiligenlevens, annalen, kronieken en andere in Nederland geschreven verhalende bronnen* (The Hague, 1981), no. 275.

9   As he recalled later, in 1525; Ep 1581A, lines 90–91. This letter is a fragmentary account to Leo X by Erasmus of his early years; it appears in *Opus epistolarum*, ed. Allen, as Ep 1436.

10   *On Disdaining the World*, in CWE LXVI.

11   Ep 447.

12   From Epp 7 and 9. On sentimentality, see Johan Huizinga, *Erasmus*, trans. F. Hopman (New York, 1924), p. 11; Peter Burke, 'Humanism and Friendship in Sixteenth-century Europe', in *Friendship in Medieval Europe*, ed. Julian Haseldine (Stroud, 1999), pp. 262–74; Alan Bray, *The Friend* (Chicago, IL, 2003) is a moving account of early modern male friendship.

13   Ep 296.

14   Ep 1347.

15   From *On the Writing of Letters* (*De conscribendis epistolis*), trans. Charles Fantazzi, CWE XXV, p. 136; also, in the same passage, 'I have no patience with those who say that sexual excitement is shameful and that venereal stimuli have their origin not in nature, but in sin. Nothing is so far from the truth.'

16   The date for his ordination is usually given as 1492; Koen Goudriaan gives an excellent explanation for the revised date in 'New Evidence', pp. 205–10.

17   *Adages* III iii 1; see also Erika Rummel, *The Humanistic–Scholastic Debate in the Renaissance and the Reformation* (Cambridge, MA, 1995).

18   Ep 64; in Diogenes Laertius, *Lives of the Philosophers*, I, 110, Epimenides slept for 57 years.

19 *The Antibarbarians*, trans. Margaret Mann Phillips, in CWE XXIII, pp. 1–122; quotations from pp. 3, 31.

20 Ibid., pp. 47, 64, 72, 82.

21 Ibid., p. 104; the extraordinary decadence of Sardanapalus, the king of Assyria, is described in Diodorus Siculus' *Library of History*, 11, 23.

22 Ep 45.

23 Ep 103.

24 Ep 104.

25 *A Short Debate Concerning the Distress, Alarm and Sorrow of Jesus* (*Disputatiuncula de taedio, pavore, tristicia Iesu*), trans. Michael J. Heath, in CWE LXX, p. 66.

26 Ep 118.

2 Publication, 1500–1516

1 Ep 380, 26 December 1515, from Udalricus Zasius, a legal scholar in Freiburg, who tells Erasmus he is '*Summus doctrinarum princeps*'.

2 The 'theft' is described in Ep 119. Erasmus said he lost around £20. As a comparison, the well-paid master of St Paul's School, founded by John Colet in 1509, was paid 52 marks or just under £40 a year, and the assistant master received half that; see the school statutes in J. H. Lupton, *A Life of John Colet, D.D.* (London, 1909), p. 284.

3 Ep 128.

4 Epp 123, 124.

5 *Gathering of Adages*, trans. John Grant, in CWE XXX, p. 4.

6 Ibid., nos. 54, 66, 274, 374.

7 Ibid., no. 172.

8 Ibid., no. 164.

9 See the *Oxford English Dictionary*, 'tiger', n.12a (all with twentieth-century citations), www.oed.com, accessed 9 September 2020.

10 *Gathering of Adages*, no. 58.

11 A reliance on Vergil cannot however be firmly established. See Miekske L. van Poll-van de Lisdonk, 'Humanists, Letters and *Proverbia*: Some Aspects of Erasmus' First Collection of Proverbs', *Erasmus of Rotterdam Society Yearbook*, XXVI (2006), pp. 11–12; see also Dana Sutton in the introduction to his edition and

translation of Vergil's *Adagiorum libellus* (1521 edn), at
www.philological.bham.ac.uk.

12 Van Poll-van de Lisdonk, 'Humanists, Letters and *Proverbia*', p. 11.

13 Ep 151.

14 Ep 152.

15 Ibid.

16 *Enchiridion*, trans. Charles Fantazzi, in CWE LXVI, p. 24.

17 Heiko A. Oberman, *The Reformation: Roots and Ramifications*, trans.
Andrew Colin Gow (London, 1994 [2004]), p. 72; from an essay
first published in German in 1984.

18 Ibid., pp. 61, 106, 109.

19 Ross Dealy, *The Stoic Origins of Erasmus' Philosophy of Christ* (Toronto,
2017), pp. 263ff.

20 Ep 181, lines 53–9.

21 *Enchiridion*, trans. Fantazzi, in CWE LXVI, pp. 61, 65.

22 Ibid., pp. 126, 127.

23 Ibid., p. 127.

24 Ep 858.

25 Ibid., lines 95–6.

26 *Panegyricus*, trans. Betty Radice, in CWE XXVII, p. 6.

27 Ibid., p. 19.

28 Ep 1341A, line 1748.

29 On Valla, in addition to CE, see the short article by Lodi Nauta in
the online *Stanford Encyclopedia of Philosophy*, with bibliography, at
https://plato.stanford.edu, and Nauta's *In Defense of Common Sense:
Lorenzo Valla's Humanist Critique of Scholastic Philosophy* (Cambridge, MA,
2009), an aspect of Valla that became central to Erasmus's work.
Jerry Bentley's *Humanists and Holy Writ: New Testament Scholarship in the
Renaissance* (Princeton, NJ, 1983) is still a good introduction to the
scholarship of Valla and Erasmus.

30 Bentley, *Humanists and Holy Writ*, p. 41.

31 Ibid., p. 46.

32 Ep 182, line 145.

33 Ep 185.

34 Ep 1341A, lines 152–6.

35 Ep 199.

36 Ep 187.

37 The 246-line poem is found in Latin and English, edited by Harry
    Vredeveld and translated by Clarence Miller, in CWE LXXXV–LXXXVI,
    pp. 13–25.

38 CWE XXX, no. 132; in the full sequence of *Adages* it is 1 i 28.

39 Ep 189; the expression 'too late to spare' later appeared in *Adages* 11
    ii 64.

40 Sir Thomas Elyot, *The Castel of Helthe*, fols. 10v–11r, cited in Creighton
    Gilbert, 'When Did a Man in the Renaissance Grow Old?', *Renais-
    sance Studies*, XIV (1967), p. 13. For many ancient and medieval writers
    there were four stages: childhood, youth, old age and decrepitude
    (what Dante called 'senio'), which comes at the age of sixty.

41 Percy S. Allen, *The Age of Erasmus: Lectures Delivered in the Universities
    of Oxford and London* (Oxford, 1914), p. 264.

42 For instance, Germain de Brie in Ep 569, lines 79–80: 'Erasmus . . .
    wins the palm against all men on both sides of the Alps.'

43 Ep 253.

44 Paul Grendler, 'How to Get a Degree in Fifteen Days: Erasmus'
    Doctorate of Theology from the University of Turin', *Erasmus
    of Rotterdam Society Yearbook*, XVIII (1998), pp. 40–69.

45 Ibid., pp. 55, 64.

46 Martin Lowry's *The World of Aldus Manutius: Business and Scholarship
    in Renaissance Venice* (Oxford, 1979) is still a good introduction.

47 Ep 296, line 157.

48 Jean-Claude Margolin, 'À propos des *Nova Reperta* de Stradan',
    in *Esthétiques de la nouvauté à la Renaissance*, ed. François Laroque and
    Franck Lessay (Paris, 2001), pp. 1–28 with plates (translation
    author's own).

49 Martin Davies, *Aldus Manutius: Printer and Publisher of Renaissance Venice*
    (Tempe, AZ, 1999), p. 58.

50 December 1508, Ep 212 to Aldus.

51 James McConica, 'The Riddle of Terminus', *Erasmus in English*, 11
    (1971), pp. 2–7.

52 Ep 215.

53 Ep 222, translation slightly adjusted; see also Ep 337, lines 135–46,
    and *Adagia* 11 ii 40, with a short discussion of the origin of the book.

54 *The Praise of Folly*, trans. Betty Radice, in CWE XXVII, ed. A.H.T. Levi,
    p. 101.

55 Ibid., p. 136.

56 Ibid., p. 106.

57 Ibid., p. 143; Erasmus cites Pseudo-Cato, *Distichs*, II, 19; Cicero, *Ad familiares*, Book IX, letter 22 (section 4); Ecclesiastes 1:15 and 1:17; and Proverbs 15:21.

58 Ibid., p. 144, citing 2 Corinthians 11:23.

59 Ibid., p. 146, citing Paul from 1 Corinthians 4:10 and 3:18.

60 Ibid., p. 148.

61 Ibid., p. 151.

62 Ibid., p. 152.

63 Ibid., pp. 152–3.

64 Ibid., p. 153.

65 There are many discussions of *Praise of Folly*; two outstanding interpretations are by Michael Screech, *Ecstasy and 'The Praise of Folly'* (London, 1980) and J. M. Coetzee, 'Erasmus' *Praise of Folly*: Rivalry and Madness', *Neophilologus*, LXXVI (1992), pp. 1–18.

66 Erasmus, *Encomium moriae* [1515 facsimile], ed. Heinrich Alfred Schmid, trans. Helen H. Tanzer (Basel, 1931), vol. II, p. 30, n. 1.

67 *Copia: Foundations of the Abundant Style*, trans. Betty I. Knott, CWE XXIV, pp. 348, 354.

68 Ibid., p. 356.

69 For Erasmus, the French writers and a full explanation of the theoretical implications, see Terence Cave, *The Cornucopian Text: Problems of Writing in the French Renaissance* (Oxford, 1979).

70 Ep 225 to John Colet.

71 Thanks to Professor Richard Rex of the Faculty of Divinity at the University of Cambridge for this information.

72 Ep 226.

73 Ep 230.

74 Ep 237.

75 Ep 248.

76 Ep 270.

77 Ep 256.

78 Ep 266.

79 The debate over authorship is laid out by Michael Heath in CWE XXVII, ed. A.H.T. Levi, pp. 156–67; on the involvement of Ulrich von Hutten see Silvana Seidel Menchi, 'Julius, Erasmus, Hutten:

A Dialogue in Three Voices', trans. Mark Roberts, in *Erasmus and the Republic of Letters*, ed. Stephen Ryle (Turnhout, 2014), pp. 63–81.

80 *Julius Locked Out from Heaven*, trans. Michael Heath, in CWE XXVII, pp. 177, 173.

81 Ep 305, lines 192–7.

82 *Dulce bellum inexpertis*, Adages IV i 1, in CWE XXXV, pp. 399–440.

83 *Scarabaeus aquilam quaerit*, Adages III vii 1, in CWE XXXV, pp. 178–214.

84 *Education of a Christian Prince*, trans. Neil M. Cheshire and Michael Heath, in CWE XXVII, ed. A.H.T. Levi, p. 212; Denis L. Drysdall, 'Erasmus on Tyranny and Terrorism: *Scarabaeus aquilam quaerit* and the *Institutio principis christiani*', *Erasmus of Rotterdam Society Yearbook*, XXIX (2009), pp. 89–102.

85 *Sileni Alcibiadis*, Adages III iii 1, in CWE XXXIV, pp. 262–82.

86 *Symposium* 216d, trans. Alexander Nehemas and Paul Woodruff, in Plato, *Complete Works*, ed. John C. Cooper (Indianapolis, IN, 1997), p. 498; see Todd W. Reeser, *Setting Plato Straight: Translating Ancient Sexuality in the Renaissance* (Chicago, IL, 2015), Chapter Six: 'Seducing Socrates: The Silenus in Erasmus and Rabelais', pp. 179–206.

87 *Handbook of the Christian Soldier*, trans. Charles Fantazzi, CWE LXVI, pp. 67–8.

88 On his preparatory work, see Ep 305 to Wimpfeling and the Strasbourg scholars, and Mark Vessey, 'Basel 1514: Erasmus' Critical Turn', in *Basel 1516*, ed. Martin Wallraff et al. (Tübingen, 2016), pp. 3–26. The following relies on essays in *Basel 1516*, an excellent account; in addition, Erika Rummel, *Erasmus' Annotations on the New Testament: From Philologist to Theologian* (Toronto, 1986); Andrew J. Brown on biblical manuscripts in ASD 6-II; H. J. de Jonge, 'Novum Testamentum a nobis versum: The Essence of Erasmus' Edition of the New Testament', *Journal of Theological Studies*, XXXV/2 (October 1984), pp. 394–413; P. F. Hoving on the *Annotations* in ASD 6-V; Grantley McDonald, *Biblical Criticism in Early Modern Europe: Erasmus, the Johannine Comma and Trinitarian Debate* (Cambridge, 2016). See also Richard Rex, 'Humanist Bible Controversies', in *The New Cambridge History of the Bible*, vol. III: *From 1450–1750*, ed. Euan Cameron (Cambridge, 2016), pp. 61–81. All Erasmus's editions of the New Testament are online at www.e-rara.com.

89 Paraphrase on Mark in CWE XLV, p. 17 (Erasmus calls Christ's
    language 'Syriace' or 'Syrian' which we would call Aramaic).
90 Ep 384.
91 All these texts are gathered together in CWE XLI, an introductory
    volume to the series of New Testament annotations; I am grateful to
    its editor, Robert Sider, for allowing me an early look at this import-
    ant work with its lengthy commentary and historical background.
92 Bart Ehrman, *The New Testament: A Historical Introduction to the Early
    Christian Writings* (New York and Oxford, 1997), p. 415.
93 Ep 421, on 19 June 1516.
94 Valentina Sebastiani, 'The Impact of Erasmus' New Testament on
    the European Market (1516–1527): Considerations Regarding
    the Production and Distribution of a Publishing Success', in *Basel
    1516*, ed. Wallraff et al., p. 232.
95 ASD 6-VI, p. 32, trans. in Marjorie O'Rourke Boyle, 'Sermo:
    Reopening the Conversation on Translating Jn 1,1', *Vigiliae
    Christianae*, XXXI/3 (1977), p. 167.
96 ASD 6-V, p. 158, trans. Rummel, in *Erasmus' Annotations*, p. 72.
97 'López Zúñiga, Diego', in CE.
98 McDonald, 'Erasmus', in *Biblical Criticism in Early Modern Europe*,
    pp. 13–55.
99 Luther's marked-up Bible is available through Annotated Books
    Online www.annotatedbooksonline.com; see also Arnoud Visser,
    'Irreverent Reading: Martin Luther as Annotator of Erasmus',
    Sixteenth Century Journal, XLVIII/1 (2017), pp. 87–109.
100 Ep 22.
101 Ep 139.
102 Ep 446.
103 Ep 396, lines 283–4
104 Ibid., lines 260–61.
105 Ibid., lines 395–402; CWE LXI, p. 13.
106 CWE LXI, p. 22.
107 Ibid., p. 24.
108 Ibid., p. 44.
109 Ibid., p. 46.
110 Ibid., p. 47.
111 Ibid., p. 62.

3 Affirmation, 1516–36

1 Ep 566.

2 Valentina Sebastiani, 'Sales Channels for Bestsellers in Sixteenth-century Europe', in *International Exchange in the Early Modern Book World*, ed. Matthew McLean and Sara Barker (Leiden, 2016), p. 5.

3 Gabriella Del Lungo Camiciotti, 'Letters and Letter Writing in Early Modern Culture: An Introduction', *Journal of Early Modern Studies*, III (2014), pp. 17–35; and for general context, Armando Petrucci, *Scrivere Lettere: Una storia plurimillenaria* (Rome and Bari, 2008), chapters 4 and 5.

4 Léon-E. Halkin, *Erasmus ex Erasmo* (Aubel, 1983), p. 150. The collections are listed in Erasmus, *Opus epistolarum*, ed. P. S. Allen (Oxford, 1906–58), vol. I, Appendix 7, pp. 593–602; what follows is in part based largely on the volume introductions to CWE by various editors, mostly James Estes; Halkin, *Erasmus ex Erasmo*; Lisa Jardine, *Erasmus, Man of Letters: The Construction of Charisma in Print* (Princeton, NJ, 1993) with a detailed and influential analysis; and, more recently, Christine Bénévent, 'La Correspondance d'Érasme: Fonctionnement, fonctions et fictions d'un réseau épistolaire', in *Réseaux de correspondance à l'âge classique (XVIe–XVIIIe siècle)*, ed. Pierre-Yves Beaurepaire et al. (Saint-Étienne, 2006), pp. 17–32.

5 The correspondent was de Brie, in December 1519; see Ep 1045.

6 Ep 1041.

7 Ep 1341A, lines 1445–7.

8 Ep 1796.

9 Ep 1341A, lines 1101–4.

10 Ep 867.

11 Ep 1206.

12 Ep 1144.

13 'Uutenhove, Karel', also known as Karel van Utenhove, in CE; his dates are not known but he was active from the 1520s until 1577.

14 Ep 2288.

15 Jan Łaski, in Ep 1341A, lines 1236ff.

16 Collections by one early editor of his letters are described in 'Barlandus, Hadrianus', in CE.

17 According to Charles Fantazzi, in his introduction to his translation of *On the Writing of Letters*, in CWE XXV, p. 3.

18 CWE XXV, p. 38; p. 20; p. 65.

19 Marc Fumaroli, *The Republic of Letters*, trans. Lara Vergnaud
    (New Haven, CT, 2018); Dierk van Miert, 'What Was the
    Republic of Letters?', in *Reassembling the Republic of Letters in the Digital
    Age*, ed. Howard Hotson and Thomas Wallnig (Göttingen, 2019),
    pp. 23–40; Hans Bots and Françoise Waquet, *La République des lettres*
    (Brussels and Paris, 1997); see also the chapter 'A Sketch Map of
    a Lost Continent: The Republic of Letters', in Anthony Grafton,
    Worlds Made by Words: Scholarship and Community in the Modern West
    (Cambridge, MA, 2009), pp. 9–34.

20 Ep 325, lines 107–8; for a general consideration of this topic, see
    Seth Lerer, *Error and the Academic Self: The Scholarly Imagination, Medieval
    to Modern* (Stanford, CA, 2002).

21 Andrew Pettegree, *The Book in the Renaissance* (New Haven, CT, and
    London, 2010), p. 86.

22 Lisa Jardine, 'Penfriends and Patria: Erasmian Pedagogy and the
    Republic of Letters', *Erasmus of Rotterdam Society Yearbook*, XVI (1996),
    pp. 1–18.

23 Though the letters of dispensation, Epp 338 and 339, are dated
    July 1515, Erasmus only found out about them the next year; in Ep
    389 Ammonio explains that locating Erasmus, who was always on
    the move, was not easy.

24 Ep 304.

25 Ep 337.

26 More to Dorp, 21 October 1515, trans. in Thomas More, *Complete
    Works*, ed. and trans. Daniel F. Kinney (New Haven, CT, and
    London, 1986), vol. XV, pp. 1–127.

27 Jardine, *Erasmus, Man of Letters*, pp. 111–22.

28 *Adages* IV i 1; The others are 'The dung-beetle pursues the eagle',
    Adages III vii 1; 'One ought to be born a king or a fool', I iii 1;
    'Sparta is your portion, do your best for her', II v 1; 'To exact
    tribute from the dead', I ix 12; 'As warts grow on the eye',
    II viii 65.

29 Ep 600, 15 July 1517.

30 On the portrait, see Lorne Campbell et al., 'Quentin Metsys,
    Desiderius Erasmus, Pieter Gillis, and Thomas More', *Burlington
    Magazine*, CXX (1978), pp. 716–25; More's response is Ep 684.

31 See Stephen K. Scher, *The Currency of Fame: Portrait Medals of the Renaissance* (New York, 1994), Erasmus at cat. no. 157; Larry Silver, 'The Face Is Familiar: German Renaissance Portrait Multiples in Prints and Medals', *Word and Image*, XIX/1–2 (2003), pp. 6–21, begins his discussion with the Metsys medal and Dürer's portrait; see also Arnoud Visser, 'Scholars in the Picture: The Representation of Intellectuals in Emblems and Medals', *Transmigrations: Essays in Honour of Alison Adams and Stephen Rawles*, ed. Lawrence Grove and Alison M. Saunders (Glasgow, 2011), pp. 139–59.

32 James McConica, 'The Riddle of Terminus', *Erasmus in English*, 11 (1971), pp. 2–7; see also Ep 2018.

33 Ep 597.

34 Jan Papy et al., *The Leuven Collegium Trilingue, 1517–1797: Erasmus, Humanist Educational Practice and the New Language Institute* (Leuven, 2018) provides many details.

35 Erika Rummel, 'Erasmus and the Louvain Theologians: A Strategy of Defense', *Nederlands Archief voor Kerkgeschiedenis/Dutch Review of Church History*, LXX (1990), pp. 2–12; see also 'Lee, Edward' in CE.

36 Ep 607.

37 Ep 843, to Maarten Lips, a supporter of Erasmus who helped him with various projects, principally the edition of St Augustine's writings; CE.

38 Erasmus, *Opuscula*, ed. Wallace K. Ferguson (The Hague, 1933), p. 250; trans. CE II, p. 312.

39 Erasmus to Lupset, mostly on Edward Lee, December 1519, Ep 1053, lines 423–35.

40 Ep 1061; in *Colloquies*, CWE XXXIX, pp. 118–20 and also n. 5; the full passage is not presented there, but the Latin is found at ASD I-III, p. 82, apparatus for line 169. Lee, whose Latin name was Leus, saw in the Latin word *ardeleo*, a variant spelling of *ardelio* or 'busybody', a reference to himself; Ari Wesseling, 'Dutch Proverbs and Expressions in Erasmus' Adages, Colloquies and Letters', *Renaissance Quarterly*, LV/1 (Spring 2002), p. 120.

41 Erasmus, *An Apologia in Response to the Two Invectives of Edward Lee*, trans. Erika Rummel, in CWE LXXII, pp. 52–3.

42 Ep 1100.

43 *A Complaint of Peace Spurned and Rejected by the Whole World*, trans. Betty Radice, CWE XXVII, p. 297.

44 On academic contestation in the Baroque and Enlightenment university, see Sari Kivistö, *The Vices of Learning: Morality and Knowledge at Early Modern Universities* (Leiden, 2014), and for the present day, Randall Collins, 'On the Acrimoniousness of Intellectual Disputes', *Common Knowledge*, VIII/I (2002), pp. 47–70.

45 *Adages* I ii 25, in CWE XXXI.

46 For more on this, see Lerer, *Error and the Academic Self*.

47 Ep 2157, May 1529, Erasmus to Alfonso de Fonseca in the dedication to the *Opera omnia* of Augustine.

48 Explained by James Estes, 'Erasmus' Illness in 1530', in CWE XVI, pp. 410–11.

49 Froben's garden, Ep 1756; that of Brisgoicus, Ep 2156.

50 Ep 2473, lines 25–6.

51 Roger Ascham, *Toxophilus*, in *English Works*, ed. W. A. Wright (Cambridge, 1904), p. 18.

52 Ep 867; the following quotations are from this letter.

53 See 'Eschenfelder, Christoph', in CE.

54 'A Marriage in Name Only, or The Unequal Match', in *Colloquies*, trans. Craig Thompson, CWE XXXIX–XL, pp. 842–59.

55 John Gleason, 'The Allegation of Erasmus' Syphilis and the Question of His Burial Site', *Erasmus of Rotterdam Society Yearbook*, X (1990), pp. 122–39.

56 Ep 1342, line 395.

57 *In Praise of Medicine*, trans. Brian McGregor, CWE XXIX, p. 40.

58 Estes, 'Erasmus' Illness in 1530', CWE XVI, pp. 410–11.

59 Epp 1223, 1238.

60 Thomas More, 'Letter to a Monk', trans. Daniel Kinney, in *Collected Works*, vol. XV, p. 297; the monk was a London Carthusian named John Batmanson, ibid., p. xli.

61 Two excellent accounts: Valentina Sebastiani, *Johann Froben, Printer of Basel: A Biographical Profile and Catalogue of His Editions* (Leiden, 2018) and Alexandre Vanautgaerden, *Érasme Typographe: Humanisme et imprimerie au début du XVIe siècle* (Geneva, 2012).

62 On the number of presses, see Sebastiani, *Johann Froben*, p. 49 n. 36
    (quoting Ueli Dill), then p. 72; for the number of titles published,
    p. 68.

63 'Zum Sessel', street address Totengässlein 3, now a pharmacology
    museum for the University, then 'Zur alten Treu', at Nadelberg 17,
    now a bookstore; on the pension, Sebastiani, *Johann Froben*, p. 68,
    n. 113 (not mentioned by Erasmus, but by the theologian and
    botanist Otto Brunfels (1488–1534), in an essay attacking him).

64 Ep 1316.

65 See Erasmus, *Colloquies*, CWE XXXIX–XL, pp. 64ff, with a useful
    commentary by Craig Thompson, the translator.

66 1532, Ep 2735; see also 'Büsslein, Margarete', in CE.

67 Fully discussed in Franz Bierlaire, *La Família d'Érasme: Contribution à
    l'histoire de l'humanisme* (Paris, 1968); see also Ann Blair, 'Erasmus
    and His Amanuenses', *Erasmus Studies*, XXXIX (2019), pp. 22–49.

68 There are articles on all these names in CE.

69 Ep 1205.

70 Ep 1790, lines 70–73.

71 Ep 2449.

72 Ep 1669.

73 'Talesius, Quirinus', in CE.

74 'Cousin, Gilbert', in CE.

75 Blair, 'Erasmus and His Amanuenses', pp. 22–49.

76 Egbertus van Gulik, *Erasmus and His Books*, trans. J. C. Grayson,
    ed. J. K. McConica and Johannes Trapman (Toronto, 2018) is an
    excellent account of the history and contents of the library.

77 Ep 31.

78 Arnoud Visser, 'Irreverent Reading: Martin Luther as Annotator
    of Erasmus', *Sixteenth Century Journal*, XLVIII/1 (2017), pp. 87–109.

79 Ep 2018.

80 Ep 2056.

81 'Łaski, Jan', in CE.

82 Erasmus to Pope Adrian VI, 1523, in Ep 1352, lines 45–6.

83 'Berquin, Louis de', in CE.

84 Jessica Wolfe, *Homer and the Question of Strife from Erasmus to Hobbes*
    (Toronto, 2015) has an excellent first chapter on 'Homer, Erasmus,
    and the Problem of Strife'.

85 Erika Rummel, *Erasmus and His Catholic Critics* (Nieuwkoop, 1989), vol. II, pp. 193–5, lists them all in an appendix and discusses most of them in the text. See also Erika Rummel, ed., *A Companion to Biblical Humanism and Scholasticism in the Age of Erasmus* (Leiden, 2008).

86 Ep 1016, lines 28–9.

87 James Tracy, *Erasmus of the Low Countries* (Berkeley, CA, 1996), p. 80.

88 As noted by Erasmus in his *Contra morosos* or *Chief Points in the Arguments Answering some Crabby and Ignorant Critics*, trans. Clarence Miller, CWE XLI, p. 811 (thanks to Erika Rummel for this citation).

89 'Lefèvre d'Étaples', in CE.

90 Collins, 'On the Acrimoniousness of Intellectual Disputes', p. 48.

91 The story of Luther has been told many times; for specifics in relation to Erasmus, a useful start is 'Luther, Martin', in CE.

92 '*Humana praevalent in eo plus quam divina*'; Martin Luther to Johann Lange in *Luthers Werke Kritische Gesamtausgabe* (Weimar, 1883–2009), *Briefwechsel*, vol. I, p. 90, no. 35, translated in *Luther's Works*, 55 vols, ed. Jaroslav Pelikan and Helmut T. Lehmann (St Louis, MO, 1955–86), vol. XLVIII, pp. 39–41.

93 Ep 947, lines 40–42.

94 Ep 939, lines 69–72.

95 Ep 980, line 45.

96 Ep 1033, lines 44–6.

97 Sebastiani, *Johann Froben*, p. 62.

98 Ep 1341A, line 1365, to Botzheim, 30 January 1523.

99 *Acts of the University of Louvain against Luther: Brief Notes of Erasmus of Rotterdam for the Cause of the Theologian Martin Luther*, trans. Martin Lowry, CWE LXXI, p. 103.

100 For this debate, see Shimon Markish, *Erasmus and the Jews* (Chicago, IL, 1986), and for a stronger argument Nathan Ron, *Erasmus and the 'Other': On Turks, Jews, and Indigenous Peoples* (Cham, Switzerland, 2019).

101 CWE LXXI, pp. 106–7.

102 Lyndal Roper, *Martin Luther: Renegade and Prophet* (London, 2016), p. 183.

103 Albrecht Dürer, *Documentary Biography*, ed. Jeffrey Ashcroft (New Haven, CT, 2017), p. 582.

104 This part of the *Assertion* is given in CWE LXXVI, pp. 299ff.

105 A very quick introduction directly into these Erasmus–Luther texts is *Erasmus and Luther: The Battle over Free Will*, ed. Clarence H. Miller (Indianapolis, IN, 2012). The full texts of Erasmus's *Diatribe* and *Hyperaspistes* in Latin are in LB, vol. X, and are translated in CWE LXXVI–LXXVII. CWE LXXVI has a good background discussion by Charles Trinkaus, and at the end provides useful tables tracing the developing arguments through the books. For Luther I quote from *Luther and Erasmus: Free Will and Salvation*, ed. E. Gordon Rupp and Philip S. Watson (Louisville, KY, 1969), with the same translation as in *Luther's Works*, ed. Pelikan and Lehmann, vol. XXIII; the *De servo arbitrio* is in Luther, *Weimar Ausgabe*, vol. XVIII.

106 *Diatribe* (*A Discussion of Free Will*), trans. Peter Macardle, CWE LXXVI, p. 87.

107 Ep 1500, 30 September 1524, Melanchthon to Erasmus.

108 Ep 1523, 10 December 1524, citing from *Horace Odes*, 1.6.

109 Quoted in *Luther and Erasmus*, ed. Rupp and Watson, p. 102.

110 Ibid., 104.

111 Luther's 'Assertio 36', trans. Clarence H. Miller, CWE LXXVI, p. 306.

112 *Luther and Erasmus*, ed. Rupp and Watson, p. 112.

113 Ibid., p. 111.

114 Ibid., p. 333.

115 *Hyperaspistes 1*, CWE LXXVI, p. 103.

116 Ibid., p. 295.

117 All from numbered sections of Luther, *Weimar Ausgabe: Tischreden*, in 6 vols: eel, no. 131; Epicurean, nos 4443 and 5535; Momus no. 811; Caiaphas, no. 818; lover of Satan, no. 131; rogue, no. 1597; inflaming teacher, no. 1597; king of ambiguity, no. 3392b; starling, no. 2895a–b; bedbug, no. 3010; more harmful than Lucian, no. 2999; hater of religion, no. 3144; comic or tragic, no. 2170; fallen, no. 1597; the quotation on him as scoffer comes from no. 1319 (repeated at no. 2420); translation taken from *Conversations with Luther*, trans. Preserved Smith and Herbert Percival Gallinger (New York, 1915), pp. 108–9.

118 Luther, *Weimar Ausgabe, Briefwechsel* 7, no. 2093, lines 154–83; the text of Luther's letter is translated by Henry Cole as an appendix to Luther's *Bondage of the Will* (London, 1823), pp. 380–402.

119 Ep 2918, lines 13–15.

120 *Desiderius Erasmus of Rotterdam against a Most Slanderous Letter*
     of Martin Luther, trans. Peter Macardle, in CWE LXXVIII,
     p. 451.

121 Ibid., pp. 441, 415.

122 Ibid., pp. 438–9.

123 Ibid., pp. 458, 447, 464.

124 Ep 1528 to Johannes Caesarius, 16 December 1524.

125 Ep 2136, lines 39–45.

126 The 'House of the Whale' is on Franziskanerstrasse and is now
     a bank; Erasmus's house, 'Zum Kind Jesu' on Schiffstrasse, is no
     longer standing.

127 John Munro, 'Money, Wages, and Real Incomes in the Age of
     Erasmus', appendix to CWE XII, pp. 697–8, using Rhenish gold
     florins of 1526 valuation.

128 For an outline of his programme of publication, see Jan den
     Boeft, 'Erasmus and the Church Fathers', in *The Reception of the*
     Church Fathers in the West, ed. Irena Backus, 2 vols (Boston, MA, and
     Leiden, 2001), pp. 538–73.

129 *On Good Manners for Boys*, trans. Brian McGregor, CWE XXV,
     pp. 273–89, with nose-picking at 274, farting, urination and
     so on, pp. 277–8; Norbert Elias, *The Civilizing Process: Sociogenetic*
     and Psychogenetic Investigations [1939], revd edn, trans. E. Jephcott
     (London, 2000), pp. 48ff.

130 'Cyclops, or The Gospel-bearer', in *Colloquies*, trans. Craig
     Thompson, CWE XXXIX, pp. 869–70. Thompson provides a vast
     commentary on the dialogues.

131 Scenes from 'The Funeral' (*Funus*), 'Sympathy' (*Amicitia*),
     'Knucklebones' (*Astragalismos*) and 'Charon', in CWE XXXIX–XL.

132 CWE XXXIX–XL, p. 716.

133 Ibid., p. 705.

134 Ibid., p. 704.

135 Ibid., p. 501.

136 'More, Margaret' and 'Pirckheimer, Charitas', in CE.

137 CWE XXXIX–XL, pp. 504–5.

138 Ibid., p. 353.

139 Ibid., p. 356.

140 Brian Vickers, 'Leisure and Idleness in the Renaissance: The Ambivalence of *Otium*', *Renaissance Studies*, IV/I (1990), pp. 1–37, and IV/2 (1990), pp. 107–54.

141 *CWE* XXXIX–XL, p. 194; on the opposite page there is an image of the Copenhagen manuscript, showing that Eramus added the passage '*Sancte Socrates ora pro nobis*' as an afterthought.

142 Luther in *Luthers Werke, Tischreden* no. 817; similar comments recorded elsewhere.

143 *The Ciceronian*, trans. Betty I. Knott, in *CWE* XXVII–XXVIII, p. 351.

144 Ibid., p. 439; on Longueil, see ibid., pp. 430–31 and the entry in *CE*.

145 Ibid., p. 441.

146 Ibid.

147 Ibid., p. 445.

148 Ibid., p. 447.

149 Rummel, *Controversies*, vol. II, 141, citing B6R, E6R, from the *Oratio pro Marco Tullio Cicerone contra Desiderium Erasmum* (1531). See also 'Scaliger, Julius Caesar', in *CE*.

150 'Ah, quid me linquis, Erasme / ante meus quam sit conciliatus amor', in *Heroes* (Lyon, 1539), p. 23.

151 *Nicomachean Ethics*, 1115a26.

152 *Preparing for Death*, trans. John N. Grant, in *CWE* LXX, p. 393.

153 Ibid., p. 426.

154 Ibid., pp. 436–40.

155 Ibid., p. 446.

156 For this work, see Thomas P. Scheck, *Erasmus's Life of Origen* (Washington, DC, 2016), with a translation of Erasmus's short biography and assessment of Origen and Scheck's valuable introduction to the importance of Origen in Erasmus's theology.

157 The address is Bäumleingasse 18; the building today houses several small businesses, with Galerie Knoell downstairs and the Erasmushaus bookstore adjoining.

158 Quoted by Thompson in *CWE* XXXIX–XL, p. 1129, from Allen, ed., *Opus epistolarum,*, I, pp. 53–4, from the prefatory letter by Beatus Rhenanus to the Origen edition that was published posthumously (the form 'Liever Got' is how it appeared in his text); for a full and detailed account, see Beat Rudolf Jenny,

'Tod, Begräbnis, und Grabmal des Erasmus von Rotterdam', *Basler Zeitschrift für Geschichte und Altertumskunde*, 86 (1986), pp. 61–104.

159 Thompson in CWE XXXIX–XL, p. 1132.

160 Chrysoglottis in 'The Godly Feast', *Colloquies*, in CWE XXXIX–XL, p. 192; see also *De praeparatione ad mortem* in CWE LXX, p. 395 ('We are travellers in this world, not permanent residents; we are not living in our homeland, but are visitors in a foreign land, lodging at inns or, to express the idea more clearly, living away from home in nothing more permanent than tents').

161 Munro, 'Money, Wages, and Real Incomes in the Age of Erasmus', in CWE XII, pp. 697–8.

162 A substantial history is provided in the three-volume study by Bruce Mansfield, *Phoenix of His Age: Interpretations of Erasmus, c. 1550–1750; Man on His Own: Interpretations of Erasmus, c. 1750–1920; Erasmus in the Twentieth Century: Interpretations, c. 1920–2000* (Toronto, 1979, 1992 and 2003).

4 The Spirit of a Scholar

1 See the essay by James Elkins, 'How Long Does It Take to Look at a Painting?', available at www.huffpost.com, accessed 21 September 2020, based on J. K. Smith and L. F. Smith, 'Spending Time on Art', *Empirical Studies of the Arts*, XIX/2 (2001), pp. 229–36, and a follow-up study: L. F. Smith, J. K. Smith and P.P.L. Tinio, 'Time Spent Viewing Art and Reading Labels', *Psychology of Aesthetics, Creativity, and the Arts*, XI/1 (2017), pp. 77–85.

2 William Heckscher, 'Reflections on Seeing Holbein's Portrait of Erasmus at Longford Castle', in *Essays in the History of Art Presented to Rudolf Wittkower*, ed. Douglas Fraser, Howard Hibbard and Milton J. Lewine (London, 1967), pp. 128–48, with illustrations.

3 *Adages* III i 1; quotation from CWE XXXIV, p. 168.

4 Johann Caspar Lavater, *Physiognomische Fragmente, zur Beförderung der Menschenkenntniß und Menschenliebe* (Leipzig, 1776), vol. II, pp. 267–8, as cited in Bruce Mansfield, *Man on His Own: Interpretations of Erasmus, c. 1750–1920* (Toronto, 1992), p. 104; Mansfield argues that Lavater employed a Protestant lens in his account of Erasmus.

5 See Harry Berger Jr, 'Fictions of the Pose: Facing the Gaze of Early Modern Portraiture', *Representations*, XLVI (1994), pp. 87–120.

6 Ep 337, the letter to Martin Dorp in which Erasmus defended his *Praise of Folly*.

7 Wallace Stevens to Henry Church, 1942, in *Letters*, ed. Holly Stevens (New York, 1966), p. 409, where he proposes that otherwise Erasmus must have been 'a very dull person in reality'; pointed out to me by Fred Unwalla.

8 Ep 1451; compare his claim in 'The Religious Banquet': even though 'a picture grows old', 'it's longer-lived than we are, and age commonly adds to it a grace we lose'; *Colloquies*, in CWE XXXIX, p. 179.

9 Nathan Ron, *Erasmus and the 'Other': On Turks, Jews, and Indigenous Peoples* (Cham, Switzerland, 2019) provides a more stringent assessment.

10 Johann Reuchlin (1454–1522) was an outstanding scholar who turned to the study of Hebrew, and for that was vehemently attacked and was subject to inquisitorial investigation. Because he was defended by Lutheran supporters, even after he was acquitted by the court he remained a controversial figure. Erasmus, who cautiously defended Reuchlin, relied on him for his expertise in Hebrew and their shared commitment to humanist scholarship. See CE 'Reuchlin, Johann'.

11 'Adrianus, Matthaeus', in CE.

12 Peter Sloterdijk, 'Rules for the Human Zoo: A Response to the Letter on Humanism', trans. Mary Varney Rorty, *Environment and Planning D. Society and Space*, XXVII (2009), pp. 302–33, the source of all subsequent quotations.

13 Thanks to Ian Porter, in conversation, for his constant reminders of this role.

14 Letter of 1519 to the readers of the *Familiarum colloquiorum formulae* in Ep 1041, lines 15–16; then to the Swiss Reformer Huldrych Zwingli (1484–1531) in Ep 1314. See also 'My home, in my own opinion, is wherever I keep my library and such possessions as I have', in 1518 to Mark Lawerijns, or Marcus Laurinus, Ep 809, lines 134–5; and 'Wherever a man is well treated, that is his homeland', in 1529 to Schets in Ep 2159, quoting Aristophanes, *Plutus*, as discussed in *Adages* II ii 93 and also in Ep 2196 to Willibald Pirckheimer.

SELECT BIBLIOGRAPHY

Abbreviations

Ep Number of letters quoted in English from the *Correspondence of Erasmus*, vols I–XX of the *Collected Works of Erasmus*, various editors and translators (1974–), with two volumes still to come, one of which will be an index. The numbers, with a few exceptions, are the same as in the standard Latin text in *Opus epistolarum*, ed. P. S. Allen, Helen Mary Allen and H. W. Garrod (Oxford, 1906–58), 12 vols.

ASD *Opera omnia*, various editors (Amsterdam, 1969–). The standard scholarly edition, in progress; 9 series, 52 volumes to date.

CE Peter G. Bietenholz and Thomas B. Deutscher, eds, *Contemporaries of Erasmus: A Biographical Dictionary of the Renaissance and Reformation*, 3 vols (Toronto, 1985–7); the entries are alphabetical: vol. I (A–E); vol. II (F–M); and vol. III (N–Z).

CWE *Collected Works of Erasmus*, various editors (Toronto, 1974–); 86 volumes projected, 16 still to come.

LB *Opera omnia*, ed. J. LeClerc (Leiden, 1703–6). Ten volumes in eleven. This was the standard complete edition, supplemented by *Erasmi Opuscula*, ed. Wallace K. Ferguson (The Hague, 1933), all now largely superseded by ASD.

Works by Erasmus

Adages (*Adagiorum chiliades*)
Latin in ASD, series 6, vols I–IX; English in CWE, vols XXX–XXXVI, trans. Margaret Mann Phillips, R.A.B. Mynors et al., ed. John

Grant. Selection of these translations in *Adages*, ed. William Barker (Toronto, 2001); the full series of *Adages* was organized in three sequences: by thousands (I–V), hundreds (i–x) and I–IOO.

The Antibarbarians (*Antibarbarorum liber*)
Latin in *ASD* I-I; English in *CWE* XXIII, trans. Margaret Mann Phillips

The Ciceronian (*Ciceronianus*)
Latin in *ASD* I-II; English in *CWE* XXVIII, trans. Betty I. Knott

Colloquies (*Colloquia*)
Latin in *ASD* I-III; English in *CWE* XXXIX–XL, ed. and trans. Craig R. Thompson, based on an older translation (Chicago, IL, 1965)

Copia: Foundations of the Abundant Style (*De duplici copia verborum ac rerum*)
Latin in *ASD* I-VI; English in *CWE* XXIV, trans. Betty I. Knott

Discussion of the Freedom of the Will (*De libero arbitrio diatribe*) and *Hyperaspistes*
Latin for both in *LB* X; English in *CWE* LXXVI–LXXVII, with *Discussion* trans. by Peter Macardle, and *Hyperaspistes* by Clarence H. Miller. There is also a translation of the *Discussion* in *Luther and Erasmus: Free Will and Salvation*, trans. and ed. E. Gordon Rupp and Philip S. Watson (Philadelphia, PA, 1969)

Education of a Christian Prince (*Institutio principis christiani*)
Latin in *ASD* 4-I; English in *CWE* XXVII, trans. Neil M. Cheshire and Michael J. Heath; the same translation is used for a paperback edition, ed. Lisa Jardine (Cambridge, 1997)

Handbook of the Christian Soldier (*Enchiridion militis christiani*)
Latin in *ASD* 5-VIII; English in *CWE* LXVI, trans. Charles Fantazzi

New Testament: Texts, Annotations and *Paraphrases*
The Latin of the *Annotations* is found in *ASD* series 4 and the *Paraphrases* in series 5; English versions are in *CWE*, vols LI–LX (not yet complete) and XLII–L respectively. Erasmus's introductory materials to the New Testament are translated in *CWE* XLI,

ed. Robert Sider (2019). Sider's lengthy 'General Introduction' on the New Testament also serves as a thorough chronological treatment of Erasmus's later years. His translation of the *Ratio verae theologiae* (System of True Theology) is also published separately in *Erasmus on Literature: His 'Ratio' or 'System' of 1518–1519*, ed. Mark Vessey (Toronto, forthcoming)

The Praise of Folly (Moriae encomium)
Latin in *ASD*, 4-III; English in *CWE*, vol. XXVII, using the translation by Betty Radice, which also appears in the Penguin edition of the *Praise of Folly*, ed. A.H.T. Levi (London, 1994). Other translations in English include one by Hoyt Hopewell Hudson (Princeton, NJ, 1941) and Clarence H. Miller, 2nd edn (New Haven, CT, 2003)

Poems
These appeared in a Latin text: *The Poems of Desiderius Erasmus*, ed. Cornelis Reedijk (Leiden, 1956). The Latin was re-edited with a full commentary in *CWE*, vols LXXXV–LXXXVI, by Harry Vredeveld, and English translation by Clarence H. Miller

The Erasmus Reader, ed. Erika Rummel (Toronto, 1990). Contains short selections from many of the above works

Erasmus on Women, ed. Erika Rummel (Toronto, 1996). A selection of texts mainly from *Colloquies* and *Institution of Christian Marriage*

Further reading

Allen, Percy S., *The Age of Erasmus: Lectures Delivered in the Universities of Oxford and London* (Oxford, 1914)
—, *Erasmus: Lectures and Wayfaring Sketches* (Oxford, 1934)
Augustijn, Cornelis, *Erasmus: His Life, Works, and Influence*, trans. J. C. Grayson (Toronto, 1991)
Bainton, Roland H., *Erasmus of Christendom* (New York, 1969)
Barral-Baron, Marie, *L'Enfer d'Érasme: L'humaniste chrétien face à l'histoire* (Geneva, 2014)
Bataillon, Marcel, *Erasme et l'Espagne*, 2nd edn, 3 vols (Geneva, 1991)

Bénévent, Christine, 'La Correspondance d'Érasme: Fonctionnement, fonctions et fictions d'un réseau épistolaire', *Réseaux de correspondance à l'age classique (XVIe–XVIIIe siècle)*, ed. Pierre-Yves Beaurepaire, Jens Häseler and Antony McKenna (Saint-Étienne, 2006), pp. 17–32

Bentley, Jerry H., *Humanists and Holy Writ: New Testament Scholarship in the Renaissance* (Princeton, NJ, 1983)

Blair, Ann, *Too Much to Know: Managing Scholarly Information before the Modern Age* (New Haven, CT, 2010)

Cave, Terence, *The Cornucopian Text: Problems of Writing in the French Renaissance* (Oxford, 1979)

Charlier, Yvonne, *Érasme et l'amitié d'après sa correspondance* (Paris, 1977)

Chomarat, Jacques, *Grammaire et rhétorique chez Érasme*, 2 vols (Paris, 1981)

Christ-von Wedel, Christine, *Erasmus of Rotterdam: Advocate of a New Christianity* (Toronto, 2013)

Coelen, Peter van der, ed., *Images of Erasmus* (Rotterdam, 2008)

Coetzee, J. M., 'Erasmus' *Praise of Folly*: Rivalry and Madness', *Neophilologus*, LXVII/1 (1992), pp. 1–18

Cummings, Brian, 'Erasmus and the Invention of Literature', *Erasmus of Rotterdam Society Yearbook*, XXXIII (2013), pp. 22–54

—, *The Literary Culture of the Reformation: Grammar and Grace* (Oxford, 2002)

Eden, Kathy, *Friends Hold All Things in Common: Tradition, Intellectual Property, and the Adages of Erasmus* (New Haven, CT, 2001)

—, *The Renaissance Discovery of Intimacy* (Chicago, IL, 2012)

Goudriaan, Koen, 'New Evidence on Erasmus' Youth', *Erasmus Studies* XXXIX (2019), pp. 184–216

Grafton, Anthony, *The Culture of Correction in Renaissance Europe* (London, 2011)

—, *The Footnote: A Curious History* (Cambridge, MA, 1997)

—, *Inky Fingers: The Making of Books in Early Modern Europe* (Cambridge, MA, 2020)

—, and Lisa Jardine, *From Humanism to the Humanities: Education and the Liberal Arts in Fifteenth- and Sixteenth-century Europe* (London, 1986)

Gulik, Egbertus van, *Erasmus and His Books*, trans. J. C. Grayson, ed. J. K. McConica and Johannes Trapman (Toronto, 2018)

Hale, J. R., *Renaissance Europe, 1480–1520* (London, 1971)

Halkin, Léon-E., *Erasmus: A Critical Biography*, trans. John Tonkin
  (Oxford, 1993)
Herwaarden, Jan van, *Between Saint James and Erasmus: Studies in Late-Medieval
  Religious Life: Devotions and Pilgrimages in the Netherlands*, trans. Wendie
  Shaffer and Donald Gardner (Leiden and Boston, MA, 2003)
—, 'Erasmus and the Non-Christian World', *Erasmus of Rotterdam Society
  Yearbook*, XXXII (2012), pp. 69–83
Huizinga, Johan, *Erasmus*, trans. F. Hopman (New York, 1924)
Hutten, Ulrich von, et al., *Epistolae obscurorum virorum* [Letters of Obscure
  Men], ed. and trans. Francis Griffin Stokes (London, 1909)
IJsewijn, Jozef, 'The Coming of Humanism to the Low Countries',
  in *Itinerarium Italicum: The Profile of the Italian Renaissance in the Mirror
  of Its European Transformations*, ed. Heiko A. Oberman and Thomas
  A. Brady Jr (Leiden, 1975), pp. 193–301
Jardine, Lisa, *Erasmus, Man of Letters: The Construction of Charisma in Print*
  (Princeton, NJ, 1993)
Kraye, Jill, ed., *The Cambridge Companion to Renaissance Humanism*
  (Cambridge, 1996)
McConica, J. K., *Erasmus* (Oxford, 1991)
—, 'Erasmus and the Grammar of Consent', in *Scrinium Erasmianum*,
  ed. J. Coppens, 2 vols (Leiden, 1969), vol. II, pp. 77–99
MacCulloch, Diarmaid, *Reformation: Europe's House Divided, 1490–1700*
  (New York and London, 2003)
McDonald, Grantley R., *Biblical Criticism in Early Modern Europe: Erasmus,
  the Johannine Comma and Trinitarian Debate* (Cambridge, 2016)
Mansfield, Bruce, *Phoenix of His Age: Interpretations of Erasmus, c. 1550–1750*
  (Toronto, 1979)
—, *Man on His Own: Interpretations of Erasmus, c. 1750–1920* (Toronto, 1992)
—, *Erasmus in the Twentieth Century: Interpretations, c. 1920–2000* (Toronto,
  2003)
Markish, Shimon, *Erasmus and the Jews*, trans. Anthony Olcott (Chicago,
  IL, 1986)
Moss, Ann, *Renaissance Truth and the Latin Language Turn* (Oxford, 2003)
Nauert, Charles G., *Humanism and the Culture of Renaissance Europe*,
  2nd edn (Cambridge, 2006)
Oberman, Heiko A., *Luther: Man between God and the Devil*, trans. Eileen
  Walliser-Schwarzbart (New Haven, CT, 1989)

Overfield, James H., *Humanism and Scholasticism in Late Medieval Germany* (Princeton, NJ, 1984)

Pabel, Hilmar M., *Herculean Labours: Erasmus and the Editing of St Jerome's Letters in the Renaissance* (Leiden, 2008)

Panofsky, Erwin, 'Erasmus and the Visual Arts', *Journal of the Warburg and Courtauld Institutes*, XXXII (1969), pp. 200–227

Pettegree, Andrew, *The Book in the Renaissance* (New Haven, CT, 2010)

Phillips, Margaret Mann, *The 'Adages' of Erasmus: A Study with Translations* (Cambridge, 1964)

Ron, Nathan, *Erasmus and the 'Other': On Turks, Jews, and Indigenous Peoples* (Cham, Switzerland, 2019)

Roper, Lyndal, *Martin Luther: Renegade and Prophet* (London, 2016)

Rummel, Erika, *Erasmus* (London, 2004)

—, *Erasmus and His Catholic Critics*, 2 vols (Nieuwkoop, 1989)

—, *The Humanistic–Scholastic Debate in the Renaissance and Reformation* (Cambridge, MA, 1995)

Screech, M. A., *Ecstasy and The Praise of Folly* (London, 1980)

Sebastiani, Valentina, *Johann Froben, Printer of Basel: A Biographical Profile and Catalogue of His Editions* (Leiden, 2018)

Tracy, James D., *Erasmus of the Low Countries* (Berkeley, CA, 1996), available online at University of California Press, http://ark.cdlib.org

—, *Erasmus, The Growth of a Mind* (Geneva, 1972)

Van Engen, John, *Sisters and Brothers of the Common Life: The Devotio Moderna and the World of the Later Middle Ages* (Philadelphia, PA, 2008)

Vanautgaerden, Alexandre, *Érasme typographe. Humanisme et imprimerie au début du XVIe siècle* (Geneva, 2012)

Visser, Arnoud, 'Erasmus, the Church Fathers and the Ideological Implications of Philology', *Erasmus of Rotterdam Society Yearbook*, XXXI/1 (2011), pp. 7–31

—, 'Irreverent Reading: Martin Luther as Annotator of Erasmus', *Sixteenth Century Journal*, XLVIII (2017), pp. 87–109

—, *Reading Augustine in the Reformation: The Flexibility of Intellectual Authority in Europe, 1500–1620* (New York, 2011)

—, 'Reading Augustine through Erasmus' Eyes: Humanist Scholarship and Paratextual Guidance in the Wake of the Reformation', *Erasmus of Rotterdam Society Yearbook*, XXVIII (2008), pp. 67–90

Vocht, Henry de, *History of the Foundation and the Rise of the Collegium Trilingue Lovaniense, 1517–1550*, 4 vols (Louvain, 1951–5)

Vredeveld, Harry, 'The Ages of Erasmus and the Year of His Birth', *Renaissance Quarterly*, XLVI/4 (1993), pp. 754–809

Wallraff, Martin, Silvana Seidel-Menchi and Kaspar von Greyerz, eds, *Basel 1516: Erasmus' Edition of the New Testament* (Tübingen, 2016)

ACKNOWLEDGEMENTS

Amicorum communia omnia (Among friends all is common), the first proverb in Erasmus's *Adages*, is a summary of Erasmus's ideal of the shared humanist enterprise that remains relevant today. James McConica and the late Ron Schoeffel of the *Collected Works of Erasmus* long ago offered me undeserved citizenship in the Erasmian republic of letters, and it is largely because of them that I have been able to write this book. My debt to the many other dedicated scholars who have written about, edited or translated Erasmus will be obvious to anyone familiar with the scholarship, especially that found in the work of Percy Allen or in the volumes of the Amsterdam edition. Readers of English are extremely fortunate to have the *Collected Works of Erasmus*, initiated by Ron and led for many years by Jim, and I hope the day comes when this marvellous edition is freely available online to all readers. For reading a draft of the book I am grateful to its Jack Crowley and Elizabeth Church for their many detailed suggestions and to Erika Rummel for an Erasmian response. I am also grateful for those who supported me in various ways by writing a letter, answering an odd question, helping with the many books I needed, giving me encouragement, or asking questions: Ann Blair, Patricia Chalmers, Jim Estes, Jim Farge, Natalie Oeltjen, Richard Rex, Thomas Scheck, Fred Unwalla, John Van Engen, Adrie Van der Laan, Arnoud Visser and Germain Warkentin. My colleagues at Dalhousie University listened to a couple of talks in which I experimented with sections of my writing and their questions also helped to push things along. I had conversations with friends and family who would ask, 'Why Erasmus?' I am grateful for their questions, especially in the early days to those of Joel Zemel, and I hope this book gives them an answer. Michael Leaman and the editorial team at Reaktion Books have provided excellent advice, and I am still surprised they encouraged me to do this book. And an odder acknowledgement: for providing a congenial place to do much of the writing during the pre-COVID era I thank Laurent, Ludo and the staff of LF Bakery. For her love and lifelong support, I give special thanks to Elizabeth Church.

PHOTO ACKNOWLEDGEMENTS

The author and publishers wish to express their thanks to the below sources of illustrative material and/or permission to reproduce it. Some locations of artworks are also given below, in the interest of brevity:

From Andrea Alciato, *Emblemata cum commentariis Claudii Minois . . .* (Padua, 1621), photo William Barker: p. 22; Art Institute of Chicago: p. 251; photo William Barker: p. 188; photo courtesy Bayerische Staatsbibliothek (BSB)/ Ludwig-Maximilians-Universität, Munich: p. 92; from Georg Braun and Frans Hogenberg, *Civitates orbis terrarum*, vol. III (Cologne, 1581), photo courtesy Biblioteka Uniwersytecka we Wrocławiu: pp. 28–9; The British Museum, London: p. 167; from Isaac Bullart, *Academie des sciences et des arts, contenant les vies, & les eloges historiques des hommes illustres . . .* , vol. II (Amsterdam, 1682): p. 51; Centre for Reformation and Renaissance Studies, Victoria College, University of Toronto (photos William Barker): pp. 108, 148; Cleveland Museum of Art, OH: p. 265; © The Estate of R. B. Kitaj, reproduced with permission: p. 261; The Frick Collection, New York: p. 54; courtesy Will Flanagan, Halifax: p. 58; Historisches Museum, Basel (photo Peter Portner, CC BY-SA 4.0): p. 95; The J. Paul Getty Museum, Los Angeles: p. 10; photo courtesy Koninklijke Bibliotheek (KB), The Hague: p. 63; Kunstmuseum, Basel: pp. 6, 99, 106, 107, 192, 193, 233, 247; Longford Castle, Earl of Radnor Collection: p. 165; The Metropolitan Museum of Art, New York: pp. 18, 91, 152, 211, 228, 241; Musée du Louvre, Paris: pp. 81, 217; Museum Boijmans Van Beuningen, Rotterdam (on loan from Erasmusstichting, Rotterdam): p. 229; The National Gallery, London: pp. 116, 137, 254 (on loan from Longford Castle, Earl of Radnor Collection); Rijksdienst voor het Cultureel Erfgoed, Amersfoort/14.651

(photo J.P.A. Antonietti, CC BY-SA 3.0): p. 60; Rijksmuseum, Amsterdam: pp. 74, 215; Royal Collection Trust/© Her Majesty Queen Elizabeth II 2021: pp. 56, 112, 164, 190; Szépművészeti Múzeum, Budapest: p. 161; photos courtesy Universitätsbibliothek, Basel: pp. 89, 117, 124, 138, 139, 198.

INDEX

Page numbers in *italic* refer to illustrations